Audrey Grant's

BETTER BRIDGE

♠ ♥ ♦ ♣ ♠ ♥ ♦ ♣ ♠ ♥ ♦ ♣ ♠ ♥ ♦ ♣ ♠ ♥ ♦ ♣ ♠ ♥ ♦ ♣

Defense

CENTENNIAL PRESS

ISBN 0–8220–1668–0

Design and composition by
John Reinhardt Book Design

Centennial Press
Box 82087, Lincoln, Nebraska 68501
an imprint of Cliffs Notes, Inc.

*To the staff of the American Contract Bridge League,
and to the many bridge organizers across the country
and throughout the world. Thank you for keeping the game alive
and for providing an opportunity for so many people to meet
across the bridge table.*

Contents

Preface

For many years, I've seen people of all ages and all walks of life playing bridge. These bridge players are so obviously enjoying themselves that I've made it part of my life's work to teach and write about the game.

The best theorists in the world have shared their secrets with me, and I bring these pieces of bridge wisdom to you in a manner which I hope you will find readable.

Bridge is more than a game. It's a wonderful life skill. It's given me—as it can you—friends around the world. Anywhere you travel, being able to play a hand of bridge opens the door to meeting new people.

Here's more good news about bridge. It's healthy. The days of smoke-filled rooms of bridge players are long gone. It's accepted now that bridge exercises the mind the same way that physical activity exercises your body. That's right. Research indicates that the brain actually changes in response to the stimulus which a game like bridge provides.

This fourth book in the series is all about working with your partner to take the maximum number of tricks. It takes you beyond the first card played to a trick and shows you how to visualize the unseen cards.

You'll enjoy the game much more once you discover the techniques that allow you to use your imagination when defending a hand. You'll find yourself in a new role as detective: searching for clues, and putting them together to defeat contracts.

I like to think of the defense as a duet. The ideas in this book will bring harmony into your game. You'll end up playing as though you can see through the backs of the cards.

Audrey Grant

Acknowledgments

To my husband, David Lindop, who works hand-in-hand with me in all my bridge endeavors. Without his talent, drive, and love, these books would still be in the conceptual stage.

To my mother, Connie, who became an expert in counting up to thirteen while making sure every card was in its place.

To my dad, Alex, who writes my bridge jokes—and that's no laughing matter.

To my children, Joanna and Jason, who get involved in so many aspects of the projects—from making crepes for the bridge students to dressing up as cards.

To my brother, Brian, who has helped test much of the material used throughout this series.

To Julie Greenberg, head of the Education Department at the American Contract Bridge League, for her friendship and inspiration, and to the members of her staff for sharing their knowledge about bridge instruction.

To Henry Francis, editor of the *American Contract Bridge League Bulletin,* and his staff, who have been editing my work for years and have helped turn me into a better writer.

To Jerry Helms, the true bridge professional, who has generously shared both his teaching methods and expertise.

To Pat Harrington, whose understanding of the beginners' point of view has helped me write with more clarity to the books.

To Eric Rodwell and Zia Mahmood, world-class players, who have spent countless hours sharing their theories about the game.

To Fred Gitelman and Sheri Winestock, for showing what bridge will look like in the 21st Century.

To Michael Laughlin and Kirk Frederick, for their belief in me, together with their creative input.

To Flip Wilson, for his confidence that even my wildest promotional ideas would work out.

To the American Contract Bridge League Board of Directors, who help provide an overview of how bridge is played in all parts of the country.

To Doug Lincoln, for his vision and his ongoing support of this project.

To Jim Borthwick, who took care of all the details to bring this series to fruition.

To Michele Spence, for the many hours spent proof-reading each page of the manuscript and her cheerful disposition throughout the project.

To John Reinhardt, for combining his bridge knowledge and design talents to make each book in the series pleasing to the eye.

And of course, I'd like to acknowledge all those students, teachers, and expert players who have constantly provided inspiration and ideas in the field of bridge.

How Defenders Take Tricks

"*Most of the mistakes at the bridge table are made, not because players do not know what to do, but because they don't know when to do it.*"

—VICTOR MOLLO,
Bridge—A Case for the Defense

A book on defense is a must for any bridge player. After all, you'll be defending about half the time in any session of bridge. When you first start playing bridge, it's quite relaxing to find yourself on defense once the auction is over. It's tempting as a defender to sit back and watch to see whether or not declarer makes the contract.

As you gain experience, you'll be more active, and it will occur to you that you might have some effect on the outcome of the hand— on whether or not declarer makes the contract. You start to realize that the person sitting opposite you is on the same side. You're supposed to be working together to try to defeat the contract.

This book moves beyond the rules and the uncertainties of defense. You'll get an opportunity to use your imagination and play detective. When you can put all the clues together, it's quite a thrill. The skills of good defenders are right up there with the great detectives, like Sherlock Holmes and Columbo.

How Declarer Takes Tricks

This is a book on defense, but the first step is to start by looking at things from declarer's viewpoint to see how declarer goes about taking tricks. Imitation is the sincerest form of flattery.

How might you plan to take tricks from the following combined hands?

YOU (DECLARER)
♠ Q 10 8 5 2
♥ 7 3
♦ 8 4 2
♣ A K 6

PARTNER (DUMMY)
♠ J 9 7
♥ 10 8 4
♦ K 9 7 5 3
♣ 8 2

I'm sure you're thinking that you would never be declarer with these hands, and you're probably right. But play along for a moment. You can pretend that you're in a notrump contract and the opponents have led a club. The cards in the dummy have a shaded background indicating that they're face up on the table.*

Sure Tricks

As declarer, one of the first things you look for is the number of *sure tricks* you have between the two hands. Sure tricks are those winners you can take any time you have the lead. On this hand, you have two sure tricks, the ♣A and ♣K.

Entries play an important role when taking sure tricks. An *entry* is a winner that allows you to cross over to a specific hand. There must also be a *link card* in the opposite hand, which is the card that can be led over to the winner. Declarer notes the order in which the cards

---

*This convention is used throughout the book. The cards you see on the table—the opening lead, the dummy, and cards already played to a trick—have a shaded background. Those you can see in your hand will be set in normal type.

have to be played to make best use of the available entries. Suppose this were your holding in the club suit:

YOU (DECLARER)　　　　PARTNER (DUMMY)

♣ K 3　　　　　　　♣ A Q J 5

One of the guidelines declarer uses when taking sure tricks is to **play the high card from the short side first.** In this layout, declarer would start by winning a trick with the ♣K, high card from the short side. Then the ♣3 can be used as the link card over to dummy's three remaining winners. By playing the suit in this manner, you don't need an entry to the dummy in another suit. If you were to win the first trick with the ♣A and the second trick with the ♣K, you'd find that dummy's last two club winners were *stranded* unless you had a way to get to them.

If you have all the sure tricks you need to make the contract, all you have to do is take them. Of course, that's sometimes easier said than done. Your winners may be *blocked.* For example:

YOU (DECLARER)　　　　PARTNER (DUMMY)

♣ A K　　　　　　　♣ Q J 5 3

You have four sure tricks in the club suit, but you can't take them right away. After taking the ♣A and ♣K, you have no low club in your hand with which to cross over to the two remaining winners in partner's hand. You'll need an entry in another suit. The above club suit is blocked because there's no link card in your hand with which to cross to dummy's club winners. If there is no entry in another suit, then partner's club winners will be stranded.

As you might expect, entries will also be an important consideration when you're defending a contract.

Promotion

When there aren't enough sure tricks to make the contract—which is usually the case—declarer looks for ways to develop additional winners. One of the principle techniques declarer relies on is *promotion*—promoting lower-ranking cards into winners by driving out any higher-ranking cards in the opponents' hands. For example:

YOU (DECLARER)
♥ K 3

PARTNER (DUMMY)
♥ Q J 10 2

By leading the ♥K to drive out the opponents' ♥A, dummy's ♥Q, ♥J, and ♥10 are promoted into winners. Notice that declarer uses the same guideline of playing the high card from the short side first when promoting winners. By starting with the ♥K, if the opponents win the first trick with the ♥A, the ♥3 can be used as the link card over to dummy's three established winners. Of course, the opponents don't have to win the first trick with their ace. They can *hold up* taking their winner, which is something we'll be discussing later. Nonetheless, starting with the high card from the short side is still the best way to go about promoting winners in a suit.

Returning to the original hand, there is an opportunity for promotion in the spade suit:

YOU (DECLARER)
♠ Q 10 8 5 2

PARTNER (DUMMY)
♠ J 9 7

You have all the high cards in the suit except for the ♠A and ♠K. By driving out the opponents' ♠A and ♠K with your high cards, you could promote three winners in the suit.

While promotion is a sure-fire way of developing extra winners, there is a disadvantage. Each time you drive out one of the opponents' higher cards, you have to give up the lead. You'll need winners in other suits so that you can regain the lead once your winners are established. On the original hand, you'd want to keep your ♣A and ♣K around while promoting winners in the spade suit, so that you would have a way of regaining the lead and eventually taking your winners.

Length

Not all tricks are won with high cards. Low cards can come into play, especially when they're located in long suits. For example:

YOU (DECLARER)
♥ A K 8 7 6 5

PARTNER (DUMMY)
♥ 4 3 2

You have two sure tricks, the ♥A and ♥K. But you hold nine hearts in the combined hands, leaving the opponents with four cards in the suit. If the opponents' hearts are divided 2–2—two cards in each hand—all their hearts will be gone after you play your ♥A and ♥K, leaving you with four additional winners in the suit. You can't count on six tricks from this suit, however, since the opponents' hearts might not be divided 2–2. They could be divided 3–1, in which case, one of the opponents will have a heart left after you take your ♥A and ♥K. You can still develop three extra winners in the suit by giving up a trick to the opponents. Your remaining hearts are now winners.

The opponents' hearts might also be divided 4–0, with one opponent holding all four hearts. In that case, you would have to give up two tricks to the opponents, and would end up with two additional winners through length. The hearts won't often divide this badly, but it's comfortable to know what you might expect when thinking about getting extra tricks from length. The guideline declarer can use is that **an even number of cards in the opponents' hands can be expected to divide slightly unevenly; an odd number of cards can be expected to divide as evenly as possible**. This is expressed in the following table:

Number of Cards in the Opponents' Hands	Expected Division Between the Opponents
3	2 – 1
4	3 – 1
5	3 – 2
6	4 – 2
7	4 – 3
8	5 – 3

This is a useful piece of information to keep in mind when looking for extra tricks. For example, the diamond suit in the original hand provides some potential for developing extra winners through length:

YOU (DECLARER)
♦ 8 4 2

PARTNER (DUMMY)
♦ K 9 7 5 3

There are eight diamonds between the two hands, leaving five for the opponents. You'd expect the five diamonds to be divided as evenly as possible, 3–2, between the opponents' hands. If that's the case, you'll have two extra winners in the dummy after the suit has been played three times because neither opponent will have a diamond left.

Of course, you'll need an entry to the dummy to reach your winners once they've been established. There's no sure entry to the dummy, but perhaps the ♦K can be turned into a winner. That brings us to the next method of developing winners...

The Finesse

A *finesse* is an attempt to win a trick with a card when the defenders hold one or more higher-ranking cards in the suit. The principle behind the finesse is to **lead toward the card you hope will win a trick**.

YOU (DECLARER)	PARTNER (DUMMY)
♥ 7 6	♥ A Q

In this layout, you have one sure trick with the ♥A. To win a second trick from this combination of cards, you would start by leading a low heart from your hand toward dummy. Assuming the ♥K didn't appear, you would then play—finesse—dummy's ♥Q. Your finesse will succeed whenever the ♥K is on your left because your right-hand opponent won't be able to win the trick. You'll get two tricks instead of one. Of course, if the ♥K is unfavorably placed on your right, your finesse will lose, and you'll be back to the one sure trick you started with.

In the original hand, the diamond suit offered the possibility of developing a trick with the help of a finesse:

YOU (DECLARER)	PARTNER (DUMMY)
♦ 8 4 2	♦ K 9 7 5 3

You could lead a low diamond from your hand toward dummy's ♦K. If the player to your left holds the ♦A, you can't be prevented from establishing the ♦K as a winner. If the ♦A is played, you play a low diamond from dummy and can get a trick with dummy's ♦K when you regain the lead. If the ♦A isn't played, you finesse dummy's ♦K and win a trick immediately. Your finesse has a 50–50 chance of succeeding. It all depends on which opponent holds the ♦A.

The Trump Suit

The techniques for trick development through promotion, length, and the finesse are useful in both notrump and suit contracts. When there's a trump suit, however, additional possibilities arise. For example, if you were to make spades the trump suit on the original hand, you could get an extra trick by playing the ♣A and ♣K, and then trumping your remaining low club with one of dummy's spades.

Playing with a trump suit has advantages and disadvantages. You can use the trump suit to prevent the opponents from taking all their winners in a suit, since you can ruff—trump—their winners once you have no cards left in the suit in either your hand or in partner's hand. At the same time, you must be careful that the opponents don't use the trump suit to ruff your winners. That's why declarer usually draws trump as soon as possible.

Summing Up

So, here are the original hands we were viewing from the standpoint of declarer:

YOU (DECLARER)	PARTNER (DUMMY)
♠ Q 10 8 5 2	♠ J 9 7
♥ 7 3	♥ 10 8 4
♦ 8 4 2	♦ K 9 7 5 3
♣ A K 6	♣ 8 2

You have two sure tricks in clubs. You may be able to develop three extra tricks from the spade suit through promotion. You may be able to develop two extra tricks from the diamond suit through length, and you may be able to get a trick with the ♦K using the finesse. If there's a trump suit, you might also gain a trick by ruffing your low club in the dummy. Lots of possibilities.

Of course, with only 13 high card points between the two hands, it's unlikely that your side will actually get to play the contract. It's more likely you'll end up on defense, with the opponents choosing the contract. So let's see what difference that makes.

How Defenders Take Tricks

First the good news. As a defender, there's nothing new to learn about how tricks are taken. All the techniques available to declarer are also available to the defenders. You can take your sure tricks; you can use promotion, length, and the finesse; you can use the trump suit to obtain ruffs.

As you're probably aware, however, there is a challenge. To see this, let's return to our earlier hand and put you in the position of a defender. To keep things simple, we're going to have South as the declarer on all the hands throughout this book, with North as the dummy. You'll be defending from either the West position—as the player before, or in front of, the dummy—or the East position—as the player behind, or after, the dummy.

Here goes. We'll start you off as West in a notrump contract:

WEST (YOU)	EAST (PARTNER)
♠ Q 10 8 5 2	♠ ?
♥ 7 3	♥ ?
♦ 8 4 2	♦ ?
♣ A K 6	♣ ?

Oh, oh! Partner's hand is now hidden from you. It's no longer so easy to see where the tricks are going to come from. You can still see the two sure tricks in clubs, but the possibilities for promotion in the spade suit, or using the combined length in the diamond suit, or taking a finesse in the diamond suit, are no longer readily apparent. And if, for example, hearts is the trump suit, even the possibility of playing the ♣A and ♣K and leading the ♣6 for partner to ruff has now disappeared from view.

You need a new tool to help lift the veil hanging over partner's cards. Lacking x-ray vision, it'll have to be **visualization**. You're going to have to use your imagination to picture the unseen cards located in partner's hand. Impossible, you say? It's actually not as difficult as you might think. You already know something about partner's hand: there are only thirteen cards in it—unless there's been a mis-deal. You could also conclude that they can't all be spades, since you hold five spades yourself. Already something is starting to come into focus.

The few psychics aside, you're not going to be able to name the exact cards that partner holds, but you're going to be presented with a number of clues throughout the hand. It starts with the auction. The opponents can hardly reach a contract without giving you some information along the way. For example, if they were to bid and raise spades during the auction, you could conclude that partner probably doesn't have any of the missing spades. Or perhaps partner has bid hearts twice during the auction. You could then place about six of those in partner's hand, leaving not too much room for other long suits.

And if the opponents bid to a game contract? It might be optimistic to envision many aces and kings in partner's hand, but let's be practical! The opponents probably hold at least 26 points between them, and if you're looking at 9 or 10 points, that doesn't leave too much for partner to hold. There are only 40 high card points in the deck, and even counting extra points for distribution, partner's not going to hold many aces and kings.

You're going to get information when the dummy comes down. All of a sudden, you'll be able to see thirteen more cards that your partner can't possibly hold. There may be some disappointments, but your picture of partner's hand will start to come into focus more sharply. In fact, you can place any of the missing cards in partner's hand and have at least a 50% chance of being right—either partner holds the card, or declarer holds it.

As the play goes on, even more clues will start to come your way. Each card you see played by partner and declarer will narrow the possibilities. If declarer discards when you lead a heart, any remaining hearts you can't see in your hand or the dummy must lie in partner's hand. Even more importantly, as we'll see later, the cards partner chooses to play can be given special significance. They can be used to send signals about other features of the hand, to help you build up an image of partner's hand.

It's a two-way street. Partner will be trying to form a picture of your hand and will be relying on your signals to help fill in the details.

You're both going to be playing detective, listening and watching for clues throughout the bidding and play. It will take a while to become good at this type of detective work, but that's what this book, together with a little practice, will help you do. You'll be surprised how those hidden cards suddenly start to come into view.

Even those times when you really don't know what cards partner holds are not hopeless. The game of bridge is filled with sayings that have been passed down through the generations: lead fourth from your longest and strongest; play second hand low; cover an honor with an honor. We'll look at some of these guidelines in the next chapter, to see what they mean. Then you can use them to guide you when there's nothing better to go by. They're only guidelines, however, and it's more important to know when to use them, rather than how to use them. That's what visualization of partner's hand will provide.

Defending Against 3NT

Let's practice. We'll return to the original hand and start with an auction—that's supposed to provide some initial clues.

WEST (YOU)	NORTH	EAST (PARTNER)	SOUTH
			1NT
Pass	3NT	Pass	Pass
Pass			

Well, that wasn't much was it? Nonetheless, there's information available. South has shown a balanced hand with about 16–18 points.* North has raised directly to the game level, so probably has about 10 points, enough to give the North-South partnership a combined total of 26 points. North and South haven't shown any interest in playing in a major suit, so it's unlikely either one of them has a long major suit. Before making the opening lead, let's draw a first picture of the combined partnership hands:

WEST (YOU)
♠ Q 10 8 5 2
♥ 7 3
♦ 8 4 2
♣ A K 6

EAST (PARTNER)
♠ x x x
♥ x x x x
♦ x x x
♣ x x x

---

*Different ranges for an opening bid of 1NT are popular in different areas, but you'll always be able to ask your opponents what range they're using. We'll provide a consistent answer of 16-18 points for use throughout this book.

Not too impressive, but at least you've filled in thirteen cards that could possibly be in partner's hand. There's no indication that partner has an unbalanced hand, so you can picture a reasonably balanced distribution. There will probably be some high cards scattered here and there, but we can leave that for now. It gives you some sort of image. Throughout this book, we'll use an italic typeface to indicate the cards that you visualize in another player's hand. Each small "*x*" represents a card whose rank has yet to be determined.

You need five tricks to defeat North-South's 3NT contract. Looking at the combined hands, where are they going to come from? You have two sure tricks in clubs, but it's not very likely that the partnership has enough combined sure tricks to defeat the contract right away. North-South have about 26 combined points, and you have 9 high card points. With only 40 high card points in the deck, that doesn't leave too much room for many of those '*x*'s in partner's hand to be aces and kings. There are only about 5 or 6 points left for partner—perhaps a king and a queen. The partnership will likely have to develop the extra tricks needed to defeat the contract with the help of the standard techniques: promotion, length, and the finesse.

Should you be leading spades, hoping to promote some tricks in that suit? Should you be leading hearts or diamonds, hoping partner has some strength in one of those suits? Should you be leading clubs, hoping that partner has some length in clubs? You can't know for sure, but your image of partner's hand indicates that spades might be a good choice. That's your long suit, and even if it isn't partner's longest suit, it could well be the longest combined suit between the two hands. If partner holds a little something in the suit—the king or the jack—you may be able to promote winners, or develop tricks through length. So, as the best guess, you start off by leading a spade. Let's see how that works out when we look at the complete hand:

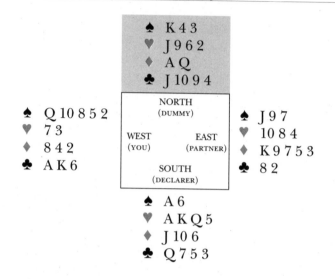

Partner's hand isn't exactly what you pictured, but it's not so far off. Partner has a king and a jack, and some cards in all the suits. If you start by leading a spade, partner has just enough to help you promote winners in that suit. Declarer will have to play the ♣A or ♣K to win a trick in the suit. Declarer has seven sure tricks: two spades, four hearts, and a diamond. To get the two extra tricks needed to make the contract, declarer will have to try to promote extra winners in the club suit. When declarer leads a club, you can win the trick and lead another spade, driving out declarer's remaining high spade. When declarer leads another club, win the trick and take your three promoted spade winners to defeat the contract.

It wasn't so impossible to come up with the winning defense, even though you couldn't see partner's cards. A little visualization got you off to the right start, and as the play moved along, things became clearer and clearer.

Defending Against 4♥

You might argue, of course, that you could fall back on the old adage, "lead fourth best from your longest and strongest." As you'll see in the next chapter, following that guideline would get you off to the lead of the ♣5, putting you in the same position of being able to defeat the contract. But suppose we were to change the auction slightly:

WEST	NORTH	EAST	SOUTH
(YOU)		(PARTNER)	
			1NT
Pass	2♣*	Pass	2♥
Pass	4♥	Pass	Pass
Pass		*Stayman convention	

North has used the Stayman convention to ask partner for a four-card major suit. South has shown a four-card heart suit, and North has put the partnership at the game level in the major suit, and you're back on lead. What happens if you start again with fourth from your longest and strongest, and lead the ♠5? Let's look at the complete hand again:

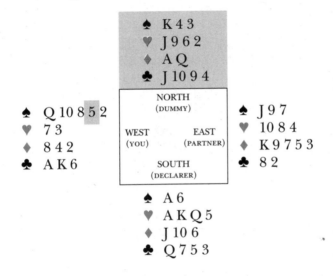

Declarer will win the first trick and play three rounds of hearts, drawing all the trump from the East-West hands. Then declarer might lead a club. You can win the trick and lead another spade to drive out declarer's other high card in the suit, establishing your three remaining spades as winners. But declarer will simply drive out your last high club. Your spade winners do you no good, because when you lead one, declarer trumps your winner with a heart. Your partner will eventually get a trick with the ♦K, but that's all. The only tricks your side wins are two club tricks and a diamond trick. Declarer makes the 4♥ contract.

Leading your long suit doesn't usually work as well against suit contracts as against notrump contracts. And that's the trouble with guidelines—you have to know when to apply them.

The only way to defeat the 4♥ contract is for you to start by leading the ♣A, ♣K, and another club for your partner to ruff. Later in the hand, partner will get a trick with the ♦K, and that'll be the fourth trick for the defense, enough to defeat the contract. How are you going to know to do this? We'll see later on how partner can signal for you to continue leading clubs once you start off by leading one.

Of course, you may have heard something about leading the top of a sequence, and that may guide you to the best opening lead on this hand—but you have to know which guideline to apply each time. That's where visualizing partner's hand can help out. You know partner doesn't have much in the way of high cards, and you can expect that establishing winners in your long suit probably won't do much good when the contract is being played in a trump suit. But you need four tricks to defeat the 4♥ contract, rather than the five you needed to defeat 3NT. That's a bonus. And you can already see a couple of sure tricks. If you lead one, you might get a better clue as to where the other two tricks are coming from once you see dummy. Unlike the defense to 3NT—where you needed your club winners as entries to establish winners in the spade suit—it's unlikely to be fatal to the defense if you start by taking one of your club winners. Once you see the dummy, and you get some help from partner's signals, you'll be in a better position to fill in those unseen cards in partner's hand. That will often lead you to the winning defense.

Turning Things Around

It might seem as though you were very lucky on this first hand to find the winning defense against the 3NT contract with only a vague idea of what to lead. But let's turn all four hands through 180 degrees to put your partner's original hand on lead. The complete hand would now look like this:

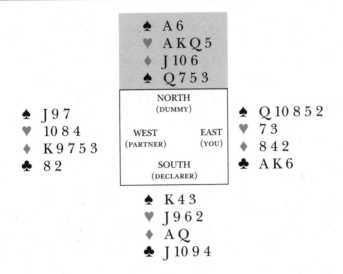

♠ A 6
♥ A K Q 5
♦ J 10 6
♣ Q 7 5 3

NORTH
(DUMMY)

♠ J 9 7   ♠ Q 10 8 5 2
♥ 10 8 4   ♥ 7 3
♦ K 9 7 5 3   ♦ 8 4 2
♣ 8 2   ♣ A K 6

WEST   EAST
(PARTNER)   (YOU)

SOUTH
(DECLARER)

♠ K 4 3
♥ J 9 6 2
♦ A Q
♣ J 10 9 4

Partner can't see your hand and won't know that you're rooting for a spade lead. Instead, partner will probably think that diamonds is the best suit for the defense to attack—hoping that you have some length and strength in that suit. Partner might be disappointed to see your actual holding in the suit, but let's see what happens if partner starts off the defense to 3NT by leading a low diamond.

The first trick is right into the jaws of declarer's ♦A–Q, and declarer will win the first trick with the ♦Q. Even with this, declarer has only eight sure tricks: two spades, four hearts, and two diamonds. Declarer will have to go after the club suit for a ninth trick. When declarer leads a club and you win the trick, you can lead another diamond, which drives out declarer's ♦A. Declarer next drives out your remaining high club, but you can lead your last diamond over to partner's ♦K. Partner takes two more diamond tricks to defeat the contract. So it really doesn't matter which of you is on lead. Declarer's contract is doomed against good defense.

We did glide over a couple of points here. You might be wondering what would happen if you'd switched to your suit, spades, rather than continuing with partner's suit, diamonds, after winning the first club trick. Declarer would make the contract. The same thing would have happened when the hands were reversed if partner had switched to diamonds after you started with spades. Returning partner's suit is useful to avoid working at cross-purposes on hands such as this.

It's also interesting to note what would happen if partner were on lead against a contract of 4♥. A diamond lead would prove disastrous. Declarer would win the first trick with the ♦Q and draw trump. Declarer would end up losing only two tricks to your ♣A and ♣K, and would make an overtrick in the 4♥ contract. Instead, partner would have to visualize that attempting to establish tricks through the length in the diamond suit is unlikely to be effective against a suit contract. Looking at only 4 high card points, however, partner might suspect that you have a couple of high cards, and could well decide to lead a short suit, clubs, hoping to make use of one of the trumps.

It's difficult from partner's side, but it's not completely out of the question that you would end up defeating the 4♥ contract in the same manner as before: by winning the first two club tricks, giving partner a club ruff, and waiting around for a trick with partner's ♦K.

You're probably starting to feel sorry for declarer by now. Don't worry. Many contracts will be impossible to defeat, while others will be a challenge even when both defenders are on their toes. But let's have some fun trying to defeat as many as we can. The coming chapters will provide ideas to assist you on defense. It'll be up to you to put your imagination to work and picture those cards in partner's hand that will help defeat the contract.

Summary

The defenders take tricks in the same manner as declarer. In both notrump and suit contracts, the defenders can make use of promotion, length, and the finesse to develop the extra winners they need to defeat the contract. In a suit contract, the defenders can also make use of the trump suit, perhaps by ruffing some of declarer's winners.

The challenge as a defender is that you can't see the cards in your partner's hand. You get a number of clues, however, from the auction, from the dummy, and from the cards partner plays during the hand. This allows you to play detective and visualize the cards in partner's hand, often giving you the information you need to defeat the contract.

Practice Hands

Hand 1.1

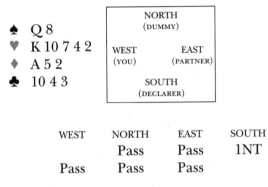

♠ Q 8
♥ K 10 7 4 2
♦ A 5 2
♣ 10 4 3

	WEST	NORTH	EAST	SOUTH
		Pass	Pass	1NT
	Pass	Pass	Pass	

You find yourself on lead against a contract of 1NT by South. How many high card points do you think will come down in the dummy? How many high card points do you think your partner might hold?

Try to visualize partner's hand. Which suit might you lead to get the partnership off to a good start? Do you think your side has a reasonable chance of defeating the contract?

Solution 1.1

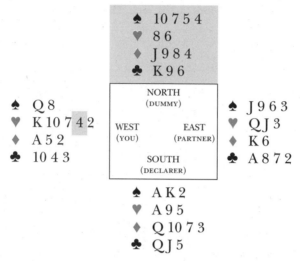

```
                    ♠ 10 7 5 4
                    ♥ 8 6
                    ♦ J 9 8 4
                    ♣ K 9 6
                         NORTH
                        (DUMMY)
♠ Q 8                                    ♠ J 9 6 3
♥ K 10 7 4 2    WEST          EAST       ♥ Q J 3
♦ A 5 2         (YOU)       (PARTNER)    ♦ K 6
♣ 10 4 3                                 ♣ A 8 7 2
                         SOUTH
                       (DECLARER)
                    ♠ A K 2
                    ♥ A 9 5
                    ♦ Q 10 7 3
                    ♣ Q J 5
```

North passed the opening bid of 1NT and is likely to hold some-where between 0 and 7 high card points. You'd expect about 4 or 5 points to come down in the dummy. Partner would have opened the bidding with 13 or more points, so must hold something in the range of 0–12 points. Since you have only 9 high card points and North-South stopped in partscore, you'd expect partner to have about 8–12 points. On the actual hand, dummy has 4 points, and your partner holds 11 points.

Without much to go on, you'd visualize partner's hand as contain-ing a scattering of cards in all the suits, much like the actual hand. The suit with the most promise from your point of view is hearts. With a little help from partner, you may be able to develop tricks through promotion or length. Since the opponents have stopped quietly in a partscore at the one level, it's quite likely the strength is fairly evenly divided between the two partnerships. That should give your side a reasonable chance of defeating the contract, especially with the ad-vantage of the opening lead. On the actual hand, a heart lead gives you a good chance of success. Partner's holding in hearts will let your side develop four tricks through promotion. Together with the ♦A and ♦K, and the ♣A, you can take seven tricks before declarer gets the seven tricks to make the contract. Declarer needs to promote winners in both diamonds and clubs to make the contract. That should give your side the opportunity to take your winners.

Hand 1.2

♠ 7 5 2
♥ 9 6 3
♦ J 10 8 6 3
♣ 8 4

```
          NORTH
         (DUMMY)

WEST              EAST
(YOU)           (PARTNER)

          SOUTH
        (DECLARER)
```

WEST	NORTH	EAST	SOUTH
		1♠	1NT
Pass	3NT	Pass	Pass
Pass			

It's not surprising that you don't have a very good hand with all the bidding that's going on around you. It's your lead against the opponents' 3NT contract. Your best suit is diamonds. Will that be the best suit to lead for the partnership, or are there other considerations? What sort of picture do you have of partner's hand?

Solution 1.2

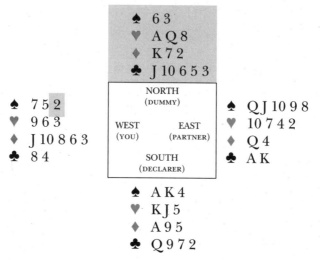

```
              ♠ 6 3
              ♥ A Q 8
              ♦ K 7 2
              ♣ J 10 6 5 3

                   NORTH
                   (DUMMY)
  ♠ 7 5 2                              ♠ Q J 10 9 8
  ♥ 9 6 3       WEST      EAST         ♥ 10 7 4 2
  ♦ J 10 8 6 3  (YOU)    (PARTNER)     ♦ Q 4
  ♣ 8 4                                ♣ A K
                   SOUTH
                 (DECLARER)

              ♠ A K 4
              ♥ K J 5
              ♦ A 9 5
              ♣ Q 9 7 2
```

Partner has opened the bidding 1♠, so you can expect partner to have at least 13 points and a five-card or longer spade suit.* You can't expect partner to hold much more than 13 points, since the opponents have reached a game contract. Partner won't hold a second suit longer than spades, and you might picture partner holding two or three cards in each of the other suits. Partner's high cards won't all be in the spade suit; otherwise, it's unlikely the opponents would have elected to play in notrump. So you might find some help for your diamond suit. On the actual hand, partner does have enough strength in the diamond suit to help you develop winners in that suit if you choose to lead it. It won't do you much good, however, since you have no entry back to your winners once they're established.

A better option is to lead partner's suit, spades, and hope to develop enough tricks in that suit. That's what would happen on the actual hand. Your spade lead would allow partner to drive out one of declarer's high spades. Declarer has seven sure tricks: two spades, three hearts, and two diamonds. Declarer will have to try to promote extra tricks in the club suit to make the contract. When declarer leads a club, partner can win the trick and drive out declarer's remaining high spade. When declarer leads another club, partner will win the trick and be able to take three promoted spade winners.

*Throughout the book, we'll assume that the partnership style is that of *five-card majors*, requiring a five-card or longer suit to open the bidding 1♥ or 1♠.

Hand 1.3

♠ K Q J
♥ 7 5
♦ K 8 7 4 2
♣ A 4 2

```
          NORTH
         (DUMMY)

WEST              EAST
(YOU)           (PARTNER)

          SOUTH
        (DECLARER)
```

West	North	East	South
			1♥
Pass	3♥	Pass	4♥
Pass	Pass	Pass	

You're on lead again. This time the contract is 4♥. What sort of hand do you expect partner to hold after this auction? Having visualized partner's hand, which suit do you think you should be leading?

Solution 1.3

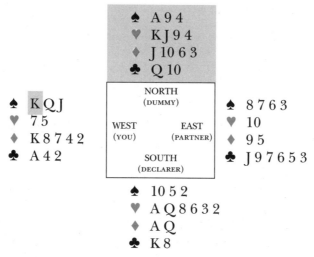

The opponents have bid up to the game level, so they should have at least 26 combined points. You hold 13 high card points. There are 40 high card points in the deck; that doesn't leave too much for partner. It looks like you're going to have to get most of the tricks yourself if you plan to defeat this contract.

You already have one sure trick, the ♣A, and you should be able to promote two more winners in the spade suit. If you can also get a trick from the ♦K, you may not need any help from partner. That gives you the clue to the best opening lead. Lead a spade, to establish two winners in that suit. You want to keep your ♣A as an entry to your spade winners, and you'll have to hope something good happens in the diamond suit to allow you to get a trick with your king.

On the actual hand, a spade lead defeats the contract. After winning the ♠A, declarer will draw trump and then has little choice but to lead a diamond from dummy and try the diamond finesse. When the finesse loses to your ♦K, you can take your two established spade winners and the ♣A to defeat the contract.

With partner holding so little in the way of high cards, an original diamond lead would be instantly fatal. Declarer would win the first trick with the ♦Q, and you'd never get a diamond trick. Also, if you didn't lead spades early on, declarer could establish two diamond winners in dummy by driving out your ♦K and use them to discard two small spades from declarer's hand.

Hand 1.4

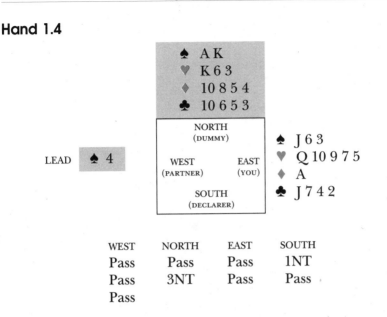

WEST	NORTH	EAST	SOUTH
Pass	Pass	Pass	1NT
Pass	3NT	Pass	Pass
Pass			

The contract is 3NT, but this time you're sitting East and it's partner who makes the opening lead. Partner leads the ♠4. You might
have preferred a heart lead, but perhaps partner didn't quite picture all the cards in your hand when going through the visualization
process.

Declarer wins the first trick in dummy and leads a diamond. Can
you see through the backs of partner's cards? What do you plan to
do after winning this trick with your ♦A?

Solution 1.4

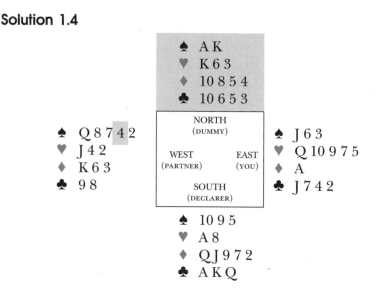

```
              ♠ A K
              ♥ K 6 3
              ♦ 10 8 5 4
              ♣ 10 6 5 3
                   NORTH
♠ Q 8 7 4 2       (DUMMY)        ♠ J 6 3
♥ J 4 2                          ♥ Q 10 9 7 5
♦ K 6 3      WEST      EAST      ♦ A
♣ 9 8      (PARTNER)  (YOU)      ♣ J 7 4 2
                  SOUTH
                (DECLARER)
              ♠ 10 9 5
              ♥ A 8
              ♦ Q J 9 7 2
              ♣ A K Q
```

You hold 8 high card points and can see 10 more in the dummy. Declarer has 16–18 points for the 1NT opening bid, so that leaves partner with about 5 or 6 points. You can't see partner's cards, but you might suspect that partner's longest suit is spades, since partner decided to lead one as the best hope for defeating the contract.

After winning a trick with the ♦A, you might think about leading your best suit, hearts. But that would be working at cross-purposes with your partner. It's probably better to carry on with partner's original idea and lead back another spade.

That works well on the actual hand. Your spade lead removes dummy's remaining high card in the suit. Declarer doesn't have enough tricks for the contract without promoting extra winners in the diamond suit. When declarer leads another diamond, partner wins the trick with the ♦K and plays the ♠Q. That removes the spades from all the other hands, and partner's last two spades have become winners through length. Your side ends up with five tricks—three spades and two diamonds—just enough to defeat the contract.

If you were to lead a heart, rather than a spade, after winning the ♦A, the defense would lose the race. Declarer would be able to promote three diamond winners before your side was ready to take any tricks in either hearts or spades. Declarer would end up taking ten tricks—more than enough to fulfill the contract.

The Top Ten List
Part I

"Ideals are like the stars; you will not succeed in touching them with your hands. But like the seafaring man on the desert of waters, you choose them as your guides, and following them you will reach your destiny."

—CARL SHURZ,
Boston Address, [1859]

Before the days of bridge, people used to play a game called whist. Whist was similar to bridge in that tricks were won in the same manner and you worked with the person opposite you as a partner. There was no auction, however, and there was no dummy placed face up on the table. As you might imagine, it was quite a challenge to figure out where your tricks were coming from.

In spite of these obstacles, the players of those days knew all about developing tricks through promotion, length, finesses, and ruffing. All the techniques common to the declarers and defenders of today, were in use at the whist table. How did partnerships manage to work together successfully under those conditions? There was a set of guidelines for play in each position—when leading to a trick, when playing the second card to a trick, and so forth. Many of these guidelines were passed down from generation to generation, even after the game had changed from whist to bridge.

There's no substitute for using your imagination when defending, but that's no reason to ignore the wisdom of the past. The next two chapters cover ten of the guidelines that are still in popular use today when defending a hand. They all have some value, provided you follow them only when you have nothing better to guide you. Here are the guidelines that are there to help you choose both the suit and the card to lead in various situations.

1. Fourth from Longest and Strongest

You're on lead against a notrump contract. The popular saying is to lead "fourth highest from your longest and strongest." This is the oldest guideline in the game and was first published in Edmund Hoyle's *A Short Treatise on Whist* in 1742.* For example, suppose the opponents have reached a contract of 3NT, and this is your hand:

♠ 8 3
♥ K 9 7 6 2
♦ A J 8 3
♣ Q 10

With nothing else to go on, pick your longest suit, hearts, and lead your *fourth highest* card in the suit, the ♥6. Notice that fourth highest means the fourth card down from the top.

Leading a heart from this hand is sound advice. Your side won't often have enough sure tricks to defeat the contract, and you'll need

*The full name of this book is actually the longest title of any book about cards: *A Short Treatise on the Game of Whist, Containing the Laws of the Game, and also Some Rules Whereby a Beginner May, with Due Attention to Them, Attain to the Playing It Well*. The book was likely the 18th Century's best seller and gave rise to the expression "according to Hoyle" when referring to any precise approach.

to develop tricks. You don't know for certain which is the longest combined suit in the partnership hands, but by picking your longest suit, you can't go far wrong. If partner has high cards in hearts to help you out, you should be able to promote winners. Even if partner has only some length in the suit, you should be able to develop winners through length if your side keeps leading the suit. Usually, it will be a combination of promotion and length that will develop the tricks you need. Once you've developed the winners, declarer won't be able to stop you from taking them when you gain the lead, since there's no trump suit. Hold on to your high cards in the other suits so that you can regain the lead.

When you have a choice of suits, the guideline suggests that you pick the strongest suit. For example:

♠ K 10 8 2
♥ Q 7 3
♦ A 3
♣ J 9 5 4

Your longest suits are spades and hearts. With a choice, pick spades because the suit contains more strength. Lead the ♠2, your fourth highest. You need less help from partner to establish winners when you lead the stronger suit. The less you need from partner, the more likely you are to find it!

Why fourth highest? That was the conventional agreement in the days of whist, and it has merit. You usually don't want to lead your highest cards in the suit. You want to save those as entries or to trap declarer's high cards. Also, by leading fourth highest, partner can often tell exactly how many cards you hold in the suit—and that will improve partner's visualization of your hand. For example, suppose you lead the ♠2 from the above hand. Look at things from partner's perspective:

WEST (YOU)   EAST (PARTNER)
♠ *x x x* 2
♥ *x x x*
♦ *x x x*
♣ *x x x*

Partner has seen only one card from your hand, yet can picture that you don't hold any five-card or longer suits and you hold exactly four spades.

Why? First, try to lead the ♠2 as the fourth highest from a five-card or longer suit. It can't be done. When you lead the ♠2, it shows specifically a four-card suit. Notice how partner can visualize your holding of exactly three cards in spades that are higher than the ♠2.

Second, since you've lead your longest suit against the notrump contract, you have no suit in your hand that is longer than your four-card spade suit. How quickly your hand starts to come into focus for partner.

Partner could draw the same conclusion even if the card you led was not the ♠2 but all the lower-ranking spades could be seen. For example, if you led the ♠4, and partner held the ♠2 and could see the ♠3 in dummy—or the ♠3 was played to the first trick by declarer—partner would know you'd led your lowest spade from a four-card suit.

Similarly, if you were to lead the ♥6—from a suit such as ♥ K 9 7 6 2—and later played the ♥2, partner would know you started with at least five cards in the suit. Your fourth highest card wasn't the lowest card you held in the suit.

Not all players pay that much attention to the low cards that are led by partner, but you can see that there is a wealth of potential information contained in that fourth highest lead. No wonder the whist players were able to take tricks effectively even without an auction or a dummy. Fourth highest leads also play a part in the rule of eleven which we'll come to in a later chapter.

Nowadays, some players prefer to lead the third highest or fifth highest card from long suits, or to lead the lowest-ranking card from their long suit against a notrump contract. Each of these leads has advantages and disadvantages, but you get the general idea. With nothing better to guide you, lead a low card from your longest and strongest suit against a notrump contract. If partner has bid a suit during the auction, or the opponents have bid your longest suit, then you do have some information to go on, and you can steer away from following the guideline.

Although fourth highest leads are most commonly used against notrump contracts, you would also lead your fourth highest card if you're leading a low card from a long suit against a trump contract.

For example, you would lead the ♦3 from ♦ Q 9 7 3 and the ♣4 from ♣ K 10 8 4 2.

2. Top of a Sequence

Suppose you decide that the best chance for defeating the contract is to promote winners in diamonds and this is your holding in the suit:

♦ K Q J 4

You have three cards in *sequence.* From your point of view, it doesn't much matter whether you lead the ♦K, ♦Q, or ♦J. They are all *equal honors.* Any one of them could serve the same purpose of driving out the ♦A. As a defender, you want to paint as clear a picture as possible of the cards you hold for partner's sake. The long-standing agreement is that you lead **the top card from a sequence.** Lead the ♦K. This lets partner know that you hold the next lower-ranking card, the ♦Q, but you don't hold the next higher-ranking card, the ♦A.

To see how useful this agreement is, suppose your partner leads the ♥Q against the opponents' contract of 3NT, and these are the hearts you can see:

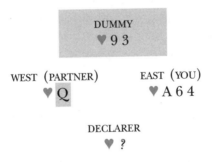

The lead of the ♥Q tells you that partner doesn't hold the ♥K, the next higher-ranking card. That wouldn't be much news if you could see the ♥K in the dummy or in your own hand. But here you can't, so declarer must hold that card. Partner's lead told you about one of the cards hidden in declarer's hand. Furthermore, you know that partner holds the ♥J, the next lower-ranking card, and probably the ♥10 as well. You can picture the complete layout of the heart suit as something like this:

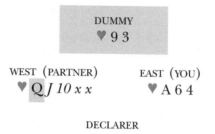

DUMMY
♥ 9 3

WEST (PARTNER) EAST (YOU)
♥ Q J 10 x x ♥ A 6 4

DECLARER
♥ K x x

You really are starting to see through the backs of the cards! The guideline of leading the top of a sequence is a very useful partnership agreement for the defenders.

So far, we've looked at only two guidelines, but it's easy to see how you might be faced with conflicting pieces of advice. Suppose you have to make the opening lead against a notrump contract from this holding:

♣ K Q J 7 2

Do you lead the top of a sequence, the ♣K, or fourth highest, the ♣7? There's no right answer; you have to visualize the possible layout of the club suit around the table. If you make the reasonable assumption that the remaining clubs are divided fairly evenly among the other three hands, it makes sense to lead the ♣K. For example, this might be the complete layout:

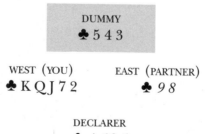

DUMMY
♣ 5 4 3

WEST (YOU) EAST (PARTNER)
♣ K Q J 7 2 ♣ 9 8

DECLARER
♣ A 10 6

If you were to lead the ♣7, fourth highest, declarer would win the first trick with the ♣10 and still have the ♣A left as a second trick in the suit. By leading the ♣K, you'll drive out declarer's ♣A, and will restrict declarer to one trick in the suit, since declarer's remaining clubs will fall under your ♣Q and ♣J.

If you have reason to suspect that declarer holds four or more clubs—perhaps declarer has bid the suit during the auction—it might well work out better to lead a low club. For example:

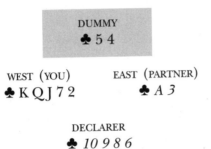

DUMMY
♣ 5 4

WEST (YOU)   EAST (PARTNER)
♣ K Q J 7 2   ♣ A 3

DECLARER
♣ 10 9 8 6

If you lead the ♣K in this situation, you won't be able to take your five club tricks right away. If partner plays the ♣3 on the first trick, the suit will be blocked. Partner can win the second trick with the ♣A, but will need to find an entry back to your hand so that you can take the rest of the club tricks. If, instead, you lead the ♣7, partner can win the first trick with the ♣A and lead back the ♣3. The defense can quickly take the first five tricks in the suit.

That's why there's no hard-and-fast rule to tell you what to do. You have to decide which guideline to follow based on the information you have available. The situation becomes even more challenging when you hold a *broken sequence* or an *interior sequence*. A broken sequence is one in which you have only two touching cards but are missing the next lower-ranking card although you do have the one after that. For example: ♥ K Q 10 7, ♥ Q J 9 6 4 2, or ♥ J 10 8 7 5. An interior sequence is one in which you hold a higher-ranking card that's not part of the sequence. For example: ♦ A Q J 10, ♦ K J 10 9 5, ♦ K 10 9 8.

Leading Against Notrump Contracts

With nothing much to go on, use the following approach when leading your long suit against a notrump contract:

- Lead the top of the touching cards from a three-card or longer sequence, a broken sequence, or an interior sequence (♣ J 10 9 6, ♣ Q J 9 4 2, ♣ A J 10 9 7); otherwise, lead fourth highest (♠ K 9 7 5̲ 2, ♠ A J 6 3̲, ♠ Q J 7 4̲ 3).

Leading Against Suit Contracts

When leading against a suit contract, there are some other considerations. It's usually not a good idea to lead a low card from a suit headed by the ace. Because of the effect of the trump suit, you may end up never getting a trick with your ace, even if you regain the lead. It's also less important to establish long suits through length. You often want to promote your winners as quickly as possible, before declarer has an opportunity to trump them. With nothing much to go on when leading against a suit contract, therefore, the following approach can be used when you've picked the suit you're going to lead:

- Lead the ace, if you hold it (♥ A̲ 8 6 4, ♥ A̲ Q J 7 3); lead the top of touching cards from a sequence headed by an honor (♦ K̲ Q 4, ♦ Q̲ J 8 6 2, ♦ J̲ 10 7 4); otherwise, lead fourth highest (♣ K J 7 5̲, ♣ Q 9 6 4̲ 2) or low from a three-card suit (♠ K 9 4̲, ♠ 10 8 3̲).

The lead of an ace against a suit contract can create confusion. It would be the top of a sequence if your suit is headed by both the ace and the king. But you might also lead an ace when you don't hold the king because, as one saying goes, you "never lead away from an ace against a suit contract." For this reason, players used to lead the king from a suit headed by the ace and king—so the lead of an ace specifically denied possession of the king. This practice, however, creates confusion when the king is led. Is it the top of a sequence headed by the king, or is it from a sequence that includes the ace? Most modern partnerships prefer to simplify the guideline by leading the top of a sequence—leading the ace from a sequence headed by the ace and king. Partner has to be aware that there may be times you'll lead an ace without the king—when you don't want to lead away from the ace and risk losing the sure trick.

Incidentally, the guideline about never leading away from an ace against a suit contract is just that, a guideline. It's usually a good rule to follow, since it might cost your side a trick, but there are always exceptions. Players occasionally underlead—lead away from—an ace, and it can often mislead even the best of declarers during the play of the hand. Of course, it may mislead partner as well, and therein lies some danger. But you should do what you think is best on any given hand.

The lead of a low card from a three-card suit (♠ K 9 <u>4</u>) could also create a misunderstanding. Naturally, you can't lead fourth highest when you only have three cards in the suit. Some partnerships prefer to lead the top of three cards when you don't hold an honor in the suit (♠ <u>8</u> 6 3). This is referred to as *top of nothing*. This can cause partner some confusion because you would also lead the top card from a doubleton (♠ <u>8</u> 3). Other partnerships prefer to lead the middle of three low cards (♠ 8 <u>6</u> 3), then follow by playing the higher card (♠8) and finally the lower card (♠3). This is referred to as *MUD*—Middle, Up, Down. It lets partner know you don't have a doubleton, but can still lead to confusion. If you want to keep things simple, I'd suggest you lead your lowest card from a three-card suit, whether or not it contains an honor. You'll have one less rule to remember.

3. Leading Partner's Suit

"Lead partner's suit," is a piece of advice that's designed to help you out when you have to make the opening lead. That's not such a bad idea. If partner has bid a suit during the auction, then that's a clue. It's reasonable to expect partner to have some length and strength in the suit, so unless you have something else that is clearly better to lead, why not work with partner to develop tricks in a suit you both know something about?

Many players feel that leading partner's suit is also a safe lead in that you can hardly be blamed if it doesn't work out well. If partner didn't want the suit led, why bid it? If you choose not to lead partner's suit, and it turns out that leading partner's suit would have defeated the contract, you may feel some remorse. Of course, that shouldn't be the deciding factor. You should be trying to visualize the cards you can't see, and put that together with what you can see, when making your decision. As an example, consider the following hands that you might hold after the auction goes like this:

WEST	NORTH	EAST	SOUTH
(YOU)		(PARTNER)	
	1♦	1♥	1NT
Pass	3NT	Pass	Pass
Pass			

♠ Q 9 7 6 5 3
♥ 10 6
♦ 7 5
♣ J 8 2

Although your best suit is spades, it makes more sense to lead a heart from this hand. You'd need a lot of help from partner to establish winners in your spade suit, and even then there's no sure entry to your hand so that you could take your winners. Partner's overcall should show a decent five-card or longer heart suit, and partner may have some other high cards as well. Leading a heart should help partner establish some winners in that suit, and partner may be able to regain the lead holding one or two high cards in the other suits.

♠ 9 6 4 2
♥ 5
♦ A 7 3
♣ K Q J 9 4

With this hand, it makes more sense to lead the ♣K. Hopefully, you can drive out the ♣A and establish four winners in the suit. Your ♦A will be an entry to allow you to take your established winners. There's no guarantee. Even after the ♣A is driven out, you may only be able to take your two club winners if one of the opponents has length in the club suit, but it's certainly a more reasonable attempt than automatically leading partner's suit.

Since you may not have much length in partner's suit when you lead it, use the following guidelines:

- Lead the top card from a doubleton (♥ <u>10</u> 6, ♥ <u>K</u> 4); lead the top of touching honors (♦ <u>Q</u> J 6, ♦ <u>J</u> 10 4 2); otherwise, lead low (♣ K 6 5 <u>4</u>, ♣ Q 7 <u>3</u>, ♣ 10 6 <u>2</u>).

If partner leads a suit and you subsequently win a trick, another popular piece of advice is to "return partner's suit." Again, this is generally good advice. The defenders don't want to work at cross-purposes.

In the first chapter, there was an example of a hand that could be defeated if you led your longest suit and both partners continued leading the suit at every opportunity. It could also be defeated after the lead of partner's longest suit provided you kept leading the same suit. The contract couldn't be defeated if you each tried to establish your own suit. That's the idea. Partner's opening lead has set the defense along a path. Unless you can clearly see a better route, it's best not to keep switching tactics.

Returning partner's suit is a guideline, not a command. Partner made the opening lead with something in mind, but you'll have more information available once the dummy is placed face up on the table and you see all the cards played to the first trick. You'll have a clearer image of the cards in partner's hand than partner had of the cards in your hand when making the opening lead. It may be easier for you to see a better opportunity to defeat the contract by switching to another suit when you gain the lead.

If you're returning partner's suit, you lead back the same card you would normally lead from your remaining holding in the suit. For example, suppose you hold ♥ A 7 3, partner leads a low heart, and you win the first trick with your ♥A. Lead back the ♥7, top of a doubleton, from your remaining ♥ 7 3. If you originally held ♥ A 7 3 2, you would return the ♥2, low from your three remaining cards, ♥ 7 3 2.

4. Lead Through Strength

"Lead through strength and up to weakness" is an expression you may have heard from other bridge players. The theory behind this statement can be seen in the following layout:

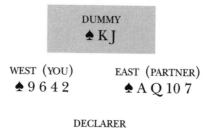

DUMMY
♠ K J

WEST (YOU) EAST (PARTNER)
♠ 9 6 4 2   ♠ A Q 10 7

DECLARER
♠ 8 5 3

The opponents strength in the spade suit is in the dummy, and the weakness is in declarer's hand. For the defenders to get all the tricks to which they are entitled in this situation, it's important that you lead the suit for your side. You lead a spade through the strength in the dummy, up to the weakness in declarer's hand. When you lead a spade, it doesn't matter which spade declarer plays from the dummy; partner can win the trick and your side takes all the spade tricks. Essentially, your side is cooperating in taking a finesse.

It wouldn't be as effective if partner had to lead this suit for your side. Partner would be leading through the weakness in declarer's hand up to the strength in dummy. Whichever spade partner leads, declarer will get a trick with one of dummy's high cards.

Here's an example of this principle at work in a complete hand. The opponents reach a contract of 4♠, and your partner leads the ♥4.

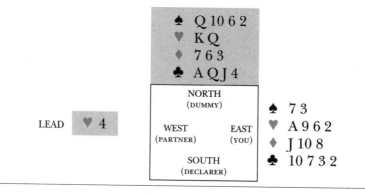

♠ Q 10 6 2
♥ K Q
♦ 7 6 3
♣ A Q J 4

NORTH
(DUMMY)

LEAD ♥ 4

WEST EAST
(PARTNER) (YOU)

SOUTH
(DECLARER)

♠ 7 3
♥ A 9 6 2
♦ J 10 8
♣ 10 7 3 2

Declarer plays the ♥Q from dummy and you win the first trick with the ♥A. One of your guidelines is to return partner's suit. That doesn't look as though it would be very effective on this hand. Partner didn't lead a diamond originally, so partner probably doesn't have a strong sequence such as ♦ A K Q. Declarer probably holds at least one of those cards. Nonetheless, if you're going to defeat this contract, it looks as though you'll need to take some tricks in the diamond suit. Looking at the weak diamonds in dummy, you have an opportunity to lead through declarer's assumed strength, up to the weakness in dummy. You switch to the ♦J, top of your touching honors, and this is the complete hand:

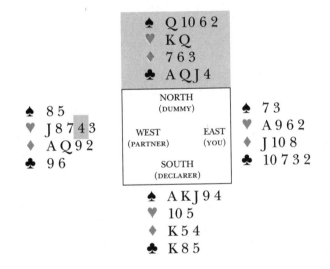

```
                  ♠ Q 10 6 2
                  ♥ K Q
                  ♦ 7 6 3
                  ♣ A Q J 4
                      NORTH
  ♠ 8 5             (DUMMY)        ♠ 7 3
  ♥ J 8 7 4 3                      ♥ A 9 6 2
  ♦ A Q 9 2    WEST      EAST      ♦ J 10 8
  ♣ 9 6      (PARTNER)   (YOU)     ♣ 10 7 3 2
                      SOUTH
                    (DECLARER)
                  ♠ A K J 9 4
                  ♥ 10 5
                  ♦ K 5 4
                  ♣ K 8 5
```

When you return a diamond, declarer's ♦K is trapped, and the defense can take three diamond tricks to go along with the ♥A. That defeats the contract. Had you led anything except a diamond, declarer would win the trick and make the contract, taking five spade tricks, a heart trick, and four club tricks.

Notice how partner found the only lead to defeat the contract. A diamond lead from partner's side would not have worked. Declarer would get a trick with the ♦K. Partner suspected that you might not hold the ♦K, but hoped that you would switch to that suit if necessary. Only good cooperation between the partners will defeat contracts such as this.

Summary

Four guidelines commonly used to help decide which suit to lead are:

- Fourth highest from your longest and strongest.
- Top of a sequence.
- Lead/return partner's suit.
- Lead through strength and up to weakness.

Having chosen the suit, chose the card within the suit as follows:

- When leading your long suit against a notrump contract:
  - Lead the top of the touching cards from a three-card or longer sequence, a broken sequence, or an interior sequence (♣ J 10 9 6, ♣ Q J 9 4 2, ♣ A J 10 9 7).
  - Otherwise, lead fourth highest (♠ K 9 7 <u>5</u> 2, ♠ A J 6 <u>3</u>, ♠ Q J 7 <u>4</u> 3).

- When leading against a suit contract:
  - Lead the ace, if you hold it (♥ <u>A</u> 8 6 4, ♥ <u>A</u> Q J 7 3).
  - Lead the top of touching cards from a sequence headed by an honor (♦ <u>K</u> Q 4, ♦ <u>Q</u> J 8 6 2, ♦ <u>J</u> 10 7 4).
  - Otherwise, lead fourth highest (♣ K J 7 <u>5</u>, ♣ Q 9 6 <u>4</u> 2) or low from a three-card suit (♠ K 9 <u>4</u>, ♠ 10 8 <u>3</u>).

- When leading partner's suit:
  - Lead the top card from a doubleton (♥ <u>10</u> 6, ♥ <u>K</u> 4).
  - Lead the top of touching honors (♦ <u>Q</u> J 6, ♦ <u>J</u> 10 4 2).
  - Otherwise, lead low (♣ K 6 5 <u>4</u>, ♣ Q 7 <u>3</u>, ♣ 10 6 <u>2</u>).

The guidelines are no substitute for common sense. They will often provide you with conflicting advice, and you'll have to decide for yourself the best course of action after trying to visualize the cards in the unseen hands.

Practice Hands

Hand 2.1

	NORTH (DUMMY)	
WEST (YOU)		EAST (PARTNER)
	SOUTH (DECLARER)	

♠ A Q 7
♥ Q J 3
♦ Q 10 8 6 3
♣ 6 2

WEST	NORTH	EAST	SOUTH
	Pass	Pass	1NT
Pass	3NT	Pass	Pass
Pass			

You have to find a lead against South's 3NT contract. Which suit do you plan to lead? Why? Which card do you plan to lead?

Solution 2.1

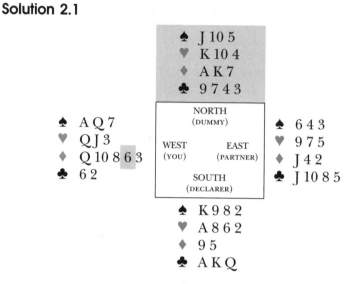

Partner can't have too much. You have 11 high card points, and the opponents should have at least 26 to bid a game. Leading top of touching cards is often a good idea, but leading the ♥Q on this hand is unlikely to be effective. Even if partner has length in hearts, it's doubtful partner also has an entry with which to take any winners that might be established.

Although most of your strength lies in the spade suit, it's better to fall back on the tried and true formula of leading fourth highest from your longest suit. Your long suit is diamonds, and the fourth highest card is the ♦6, so that's the lead you make. Here it works like a charm. Partner has very little, but just enough to help you out. Declarer has seven sure tricks and will try to develop two extra tricks from the spade suit. After winning a diamond trick, declarer will probably lead the ♠J from dummy and try the finesse, hoping East holds the ♠Q. The finesse loses, and you win the trick. Another diamond lead drives out declarer's remaining high diamond. When you get a trick with your ♣A, you can take your established diamond winners to defeat the contract.

A lead of the ♥Q would have been instantly fatal. Declarer could win with the ♥A, lead a low heart toward dummy, and finesse dummy's ♥10. When this wins and the hearts divide 3–3, declarer has nine tricks: four hearts, two diamonds, and three clubs. That's one of the dangers in leading the top of a two-card sequence against a notrump contract, especially from a short suit.

Hand 2.2

```
          ┌─────────────────────┐
♠  10 6 4 │       NORTH         │
          │      (DUMMY)        │
♥  10 3   │                     │
          │ WEST        EAST    │
♦  J 10 9 6 4 (YOU)     (PARTNER)│
          │                     │
♣  8 7 2  │      SOUTH          │
          │    (DECLARER)       │
          └─────────────────────┘
```

WEST	NORTH	EAST	SOUTH
		1♥	1♠
Pass	4♠	Pass	Pass
Pass			

You don't have much of a hand, but it's up to you to find the best opening lead for your side. Are there any clues? What card do you lead? Are there any cards in your hand with which you expect to win a trick?

Solution 2.2

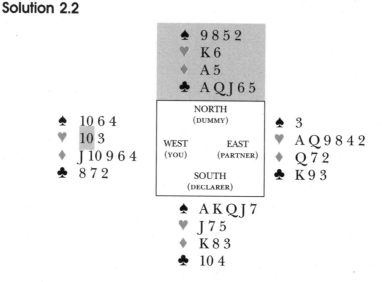

```
                    ♠ 9 8 5 2
                    ♥ K 6
                    ♦ A 5
                    ♣ A Q J 6 5
                       NORTH
                       (DUMMY)
♠ 10 6 4                                  ♠ 3
♥ 10 3         WEST          EAST          ♥ A Q 9 8 4 2
♦ J 10 9 6 4   (YOU)        (PARTNER)      ♦ Q 7 2
♣ 8 7 2                                    ♣ K 9 3
                      SOUTH
                    (DECLARER)
                    ♠ A K Q J 7
                    ♥ J 7 5
                    ♦ K 8 3
                    ♣ 10 4
```

This is an interesting hand. Although difficult to see at first, the contract can be defeated thanks to your ♠10. That's only if you get off to the right start. Although it's tempting to lead the top of your sequence in diamonds, first listen to the auction for any clues. Partner opened the bidding 1♥, and a useful piece of advice is to lead partner's suit unless there's clearly something better to do. Since it's not easy to see how leading a diamond will defeat the contract, fall back to the guidelines and lead a heart. With a doubleton in partner's suit, lead the top card, the ♥10.

Let's see how this works out. With the ♥K in dummy, you're off to a good start. If declarer chooses to play a low heart from dummy, partner will know to play the ♥Q to win the trick. If you held the ♥J, you would have led it as the top card in a sequence. If you don't have it, declarer must have it. After winning the first trick, partner has to decide what to do next. Partner can count on two heart tricks and likely a third trick with the ♣K. A fourth trick could be promoted if you have the ♦K, and partner might consider leading that suit. But your lead might give partner a better idea. As long as you have only two hearts, all you need is a spade higher than dummy's ♠9 to defeat the contract. Partner can take the first two heart tricks and lead a third round of the suit. Declarer plays the ♥J on the third round, and you get to trump with the ♠10. There's nothing declarer can do. Partner eventually gets a trick with the ♣K, and the contract is defeated.

Hand 2.3

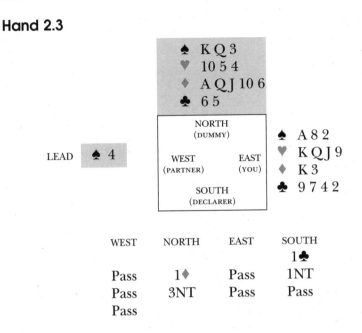

			♠ K Q 3
			♥ 10 5 4
			♦ A Q J 10 6
			♣ 6 5

	NORTH (DUMMY)	
LEAD ♠ 4	WEST (PARTNER)	EAST (YOU)
	SOUTH (DECLARER)	

♠ A 8 2
♥ K Q J 9
♦ K 3
♣ 9 7 4 2

WEST	NORTH	EAST	SOUTH
			1♣
Pass	1♦	Pass	1NT
Pass	3NT	Pass	Pass
Pass			

Partner leads the ♠4 against South's 3NT contract, and declarer plays dummy's ♠Q on this first trick. After winning this trick with the ♠A, what do you intend to do next? How many spades does partner have?

Solution 2.3

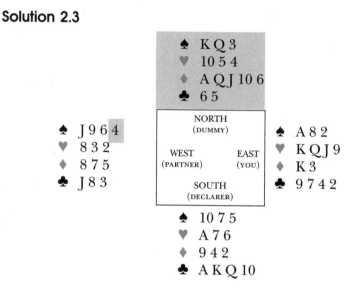

```
              ♠ K Q 3
              ♥ 10 5 4
              ♦ A Q J 10 6
              ♣ 6 5
                    NORTH
                   (DUMMY)
♠ J 9 6 4                            ♠ A 8 2
♥ 8 3 2        WEST      EAST        ♥ K Q J 9
♦ 8 7 5       (PARTNER)  (YOU)       ♦ K 3
♣ J 8 3                              ♣ 9 7 4 2
                    SOUTH
                 (DECLARER)
              ♠ 10 7 5
              ♥ A 7 6
              ♦ 9 4 2
              ♣ A K Q 10
```

When partner leads a suit and you win a trick, the guideline is to return partner's suit. It's only a guideline, however, so take a moment to visualize the hidden hands. You have several clues: the auction, the opening lead, the cards in dummy, and the cards in your hand. The auction tells you partner doesn't have much. Partner's lead is likely fourth highest from longest and strongest. Obviously, partner doesn't have much strength in the suit, since you can see the ♠A, ♠K, and ♠Q. Less obviously, partner started with only four cards in the suit. Partner led the ♠4. You can see the ♠3 in dummy and the ♠2 in your hand. That leaves partner with only the three cards that are higher than the ♠4.

If you return a spade, you may be able to help partner develop two winners in the suit—as is the case on the actual hand—but that won't be enough to defeat the contract. Looking at your hand and the dummy, you can see that declarer is likely to play diamonds to establish extra winners. You'll get a trick with the ♦K to go along with the three tricks you establish in spades, but that's all for your side. By then, declarer will have the nine tricks needed for the contract. There's a clear alternative to returning partner's suit. After winning the ♠A, switch to hearts, leading the ♥K, to drive out the ♥A. Even if declarer doesn't win the first trick, keep leading high hearts until the ♥A is gone. You develop three winners in the suit to go along with the trick already won with the ♠A. When you get a trick with your ♦K, that'll be enough to sink the contract.

Hand 2.4

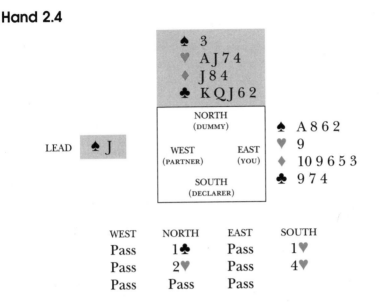

WEST	NORTH	EAST	SOUTH
Pass	1♣	Pass	1♥
Pass	2♥	Pass	4♥
Pass	Pass	Pass	

The contract is 4♥, and you're sitting in the East position. Partner makes an opening lead of the ♠J. How do you visualize the layout of the spade suit? Where are your side's tricks likely to come from? How do you plan to defend?

Solution 2.4

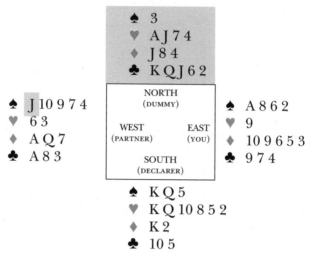

```
                    ♠ 3
                    ♥ A J 7 4
                    ♦ J 8 4
                    ♣ K Q J 6 2
                    NORTH
                    (DUMMY)
♠ J 10 9 7 4                              ♠ A 8 6 2
♥ 6 3         WEST         EAST           ♥ 9
♦ A Q 7     (PARTNER)     (YOU)           ♦ 10 9 6 5 3
♣ A 8 3                                   ♣ 9 7 4
                    SOUTH
                    (DECLARER)
                    ♠ K Q 5
                    ♥ K Q 10 8 5 2
                    ♦ K 2
                    ♣ 10 5
```

Partner's lead of the ♠J is likely the top of a sequence. Partner will have the next lower-ranking card, the ♠10, but not the next higher ranking card, the ♠Q. Partner could hold the ♠K, if partner were leading top from an interior sequence, such as ♠ K J 10 9. It's likely that declarer holds that card as well. Even if partner does hold the ♠K, it won't do the defense much good because of the singleton spade in the dummy. You have one sure trick in spades. It's unlikely your side has any heart tricks. If partner holds the ♥K or ♥Q, declarer can avoid losing a heart trick by taking a finesse. You'll need partner to hold some strength in diamonds, and hopefully the ♣A as well, if you're to defeat the contract.

Partner is unlikely to hold a strong sequence in diamonds, such as the ♦A K; otherwise, partner might have led a high diamond originally. Diamonds may be such that partner can't lead the suit without giving up a trick. Win the first trick with the ♣A, and lead back a diamond. You're leading through whatever strength declarer has in diamonds and up to dummy's weakness. If you were to lead back a club, that would be into dummy's strength. On the actual hand, a diamond lead from your side defeats the contract. Partner wins two diamond tricks with the ♦A and ♦Q, since declarer's ♦K is trapped, and takes the setting trick with the ♣A. If you don't lead back a diamond, declarer makes the contract. Partner can't do anything but take two tricks, one with the ♦A and one with the ♣A. A diamond lead from partner's side would let declarer win a trick with the ♦K.

The Top Ten List
Part II

"If we would guide by the light of reason, we must let our minds be bold."

—JUSTICE LOUIS DEMBITZ BRANDEIS,
[1932]

It's not only deciding which suit to lead and which card to lead that presents a challenge on defense. You frequently have to decide which card to play to a trick when declarer or partner has led the suit. Once again, there are many sayings that have been passed down to guide you along the path. This chapter presents six of them to add to your top ten list.

The sayings are only a guide, since there are many situations in which more than one piece of advice seems to apply. By understanding the principles behind the catchphrases, you can decide for yourself whether or not it's a good time to follow a particular adage.

5. Second Hand Low

"Second hand plays low to a trick" is a well-known expression dating from the days of whist. It has its merits. Here's a typical situation. Declarer leads a low heart toward dummy's ♥Q, and you have to decide which card to play in this situation:

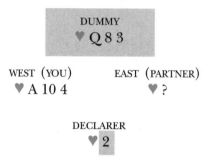

You can get a sure trick by playing your ♥A, you can play the ♥10 to force declarer to play dummy's ♥Q, or you can play the ♥4, and wait to see which card declarer plays from the dummy. The guideline suggests that, as the second player to the trick, you should play the ♥4—second hand low. It's only a guideline, and if you can see that by playing your ♥A you will be able to defeat the contract, you should ignore the guideline and take your trick. If you're not sure what to do, however, the guideline is there to help you out.

The principle behind playing a low card in this position is that you don't want to use a high card, such as the ace, to capture only low cards from the opponents. You'd prefer to wait and capture a big card, such as the king, with your ace. Also, partner plays last to the trick, so there's no need for you to go out of your way to win the trick. Let declarer make the decision about which card to play next, before partner has to chose a card to play.

The complete layout of the heart suit might be something like this:

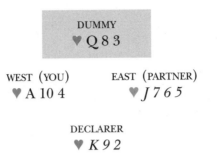

If you hop up with your ♥A when declarer leads the ♥2 toward dummy, declarer will play the ♥3 and later get two tricks from the suit—one with the ♥K and one with the ♥Q. If, instead, you play low, the ♥4, declarer will have to play dummy's ♥Q to win the trick, leaving the following cards in the suit:

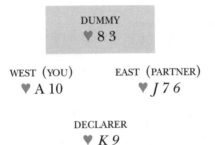

Now declarer won't be able to get a second trick from the suit—as long as the defenders are careful—because your ♥A is poised to capture declarer's ♥K.

Notice that it also wouldn't be a good idea to sacrifice your ♥10 on the first round of the suit because that would leave the following cards after declarer wins the trick with dummy's ♥Q:

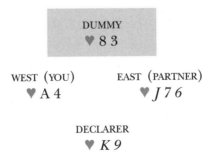

Declarer could now lead a low heart from dummy and finesse the ♥9, forcing you to win the trick with the ♥A. Again declarer would end up with two tricks in the suit. So, low means low.

Would playing second hand low have made any difference if partner held the ♥K, rather than declarer? It might if this were the complete layout:

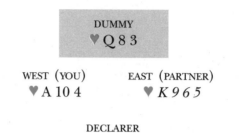

DUMMY
♥ Q 8 3

WEST (YOU)   EAST (PARTNER)
♥ A 10 4   ♥ K 9 6 5

DECLARER
♥ J 7 2

If you play the ♥A on the first round of the suit, declarer will have the ♥Q and ♥J left, which can be used to promote a trick in the suit. By playing second hand low, partner can capture dummy's ♥Q with the ♥K. Your remaining hearts will prevent declarer from taking any tricks in the suit.

The concept of second hand low applies whether declarer is leading toward dummy or from the dummy. In the last layout, if declarer were to start the suit by leading the ♥3 from dummy, partner should follow the principle of second hand low and play a low heart rather than the ♥K. This will prevent declarer from taking any tricks in the suit.

There are lots of exceptions—and we'll come across some of them later on—but when you're not sure about the exact location of the high cards that you can't see, second hand low is a useful piece of advice.

6. Third Hand High

The concept of "third hand high" is similar to that of "second hand low." When you're playing the third card to a trick, it's the last chance for your side to win the trick. You usually want to give it your best effort. A typical situation is the following. Suppose your partner leads a low diamond against declarer's notrump contract, and these are the diamonds that you can see:

When declarer plays a low diamond from dummy, you have to decide which card to play. You can't see the other high cards in either partner's hand or declarer's hand, although you might be able to visualize that both of them hold some of the unseen cards. With nothing else to guide you, the best choice is the ♦K—third hand high—attempting to win the trick for your side.

The reasoning behind this play is that the full layout might be something like this:

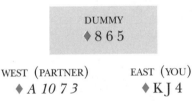

If you play the ♦4, or make a half-hearted attempt to win the trick by playing the ♦J, declarer will be able to win a trick. By playing the ♦K, you win the trick. You can now return the ♦J—leading the top card from your remaining doubleton—and declarer's ♦Q is trapped. Whether or not declarer plays the ♦Q on this trick, your side will take the first four tricks.

What if declarer held the ♦A and partner held the ♦Q?

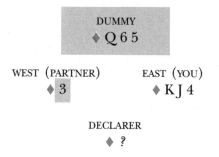

DUMMY
♦ 8 6 5

WEST (PARTNER)   EAST (YOU)
♦ Q 10 7 3   ♦ K J 4

DECLARER
♦ A 9 2

Playing the ♦K does no harm. It promotes partner's ♦Q into a winner, and your side will later be able to get three tricks in the suit. You're protecting your side's interests by playing third hand high.

There are as many exceptions to third hand high as there are to second hand low. For example, you usually won't want to play a high card if the card partner led is already going to win the trick. Or suppose we modified our earlier layout:

DUMMY
♦ Q 6 5

WEST (PARTNER)   EAST (YOU)
♦ 3   ♦ K J 4

DECLARER
♦ ?

If a low card is played from dummy, you would only need to insert the ♦J, to try to win the trick. If partner has the ♦A, your ♦J will win. If declarer has the ♦A, your ♦J will make declarer play the ♦A to win the trick, and you'll still have the ♦K poised nicely over dummy's ♦Q.

We'll look at other exceptions to third hand high in the upcoming chapters, but it's a useful guideline when you're not sure what else to do.

7. Cover an Honor

The expression "cover an honor with an honor" can be illustrated by considering this layout:

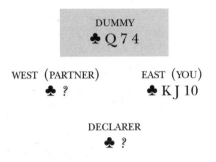

If declarer were to lead the ♣Q from dummy, you would cover an honor with an honor by playing the ♣K. That's easy enough to see here, because if declarer wins the trick with the ♣A, your ♣J and ♣10 will be promoted into winners. That's the idea of covering. You make declarer use up two high cards while you play only one, and you promote the lower-ranking cards in the suit into winners for your side.

The situation is a little more complicated when you can't see the lower-ranking cards that are about to be promoted. For example:

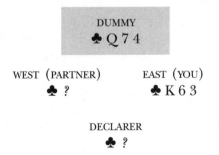

Now when declarer leads the ♣Q is it still worthwhile to cover with the ♣K? The guideline says yes, if there's any hope of promoting winners for your side. You need to visualize the cards your partner could hold in the suit. If you're an optimist, you might picture something like this:

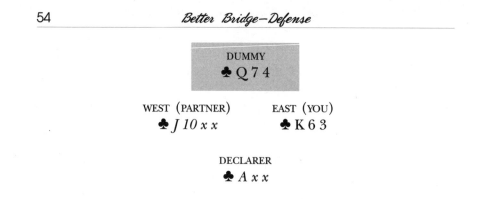

By covering the ♣Q with the ♣K, you force declarer to play the ♣A and promote both partner's ♣J and ♣10 into tricks. You don't have to be that optimistic, however. Something like this would be enough:

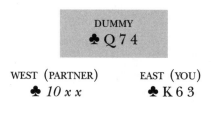

When you cover the ♣Q, declarer can win the trick with the ♣A and take a second trick with the ♣J. But now partner's ♣10 has been promoted into the highest remaining club. If you didn't cover, declarer would win the first trick and could then lead a low club from dummy and finesse the ♣J. When declarer plays the ♣A, your ♣K falls, and declarer takes all four tricks in the suit.

There's no point in covering if it's apparent that there's nothing to promote in partner's hand. That might be the case if declarer had bid clubs several times during the auction and was known to have six or seven of them. Or the cards you can see might be something like this:

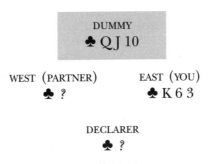

DUMMY
♣ Q J 10

WEST (PARTNER)   EAST (YOU)
♣ ?   ♣ K 6 3

DECLARER
♣ ?

Here there's no point in covering the ♣Q, since the only cards that will be promoted are dummy's ♣J and ♣10.

As you may have noticed, you can't rely on the guidelines by themselves. Covering an honor with an honor conflicts with the guideline of second hand low. You'll have to look at each situation and decide which guideline best applies. Hopefully, the discussions throughout this book will help to clarify most of the situations.

8. High Cards Encourage

A useful device for the defenders is the use of *signals*. You've already seen some types of signals. The lead of the top of touching high cards is a form of signal, since it shows partner that you hold the next lower-ranking card but not the next higher-ranking card. The lead of your fourth highest card is another form of signal. Another very important signal is the *attitude signal*.

An attitude signal is used to tell partner whether or not you like a specific suit. The general agreement is that **high cards encourage and low cards discourage**. This is typically used in this type of situation:

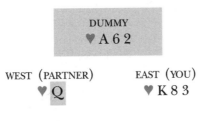

DUMMY
♥ A 6 2

WEST (PARTNER)   EAST (YOU)
♥ Q   ♥ K 8 3

DECLARER

Partner leads the ♥Q against a notrump contract and declarer wins the first trick with dummy's ♥A. You don't need to play your ♥K, but you do have a choice between playing the ♥8 or the ♥3. When you have such a choice, you play a high card to encourage partner to continue leading the suit, and you play a low card to discourage partner from leading the suit again. Here, you would play the ♥8, an encouraging card. You picture the complete layout of the heart suit to be something like this:

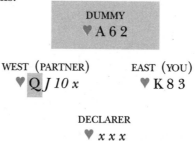

DUMMY
♥ A 6 2

WEST (PARTNER)   EAST (YOU)
♥ Q J 10 x   ♥ K 8 3

DECLARER
♥ x x x

Partner has led the top of a sequence and you have an honor of equal value. If partner regains the lead, you want partner to lead a low card to your ♥K, so that you can lead your remaining heart back to partner's remaining winners.

Unless you could see something better to do, you'd also encourage partner in this situation if you held the ♥10. You'd picture the complete layout to be something like this:

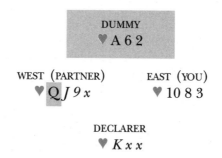

DUMMY
♥ A 6 2

WEST (PARTNER)   EAST (YOU)
♥ Q J 9 x   ♥ 10 8 3

DECLARER
♥ K x x

After partner leads the ♥Q, declarer may win the first trick with dummy's ♥A or plays a low heart from dummy intending to win the trick with the ♥K. In either case, you could encourage by playing the ♥8 to let partner know that it's safe to continue leading the suit to try to promote winners.

Contrast the above layout with this one:

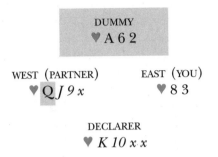

DUMMY
♥ A 6 2

WEST (PARTNER)   EAST (YOU)
♥ Q J 9 x   ♥ 8 3

DECLARER
♥ K 10 x x

Now you'd play the ♥3, your lowest heart, discouraging partner from leading hearts again because you have no help in the suit. Your signal is a suggestion, not a command. If partner holds a solid sequence, there's nothing to stop partner from continuing to lead the suit if that seems best. For example:

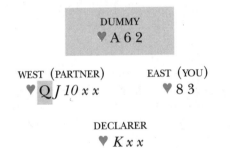

DUMMY
♥ A 6 2

WEST (PARTNER)   EAST (YOU)
♥ Q J 10 x x   ♥ 8 3

DECLARER
♥ K x x

Your discouraging card simply tells partner not to expect an equal honor from you to help establish the suit.

Attitude signals are not always clear-cut, since you may not have a choice between a high card and a low card. Suppose this is the situation:

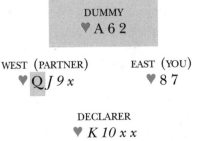

DUMMY
♥ A 6 2

WEST (PARTNER)   EAST (YOU)
♥ Q J 9 x   ♥ 8 7

DECLARER
♥ K 10 x x

You want to discourage partner, but your lowest card is the ♥7. That's the best you can do. Partner may be able to see all the other low cards and realize that you're giving a discouraging signal. If not, perhaps you'll get the lead next and be able to clarify the situation.

You can also use attitude signals when discarding. If you discard a high card in a suit, you're suggesting that you have some strength in that suit. If you discard a low card, you're suggesting the opposite. There are many uses for attitude signals, and we'll see lots of examples throughout the book.

9. High-Low to Show an Even Number

Another popular signal for the defenders is the *count signal*. The guideline used in this situation is that **high-low shows an even number; low-high shows an odd number**. The interpretation of this statement is that you can play a high card followed by a low card to show an even number of cards in a suit, such as two, four, or six. If you play a low card in a suit followed by a higher-ranking card, you're showing an odd number of cards, such as three or five.

Right away there's all sorts of possibility for confusion, since you've just seen that high cards are used to show encouragement and low cards for discouragement. Is a high card played by partner an encouraging signal or the start of a high-low signal to show an even number of cards in the suit? Hard to say. The defenders need to agree on the situations that call for attitude signals versus those that call for count signals.

Although some partnerships prefer to use attitude signals all the time and other partnerships rely solely on count signals—to avoid any possible confusion—most experienced partnerships can distinguish the type of signal required. When starting out, I'd suggest that you focus primarily on attitude signals, but there is one circumstance in which count signals can be very important.

The situation involves holding up a winner when trying to prevent declarer from taking too many tricks in a long suit. The typical case is when declarer is trying to promote winners from dummy's long suit and dummy has no entry outside the suit itself. If one of the defenders holds the ace of the suit, deciding when to play it can be important. To see an example, let's consider a complete hand.

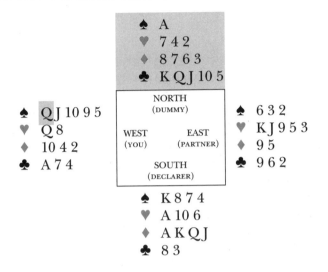

Declarer is in a contract of 3NT, and you start off by leading the
♠Q, top of a sequence in your long suit. The first trick is won with
dummy's ♠A, and partner plays the ♠2. This isn't a count signal from
partner. Partner is merely making a discouraging signal. Declarer now
leads the ♣K from dummy, and you have to decide whether or not to
win the trick with your ♣A.

If you win the first trick with the ♣A, declarer will make the contract. Declarer will end up with two spade tricks, one heart trick,
four diamond tricks, and four club tricks, for a total of eleven tricks.

Suppose you wait to win your ♣A until the third round of the suit.
Again, declarer will make the contract, even though dummy's remaining club winners are stranded. Declarer will get two spade tricks,
one heart trick, four diamond tricks, and two club tricks.

To defeat the contract, you need to take your ♣A on exactly the
second round of the suit. Declarer will then have no clubs remaining, and dummy's established clubs will be stranded. Declarer will
get two spade tricks, one heart trick, four diamond tricks, and only
one club trick. That's one trick short of the contract.

How are you to know whether to win the first, second, or third
round of clubs? You need to know exactly how many clubs declarer
holds, so that you can win the ♣A on the same trick that declarer
runs out of clubs. This is where a count signal can be useful. Partner
obviously has no interest in the club suit, so there's no purpose in
giving an encouraging or discouraging signal. Instead, partner can

give a count signal. On the first round of clubs, partner plays the ♣2, the start of a low-high signal indicating an odd number of clubs. When declarer follows suit to the first round of clubs, the only possible "odd" holdings partner could have are a singleton, or a three-card suit. That leaves declarer with either two clubs or four clubs. If declarer has four clubs, it won't matter when you take your ♣A, so you wait and see. On the next round, partner follows with the high part of the signal, confirming an original holding of three cards. That let's you work out that declarer must have started with exactly two clubs, and it's safe for you to win the second round. Dummy's club winners will now be stranded.

Had partner started with two clubs, partner would play the high club on the first round and the low club on the second round. Now you'd have to wait until the third round of the suit to take your ♣A, because declarer would have started with three cards in the suit. You'd have to hope that restricting declarer to two tricks in the club suit would be enough to defeat the contract.

You'll see other uses for the count signal later on.

10. Throw Losers, Keep Winners

The last guideline is "throw losers, keep winners." This is advice for those situations in which you have to make one or more discards, usually when declarer is taking tricks. The advice seems to go without saying—you obviously want to hold on to your winning tricks—but it's sometimes not so easy to tell your winners from your losers.

A typical situation is the following. These are the remaining cards you can see in a notrump contract, and declarer is in the dummy:

DUMMY
♥ A K Q 3
♦ A

WEST (PARTNER)   EAST (YOU)
                        ♥ J 8 4 2
                        ♣ A

DECLARER

The ♦A is led from dummy, and you need to find a discard. Your ♣A appears to be a winner, and your ♥2 appears to be a loser. Nonetheless, you need to discard the ♣A and hold on tightly to the ♥2. The reason is that the next three cards played from dummy will be the ♥A, ♥K, and ♥Q. The ♥3 will be the last card left in the dummy. If you don't have the ♥J left, dummy's ♥3 will win the last trick unless partner started with at least four hearts. You'll be helplessly discarding your ♣A on dummy's ♥3. See what's coming and discard the ♣A when the ♦A is led from dummy. You'll win the last trick with your ♥J.

Even though it hurts to throw away an ace in the above situation, you can figure out what's going to happen if you don't. The situation can be much more challenging if the remaining cards look something like this:

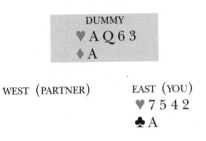

DUMMY
♥ A Q 6 3
♦ A

WEST (PARTNER)   EAST (YOU)
                      ♥ 7 5 4 2
                      ♣ A

DECLARER

When the ♦A is led from dummy, it's far more difficult to see that discarding the ♣A may be the only way to prevent declarer from taking the rest of the tricks. If you're sure that declarer, rather than partner, holds the ♥K, then that's exactly what you have to do. The complete layout might be something like this:

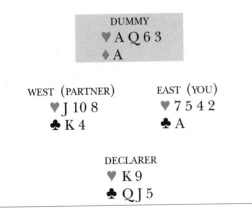

DUMMY
♥ A Q 6 3
♦ A

WEST (PARTNER)   EAST (YOU)
♥ J 10 8   ♥ 7 5 4 2
♣ K 4   ♣ A

DECLARER
♥ K 9
♣ Q J 5

If you discard your low heart on the ♦A, declarer will play a low heart to the ♥K and then lead the ♥9 back to dummy's ♥A and ♥Q. Dummy's ♥6 will win the last trick. Instead, you'll have to discard your ♣A, hoping partner can prevent declarer from winning a trick in that suit. When declarer then takes the next three heart tricks, your ♥7 will just beat out dummy's ♥6 for the last trick.

How are you going to know to do all this? Often you won't. Many contracts are made when the defenders don't hold on to exactly the right cards. The defenders have to work closely together and use their attitude and count signals to tell each other about their holdings in the suit. Frequently, only one defender can *guard* against declarer taking all the tricks in a particular suit, as in the above situation. That defender will have to carefully hold on to the suit, leaving partner to guard the other suits.

Throw losers and keep winners is good advice, but only if you can visualize the unseen cards well enough to know which are which.

Summary

Some useful pieces of advice to help decide which card to play to a trick are contained in the following sayings:

- Second hand low.
- Third hand high.
- Cover an honor with an honor.
- High cards encourage; low cards discourage.
- High-low shows an even number of cards; low-high shows an odd number.
- Keep winners and throw losers when discarding.

Each of these guidelines is based on some sound principles of defense. Nonetheless, you need to understand the basis of each, so that you will know when they apply. There's no substitute for thinking about each situation based on the clues that are available.

Practice Hands

Hand 3.1

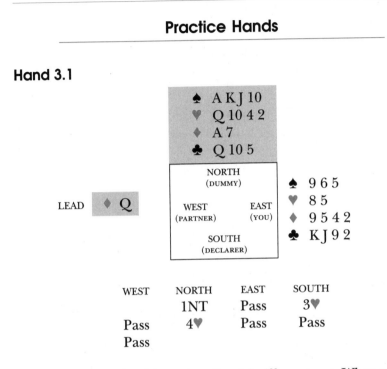

♠ A K J 10
♥ Q 10 4 2
♦ A 7
♣ Q 10 5

NORTH
(DUMMY)

♠ 9 6 5
♥ 8 5
♦ 9 5 4 2
♣ K J 9 2

LEAD   ♦ Q

WEST   EAST
(PARTNER)   (YOU)

SOUTH
(DECLARER)

WEST	NORTH	EAST	SOUTH
	1NT	Pass	3♥
Pass	4♥	Pass	Pass
Pass			

Partner leads the ♦Q against South's 4♥ contract. What cards will partner need to defeat this contract? How do you plan to help partner out?

Solution 3.1

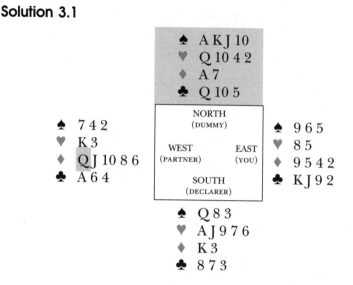

```
                          ♠ A K J 10
                          ♥ Q 10 4 2
                          ♦ A 7
                          ♣ Q 10 5
                         NORTH
    ♠ 7 4 2             (DUMMY)              ♠ 9 6 5
    ♥ K 3         WEST          EAST         ♥ 8 5
    ♦ Q J 10 8 6  (PARTNER)     (YOU)        ♦ 9 5 4 2
    ♣ A 6 4            SOUTH                 ♣ K J 9 2
                     (DECLARER)
                          ♠ Q 8 3
                          ♥ A J 9 7 6
                          ♦ K 3
                          ♣ 8 7 3
```

Partner's lead of the ♦Q let's you know that declarer must hold the ♦K, so you're not going to get any tricks from that suit. It won't do you much good if partner holds the ♣Q, since declarer can always take a finesse if that's the case. It looks as though partner's going to have a trick in the trump suit, and you're also going to need three tricks from the club suit. You'll have to hope that partner holds the ♣A.

Partner can't see the cards you hold, but you have an opportunity to help out. If declarer wins the first trick with dummy's ♦A, play your ♦2, a discouraging card. That will let partner know you don't have any interest in that suit. On the actual hand, declarer will next try the heart finesse, which will lose to partner's ♥K. Hopefully, partner will have been watching your signal and decide that there's no future in playing another diamond. Partner may come to the same conclusion that you did—the only hope for the defense is to take three tricks from the club suit.

If partner now plays the ♣A, you can announce the good news by playing the ♣9, the most encouraging card you can afford. It's like a shout for partner to continue leading the suit. Another club from partner and you take two more club tricks because dummy's ♣Q is trapped. Good cooperation by the partnership.

If partner had played a second diamond after winning a trick with the ♥K, declarer would make the contract. Declarer would end up with four spade tricks, four heart tricks, and two diamond tricks.

Hand 3.2

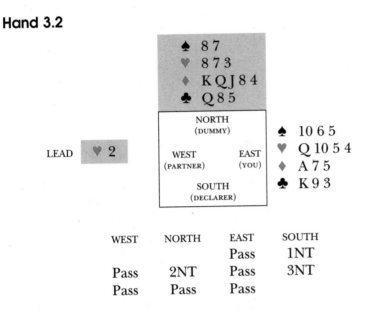

	WEST	NORTH	EAST	SOUTH
			Pass	1NT
	Pass	2NT	Pass	3NT
	Pass	Pass	Pass	

Partner's opening lead against the 3NT contract is the ♥2. How many hearts does partner have? You have three face cards, the ♥Q, ♦A, and ♣K. Do you have plans for each of them?

Solution 3.2

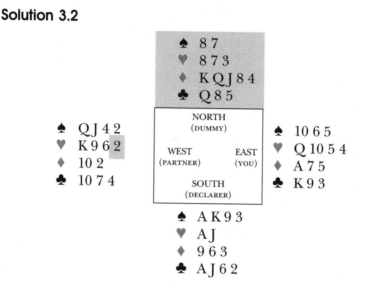

```
                    ♠ 8 7
                    ♥ 8 7 3
                    ♦ K Q J 8 4
                    ♣ Q 8 5
                    NORTH
                   (DUMMY)
♠ Q J 4 2                          ♠ 10 6 5
♥ K 9 6 2    WEST        EAST      ♥ Q 10 5 4
♦ 10 2      (PARTNER)    (YOU)     ♦ A 7 5
♣ 10 7 4                           ♣ K 9 3
                   SOUTH
                  (DECLARER)
                    ♠ A K 9 3
                    ♥ A J
                    ♦ 9 6 3
                    ♣ A J 6 2
```

Partner is likely leading fourth highest, so the ♥2 is from a four-card suit. If partner held five or more, the ♥2 couldn't be fourth highest. If partner holds both the ♥A and ♥K, you'll have an easy time defeating the contract by taking the first four heart tricks plus the ♦A. It's more likely that declarer holds at least one high heart, so you'll need to find a fourth trick elsewhere. It's not easy to see where that trick is coming from at this point, but you want to be sure you don't let the opponents get any more tricks than they're entitled.

Your first decision is in hearts. Play the ♥Q on the first trick—third hand high. After winning a trick with the ♥A, declarer will start promoting winners in diamonds. You have to decide when to take your ♦A. You want to wait until declarer has no diamonds left to reach the dummy. Partner can help you out here. When declarer leads a diamond, partner plays the ♦10, the start of a high-low to show an even number. You can work out that partner has two diamonds, rather than four diamonds. Declarer wouldn't have opened 1NT with a singleton diamond. That leaves declarer with exactly three diamonds. You need to hold up until the third round before taking your ♦A. Your final challenge comes if declarer leads the ♣Q from dummy after you duck the first two rounds of diamonds. You must play the ♣K—cover an honor with an honor—or declarer will be able to repeat the club finesse and sneak home with nine tricks: two spades, one heart, two diamonds, and four clubs.

Hand 3.3

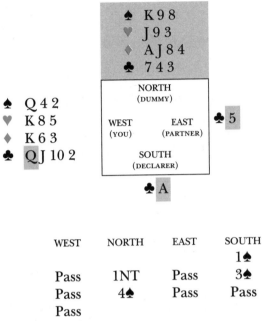

♠ K 9 8
♥ J 9 3
♦ A J 8 4
♣ 7 4 3

NORTH
(DUMMY)

WEST
(YOU)

EAST
(PARTNER)

SOUTH
(DECLARER)

♠ Q 4 2
♥ K 8 5
♦ K 6 3
♣ Q J 10 2

♣ 5

♣ A

WEST	NORTH	EAST	SOUTH
			1♠
Pass	1NT	Pass	3♠
Pass	4♠	Pass	Pass
Pass			

You elect to lead the ♣Q, top of a sequence, against South's con-tract of 4♠. A low club is played from dummy, partner plays the ♣5, and declarer wins the first trick with the ♣A.

Which player likely holds the ♣K? How many spades do you think partner has? What do you plan to do if declarer leads the ♠J at trick two? What if declarer leads the ♥4? What if declarer leads the ♦Q?

Solution 3.3

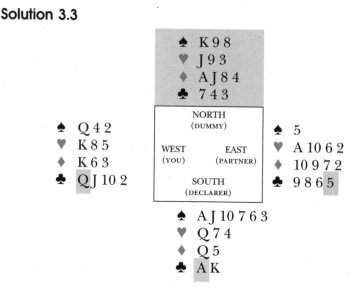

With the ♣2 in your hand, and the ♣3 and ♣4 in the dummy, the ♣5 is partner's lowest club. That's a discouraging signal. Even though declarer won the first trick with the ♣A, you suspect declarer also holds the ♣K. Declarer opened 1♠, then jumped to 3♠. It sounds as if declarer has at least six cards in the suit. With three spades in your hand and three in dummy, partner has at most a singleton. If declarer leads the ♠J, play low. There's nothing to promote for your side and it would be disastrous if partner held the singleton ♠K. When you don't cover, declarer will probably make the standard play of winning the trick with dummy's ♠K, then playing a spade back to the ♠A. With nine spades in the combined hands, it's usual to hope the ♠Q falls on the first or second trick rather than taking the finesse.

If declarer leads a low heart, play the ♥5—second hand low. On the actual hand, declarer can promote a heart winner if you win the first trick with your ♥K. Once you play low, it doesn't matter which heart declarer plays from dummy. Partner wins the trick, and the defense eventually comes to three heart tricks. If declarer leads the ♦Q, be prepared to cover with the ♦K—cover an honor with an honor. You don't know for sure whether that will promote winners for your side, but you have to hope partner holds something useful in diamonds. As it turns out, covering the ♦Q restricts declarer to two tricks in the suit. If you're very careful on this hand, your side will probably end up with one spade trick, and three heart tricks. One slip and declarer ends up with ten tricks.

Hand 3.4

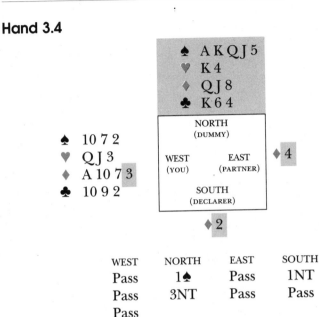

♠ A K Q J 5
♥ K 4
♦ Q J 8
♣ K 6 4

NORTH
(DUMMY)

♠ 10 7 2
♥ Q J 3
♦ A 10 7 3
♣ 10 9 2

WEST
(YOU)

EAST
(PARTNER)

♦ 4

SOUTH
(DECLARER)

♦ 2

WEST	NORTH	EAST	SOUTH
Pass	1♠	Pass	1NT
Pass	3NT	Pass	Pass
Pass			

The contract is 3NT, and you start off by leading the ♦3, fourth from your longest and strongest. Declarer plays the ♦J from dummy, which wins the trick as partner contributes the ♦4 and declarer the ♦2. Where's the ♦K?

Declarer now proceeds to take the five spade winners in the dummy. Partner follows suit for the first three rounds and then plays the ♥7 followed by the ♥8. Declarer discards the ♥2, ♦5 and ♣3 on the last three rounds of spades. You also have to find two discards on the last two rounds of spades? Which cards do you throw away? What do you plan to do when you win a trick with the ♦A?

Solution 3.4

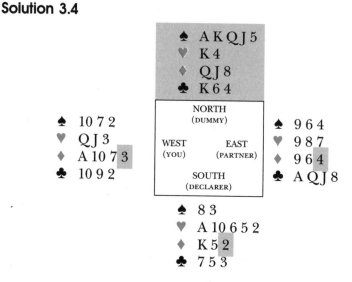

```
                    ♠ A K Q J 5
                    ♥ K 4
                    ♦ Q J 8
                    ♣ K 6 4
              ┌──────────────────┐
♠ 10 7 2      │     NORTH        │      ♠ 9 6 4
♥ Q J 3       │    (DUMMY)       │      ♥ 9 8 7
♦ A 10 7 3    │ WEST      EAST   │      ♦ 9 6 4
♣ 10 9 2      │ (YOU)   (PARTNER)│      ♣ A Q J 8
              │     SOUTH        │
              │   (DECLARER)     │
              └──────────────────┘
                    ♠ 8 3
                    ♥ A 10 6 5 2
                    ♦ K 5 2
                    ♣ 7 5 3
```

Your diamond lead hasn't worked well. When dummy's ♦J wins the first trick and partner plays the ♦4, you're fairly certain declarer has the ♦K. It looks as if diamonds aren't going to provide enough tricks. You have to hope partner holds something useful in hearts or clubs. Your first instinct might be that hearts is the most likely source of tricks. You hold the ♥Q and ♥J, and if partner holds the ♥A along with some length, you could take enough tricks in that suit to defeat the contract. Indeed, partner's first discard of the ♥7 appears to be an encouraging card. Partner's second discard of the ♥8, however, gives you pause to reconsider. If partner really wanted to make an encouraging signal in hearts, why not throw the ♥8 first? Also, why is partner discarding hearts and not clubs, if partner is expecting to take tricks in the heart suit?

Partner is making a discouraging signal in hearts by discarding a low heart followed by a higher heart. Partner must be holding on to clubs for a reason. When declarer leads a diamond, be prepared to win the ♦A and lead the ♣10. That's the only way to defeat the contract. Partner can't afford to discard a high club as an encouraging signal because all four club tricks are needed. When partner discards hearts, hold on to your hearts to prevent declarer from taking all the tricks in that suit. Also, keep at least two clubs so you can lead them through dummy's ♣K twice if necessary. Discard your low diamonds on the last two rounds of spades—they weren't going to do much good anyway.

Working Together—
To Take Sure Tricks

Sure tricks are "sure" only if you take them. As declarer, you can see where your sure tricks are coming from, although you may need to be careful about the order in which you take them. As a defender, you will often be unaware of which tricks are there for the taking. Fortunately, you're working with a partner, and the two of you will usually have the tools you need.

Sure Tricks in Notrump

Suppose you find yourself on lead against declarer's 3NT contract and this is the layout of the diamond suit:

DUMMY
♦ 6 4

WEST (YOU)   EAST (PARTNER)
♦ A K Q J 7   ♦ 9 3 2

DECLARER
♦ *10 8 5*

Not too challenging. You'd simply take your five diamond tricks
and move on to the next hand. You'd hardly expect a round of applause for your fine defense from anyone watching the game.

Unfortunately, this type of holding isn't very frequent. Your side
may often have five tricks to take, but they may be hidden from view.
Let's rearrange the diamonds a little:

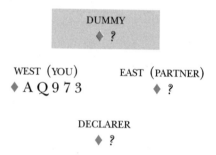

DUMMY
♦ ?

WEST (YOU)   EAST (PARTNER)
♦ A Q 9 7 3   ♦ ?

DECLARER
♦ ?

Oh, oh! This is a more typical situation. You no longer have such
a solid sequence of diamonds, and you can't see where the other
high cards in the suit are hiding. Still, you have a guideline to help
you out in this situation. You lead your fourth highest diamond and
see how it works out:

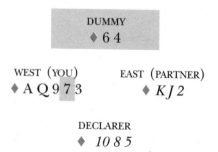

DUMMY
♦ 6 4

WEST (YOU)   EAST (PARTNER)
♦ A Q 9 7 3   ♦ *K J 2*

DECLARER
♦ *10 8 5*

No problem. Your side takes its five diamond winners. Partner will win the first trick by playing the ♦K—third hand high—and will return your suit by leading the ♦J, top of the remaining doubleton. You don't need partner to have such a strong holding in diamonds. Your lead would be equally effective if the layout were something like this:

DUMMY
♦ J 6 4

WEST (YOU)
♦ A Q 9 7 3

EAST (PARTNER)
♦ K 2

DECLARER
♦ 10 8 5

Notice that the defense is actually following the same principle as declarer when taking their tricks in this suit. They want to start by playing the high card from the short side, the ♦K in this case. That's why you start off by leading a low card. You're leading over to partner's hoped-for high card, so that partner will then have a low card—a link card—left to lead back to your length in the suit.

Of course, the diamond layout could be less friendly. Since the opponents have decided to play in notrump, it could look something like this:

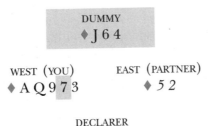

DUMMY
♦ J 6 4

WEST (YOU)
♦ A Q 9 7 3

EAST (PARTNER)
♦ 5 2

DECLARER
♦ K 10 8

Declarer will be able to win the first trick very cheaply, perhaps with the ♦8. All is not lost, however, provided the defenders continue carefully from this point. You'll have to wait until partner gains the lead, and partner will need to faithfully return your suit. The remaining cards will look like this:

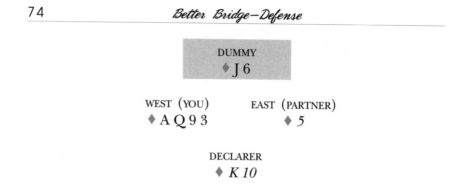

DUMMY
♦ J 6

WEST (YOU)   EAST (PARTNER)
♦ A Q 9 3   ♦ 5

DECLARER
♦ K 10

When partner leads the ♦5, declarer's ♦K is trapped. Whichever diamond declarer chooses to play, you'll be able to win the trick and take three more diamond tricks. You'll get four tricks from the diamond suit, and that's everything to which you're entitled.

Let's put you back on lead against 3NT with a slightly different holding:

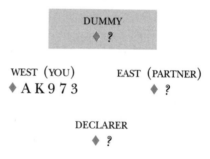

DUMMY
♦ ?

WEST (YOU)   EAST (PARTNER)
♦ A K 9 7 3   ♦ ?

DECLARER
♦ ?

One guideline is top of a sequence, but against notrump contracts this usually applies only when you have a three-card sequence, a broken sequence, or an interior sequence. It's not easy to lead a low card from this holding, but you have to visualize the expected layout. Hopefully, it will be something like this:

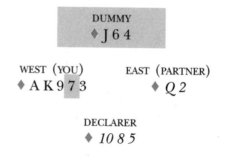

DUMMY
♦ J 6 4

WEST (YOU)   EAST (PARTNER)
♦ A K 9 7 3   ♦ Q 2

DECLARER
♦ 10 8 5

Only by leading a low diamond can the partnership take the first five tricks. If you start with the ♦A, the suit will become blocked as partner has to play the ♦2. You could continue by leading a low diamond to partner's ♦Q, but unless you have an entry in another suit, that's all you get—two of your five diamond tricks.

Leading your fourth highest diamond might get you the first five tricks when partner holds the ♦J, rather than the ♦Q. This is a possible layout you might encounter:

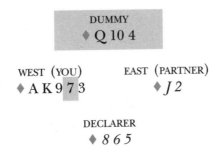

Now you and I can see that declarer can win the first trick by playing dummy's ♦Q, but few declarers would be that brilliant. You're not the only one who can't see through the backs of the cards, and declarer is most likely to assume that you've lead low from a suit headed by the ♦ A J or ♦ K J—that's twice as likely as a holding of ♦ A K. So, declarer will probably finesse dummy's ♦10. Partner will be surprised to win a trick with the ♦J, but hopefully not too surprised to return a diamond and let you take the next four tricks.

There are other possible layouts of the diamond suit which are not quite as friendly but may still result in a favorable outcome. Suppose this is the actual distribution of the diamond suit:

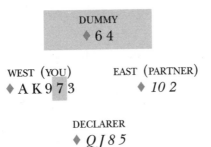

On the first trick, partner plays third hand high, the ♦10, and declarer wins the trick with the ♦J. That doesn't look like a good start, but if partner is next to gain the lead for your side, a return of the ♦2 will give your side the next four tricks, since this is the remaining layout:

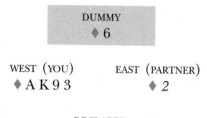

DUMMY
♦ 6

WEST (YOU)   EAST (PARTNER)
♦ A K 9 3   ♦ 2

DECLARER
♦ Q 8 5

Declarer's ♦Q won't be enough to stop you from winning all the rest of the tricks in the suit. You might also notice how ineffective it would have been if you'd originally taken your ♦A and ♦K. Declarer would get two tricks with the ♦Q and ♦J, and you'd have a difficult time developing one more winner in the suit.

Does it always work best to lead fourth highest against a notrump contract when you hold both the ace and king? Well, this could be the distribution:

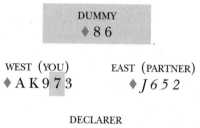

DUMMY
♦ 8 6

WEST (YOU)   EAST (PARTNER)
♦ A K 9 7 3   ♦ J 6 5 2

DECLARER
♦ Q 10

Now you might be disappointed to see declarer win the first trick with the ♦Q. But don't be too hard on yourself. Unless you have some reason to believe that the opponents don't hold many diamonds in the combined hands, your fourth highest lead will work best in the long run.

We're on a roll. Let's keep leading the long suit against declarer's notrump contract, only this time it looks like this:

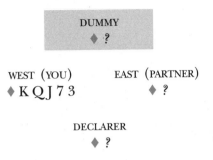

DUMMY
♦ ?

WEST (YOU)   EAST (PARTNER)
♦ K Q J 7 3   ♦ ?

DECLARER
♦ ?

Well, you'll simply lead a low diamond over to partner's ♦A, then partner can return one and you'll take your five tricks. Right? Not if this is the layout:

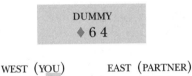

DUMMY
♦ 6 4

WEST (YOU)   EAST (PARTNER)
♦ K Q J 7 3   ♦ 9 5 2

DECLARER
♦ A 10 8

That was a little unfair—I gave partner's high diamond to declarer. Declarer wins the first trick with the ♦10 and still gets a second trick with the ♦A. It would be all right to lead a low diamond if you knew partner held the ♦A, but that's not often the case. Instead, you would start this suit by leading the ♦K, top of your three-card sequence. That way, if declarer holds the ♦A, at least you'll be able to promote two winners in the suit, and you may establish your remaining two diamonds as winners through length provided neither opponent holds more than three diamonds.

Fair enough. You'll lead the ♦K from this sequence. But what if it's partner who holds the ♦A? Will you still get your five top tricks? Probably, but it may take a little cooperation. Consider this situation:

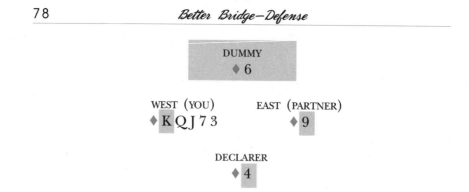

DUMMY
♦ 6

WEST (YOU)   EAST (PARTNER)
♦ K Q J 7 3   ♦ 9

DECLARER
♦ 4

You lead the ♦K, the singleton ♦6 appears in dummy, partner plays the ♦9, and declarer plays the ♦4. What's going on? Where is the ♦A? Declarer could have it and be holding up. That's fairly common. However, that ♦9 from partner looks interesting. It's a high card, so it looks as though partner is making an encouraging signal—especially since the ♦2 is nowhere to be seen. You can try to visualize the complete layout:

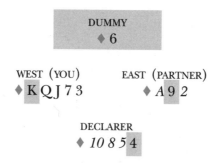

DUMMY
♦ 6

WEST (YOU)   EAST (PARTNER)
♦ K Q J 7 3   ♦ A 9 2

DECLARER
♦ 10 8 5 4

Now that you have a picture in your head, it's easier to see how you must continue at this point. Lead a low diamond to partner's ♦A. Partner will then lead the ♦2 back over to your high cards. Once again, you get the first five tricks.

Now let's put you in the East position to see how you fare when partner leads the ♦K:

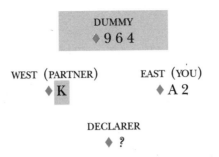

Wait a minute! Where did that ♦9 go? It's now in the dummy. Don't panic. See if you can visualize the likely layout of the diamond suit. Partner has led the top of a sequence against a notrump contract, so it should look something like this:

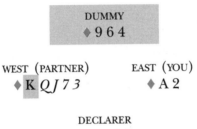

If you play the ♦2, partner's ♦K will win the trick, but the suit will now be blocked. Partner could play a low diamond over to your ♦A, but you have no link card left to get back to partner's diamond winners.

Once you visualize partner's holding, however, the solution to this dilemma becomes clear. Play your ♦A on partner's ♦K. It seems a bit extravagant, but you can now lead back your ♦2, and partner will take the next four tricks. You're back to getting the five tricks to which you were entitled. I hope you haven't heard that cliché about never playing your ace on partner's king!

Partner's diamond holding doesn't have to be quite that strong. Overtaking partner's ♦K with your ♦A would also be successful if this were the actual layout:

DUMMY
♦ 9 6 4

WEST (PARTNER)   EAST (YOU)
♦ K Q 10 7 3   ♦ A 2

DECLARER
♦ J 8 5

Partner has led the top of a broken sequence, but never mind. Once you overtake the ♦K with your ♦A, the remaining cards look like this:

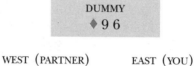

DUMMY
♦ 9 6

WEST (PARTNER)   EAST (YOU)
♦ Q 10 7 3   ♦ 2

DECLARER
♦ J 8

When you lead back the ♦2, declarer's ♦J is trapped, and partner still takes the next four tricks.

Let's make it a little more interesting. This time, partner leads the ♦Q:

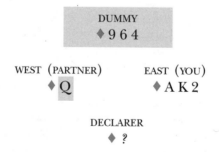

DUMMY
♦ 9 6 4

WEST (PARTNER)   EAST (YOU)
♦ Q   ♦ A K 2

DECLARER
♦ ?

Did you fill in the rest of the picture and put your ♦K on partner's ♦Q? That's the only way to take the first five tricks if this is the full layout:

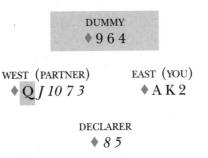

You overtake with the ♦K, play the ♦A, and lead the ♦2 back to partner's hand. If you were to play the ♦2 on the first trick, your side would win the first three tricks, but that would probably be all. Partner might have no entry outside of the diamond suit itself.

This time partner leads the ♦J:

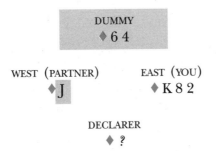

Do you play a discouraging card, the ♦2, or do you play an encouraging card, the ♦8? Actually, you shouldn't play either card. It's time for third hand high, the ♦K. The one card you know partner doesn't hold is the ♦Q. If you play anything except the ♦K, declarer will be able to win the first trick with the ♦Q. That would be unfortunate if this were the complete layout:

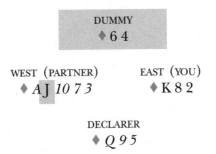

Partner was leading the top of an internal sequence. Declarer would be more than happy to get a gift trick with the ♦Q, but there's no need for that to happen if you play the ♦K on partner's ♦J. You win the trick and can return a diamond. Declarer's ♦Q will be trapped and partner will be happy to take the next four tricks.

You might be wondering whether playing the ♦K is such a great idea if partner doesn't hold the ♦A. After all, partner could simply be leading the top of a sequence:

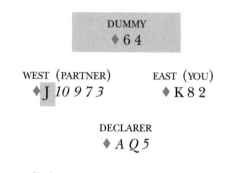

DUMMY
♦ 6 4

WEST (PARTNER)   EAST (YOU)
♦ J *10 9 7 3*   ♦ K 8 2

DECLARER
♦ *A Q 5*

It may appear a little extravagant, but there's no harm done. Declarer will win the trick with the ♦A, and both you and your partner will know where the ♦Q is located. You can still carry on promoting winners in this suit when either of you regains the lead.

Now let's have partner lead an ace against declarer's notrump contract:

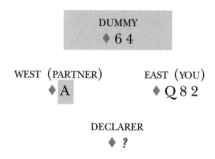

DUMMY
♦ 6 4

WEST (PARTNER)   EAST (YOU)
♦ A   ♦ Q 8 2

DECLARER
♦ ?

What's partner up to, and which card should you play? Try to visualize the type of holding from which partner would lead the ♦A. You should come up with something like this:

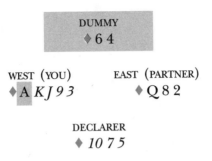

Partner is leading the top of a broken sequence. Without the ♦J, partner would probably have led fourth highest—you've seen that already. Partner would dearly like to know where the ♦Q is located. You can help out by playing the ♦8, an encouraging card. Partner can then lead a low diamond to your ♦Q, and you can play your ♦2 back to the rest of partner's winners.

Let's change this layout a bit and put you back as the opening leader:

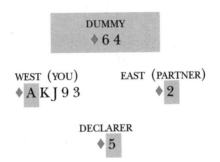

You lead the ♦A and the ♦2 appears from partner. What now? Holding the ♦Q, partner should give an encouraging signal by playing a high card, as in the previous example. The ♦2 looks like a discouraging signal, so you might visualize the layout of the suit as something like this:

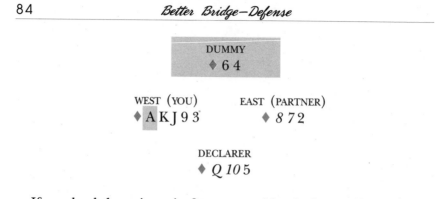

DUMMY
♦ 6 4

WEST (YOU)   EAST (PARTNER)
♦ A K J 9 3   ♦ 8 7 2

DECLARER
♦ Q 10 5

If you lead the suit again from your side, declarer will get a trick with the ♦Q. If you want to take all five tricks in the diamond suit, you'll have to be patient and look for an entry into partner's hand. Partner can then lead a diamond through declarer's ♦Q, and you'll end up taking all the tricks in the suit.

Both partners will really need to be on their toes to handle this last combination correctly. East will have to give the correct signal and draw the appropriate conclusion when West doesn't continue leading the suit. West will have to be watching for the signal, and put the knowledge to good use.

Let's see how it might work in a complete hand. As West, you're on lead after the bidding has gone:

WEST	NORTH	EAST	SOUTH
			1NT
Pass	3NT	Pass	Pass
Pass			

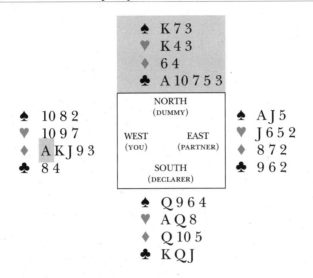

♠ K 7 3
♥ K 4 3
♦ 6 4
♣ A 10 7 5 3

NORTH
(DUMMY)

♠ 10 8 2
♥ 10 9 7
♦ A K J 9 3
♣ 8 4

WEST
(YOU)

EAST
(PARTNER)

♠ A J 5
♥ J 6 5 2
♦ 8 7 2
♣ 9 6 2

SOUTH
(DECLARER)

♠ Q 9 6 4
♥ A Q 8
♦ Q 10 5
♣ K Q J

You start by leading the ♦A, and partner plays the ♦2, a discouraging signal. You decide that it's best to look for an entry to partner's hand, and you shift to the ♥10. It turns out that this isn't where partner's entry lies, but it's not over yet. Declarer wins this trick with dummy's ♥K, as partner plays another discouraging card, the ♥2. Declarer can only count eight sure tricks—three hearts and five clubs—and decides to try leading a low spade from dummy.

The fate of the contract now rests with East. If East automatically plays second hand low, declarer will win a trick with the ♠Q. Declarer will now rattle off five club tricks and two more heart tricks to make the contract. That's a crafty play by declarer—attempting to establish a ninth trick before the defenders realize what's happening.

Partner, however, has enough clues to find the winning defense. Partner should have a picture of your diamond holding once you lead the ♦A and then shift to another suit after seeing the discouraging signal. It's unlikely that the lead of the ♥10 was an attempt to find a better suit to develop than diamonds. So, partner should hop up with the ♠A and lead back a diamond. This allows the defense to defeat the contract by two tricks. Quite a difference. It wouldn't have done any good to continue leading diamonds after partner's discouraging signal. Declarer would get a trick with the ♦Q and take the three heart winners and five club winners to make the contract. Declarer wouldn't need a trick from the spade suit.

Sure Tricks in a Trump Contract

When defending a suit contract, you can rarely take many tricks from a long suit due to the power of declarer's trump suit. That shouldn't stop you from getting the tricks to which you're entitled, although you may have to do some careful manoeuvring to get them all.

You're probably tired of all those diamonds, so here are some tricks to take in the heart suit, but with the drawback that the spade suit is trump. Here's a familiar looking holding:

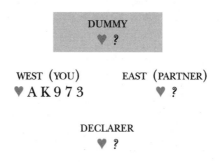

Against a notrump contract, you'd lead fourth highest from this suit, but that's not a good idea in a suit contract. The complete layout might be something like this:

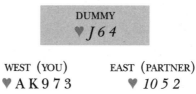

If you were to lead the ♥7, declarer would win the first trick with the ♥Q. That wouldn't be a problem in a notrump contract, because you'd now have four tricks ready to take as soon as you regained the lead. Against a suit contract, it's not so promising. Even if you immediately regain the lead, you'll only be able to take one heart trick. After that, declarer will be able to ruff your heart winners because spades are trump. Worse than that, declarer may be able discard the remaining heart on an extra winner in the dummy before you regain the lead. Now you won't even get one trick from the suit.

You're usually better off to take your ace and king, making sure that you get two sure tricks from the suit. Holdings such as the ace and king, or the king and queen, in a suit are very powerful, and you usually look for such combinations when deciding which suit to lead against a trump contract.

What if partner holds the ♥Q, and the layout looks something like this?

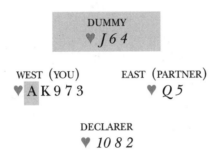

DUMMY
♥ J 6 4

WEST (YOU)   EAST (PARTNER)
♥ A K 9 7 3   ♥ Q 5

DECLARER
♥ 10 8 2

If you lead the ♥A and ♥K, partner's ♥Q will fall. That's fine. Since spades are trump, you can lead another heart to let partner win a third trick by ruffing it. You're back to three tricks.

Time for more detective work. Suppose you lead the ♥K in the following situation, and these are the cards you see:

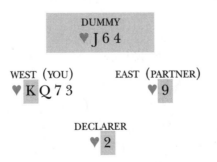

DUMMY
♥ J 6 4

WEST (YOU)   EAST (PARTNER)
♥ K Q 7 3   ♥ 9

DECLARER
♥ 2

What's going on here? Your ♥K won the trick, and partner played the ♥9. Where's the ♥A? It's a good bet that partner has it. First, the ♥9 looks like an encouraging card from partner. Second, holding the ♥A, declarer would probably have won the trick with it, since declarer could then develop another trick in the suit by leading toward dummy's ♥J. You should visualize the complete layout to be something like this:

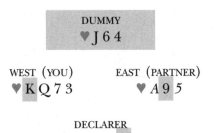

DUMMY
♥ J 6 4

WEST (YOU)   EAST (PARTNER)
♥ K Q 7 3   ♥ A 9 5

DECLARER
♥ 10 8 2

You would continue by leading the ♥3 over to partner's ♥A, and partner can return the ♥5 to your ♥Q. You quickly take the first three tricks in the suit.

Let's change the situation a little:

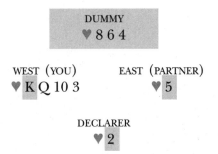

DUMMY
♥ 8 6 4

WEST (YOU)   EAST (PARTNER)
♥ K Q 10 3   ♥ 5

DECLARER
♥ 2

You again lead the ♥K which wins the first trick, but this time partner contributes the ♥5. Since you can see the ♥3 in your hand, the ♥4 in the dummy, and the ♥2 from declarer, partner's ♥5 is a low heart. Partner is sending a discouraging signal. It seems likely that declarer holds the ♥A this time, but what about the ♥J? If partner holds the ♥J, you can lead another heart to drive out declarer's ♥A and promote another winner for your side.

Actually, it would be very dangerous to lead another heart if you trust partner's signal. Put yourself in partner's shoes. When you lead the ♥K, partner can assume you also hold the ♥Q. Both the ♥A and the ♥J are equal honors as far as partner is concerned. Holding the

♥A, partner will certainly encourage you to lead the suit again, so that your side can collect its tricks. Holding the ♥J, partner should also encourage you to lead the suit again, so that you can develop another winner in the suit. Partner's discouraging signal in this situation is a warning that the actual layout is probably something like this:

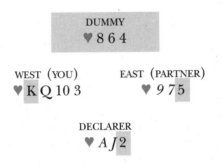

Declarer has laid a clever trap for you by not winning the ♥A on the first round.* If you lead another heart, declarer will win two heart tricks and end up with only one loser in the suit. By watching partner's signal, you can avoid the trap and switch to another suit. Hopefully, partner will gain the lead later on and lead a heart through declarer, establishing a second trick for your side.

Let's put you on the other side of the table for a while:

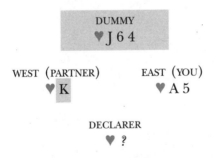

Partner leads the ♥K against declarer's spade contract, and it's up to you. Can you picture a likely layout of the unseen cards? They could be something like this:

*This ploy was commonly used in the days of whist and is called the Bath Coup. It was probably named after the town of Bath in England, which was the Las Vegas of its day.

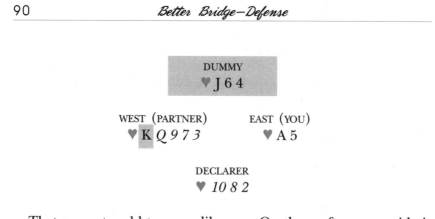

DUMMY
♥ J 6 4

WEST (PARTNER)   EAST (YOU)
♥ K Q 9 7 3   ♥ A 5

DECLARER
♥ 10 8 2

That seems to add to your dilemma. On the surface, your side is entitled to three heart tricks, but the lead of the ♥K has made things awkward. If you play the ♥5, the suit will be blocked. Partner can lead a low heart to your ♥A, but then you'll need to find another entry to partner's hand to get a trick from the ♥Q. If you overtake the ♥K with your ♥A, you can lead the ♥5 back to partner's ♥Q, but now dummy's ♥J has become a winner.

The good news is that you're playing with spades as the trump suit. If you overtake and return a heart, partner can win and lead a third round of the suit. You can trump this, and you're back to three tricks. You won't always be able to afford this. You may have no trump, or you might have a trump holding from which it would be costly to have to ruff a heart. But most of the time, you'll have a way of meeting the challenge.

Let's change the layout a little:

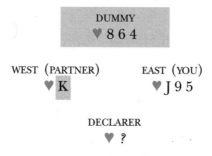

DUMMY
♥ 8 6 4

WEST (PARTNER)   EAST (YOU)
♥ K   ♥ J 9 5

DECLARER
♥ ?

Partner leads the ♥K, the ♥4 is played from dummy, and you play . . . ? Visualize the situation. It should be something like this:

DUMMY
♥ 8 6 4

WEST (PARTNER)   EAST (YOU)
♥ K Q 10 3   ♥ J 9 5

DECLARER
♥ A 7 2

Play the ♥9. You want to encourage partner to lead the suit again, whether or not declarer wins the first trick with the ♥A. This is similar to the earlier situation in which you were leading the ♥K from the other side. If you play the ♥5, partner is unlikely to continue leading the suit, being afraid that declarer holds the ♥J.

All the above examples looked at a single suit in isolation. You'll have to consider the whole hand when choosing which to play in each situation. For example, suppose you're defending with the East hand after the auction has gone:

WEST	NORTH	EAST	SOUTH
	1♦	Pass	1♠
Pass	2♣	Pass	4♠
Pass			

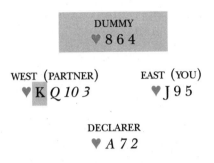

♠ Q 9 7 6
♥ 6 4
♦ A K J 10 7
♣ K 10

NORTH
(DUMMY)

LEAD ♥ A

WEST   EAST
(PARTNER)   (YOU)

SOUTH
(DECLARER)

♠ 10 4
♥ Q 9 2
♦ 8 6 3
♣ A Q 9 7 2

Partner leads the ♥A, so it looks as though partner has both the ♥A and ♥K. Holding the ♥Q, your first instinct might be to encourage partner to keep leading the suit by playing the ♥9. Looking at dummy, however, that's not the best choice when it comes to the complete hand. There are only two hearts in the dummy, so you won't get more than two heart tricks before declarer can ruff in the dummy.

The other two tricks you need to defeat the contract will probably come from the club suit, if you can persuade partner to lead clubs. The best way to do that is to give partner a discouraging signal in hearts. Play the ♥2, suggesting that you're not interested in having partner continue that suit. Looking at the dummy, partner can probably work out that the only other suit you could be interested in is clubs. As long as partner leads a club after winning the first heart trick, or after taking a trick with the ♥K, the defense will prevail. Here's the complete hand:

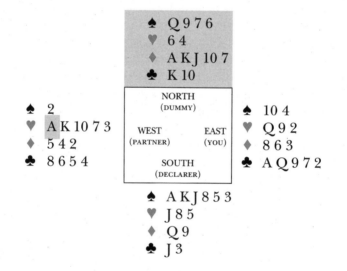

If partner does not lead a club, declarer will end up taking the rest of the tricks—six spade tricks and five diamond tricks. You might be thinking that partner should lead a club anyway, regardless of your signal. Leading a club won't always be the right defense. The complete hand could be something like this:

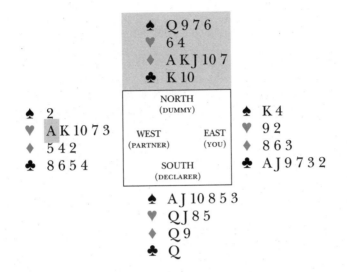

Now the only way to defeat the contract is for partner to lead a third round of hearts. Whether or not a trump is played from dummy, you can overruff with the ♠K, and take the ♣A to defeat the contract. If partner led a club after taking the ♥A and ♥K, declarer would make the contract by taking a finesse against your ♠K.

On this last hand, you would have to give an encouraging signal in hearts, even though you didn't hold the ♥Q, and partner would have to heed your signal to find the winning defense. You can't just expect partner to do the right thing. You have to use your signals to help partner out.

Summary

The defenders want to take all the tricks to which they're entitled. Since they can't see each other's hand, they must be careful to help one another out when taking their tricks. They may need to unblock the suit, and they may need to make good use of attitude signals to untangle their tricks.

Practice Hands

Hand 4.1

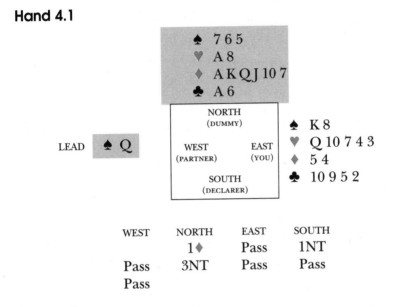

		NORTH (DUMMY)		
		♠ 7 6 5		
		♥ A 8		
		♦ A K Q J 10 7		
		♣ A 6		

				♠ K 8
LEAD	♠ Q	WEST	EAST	♥ Q 10 7 4 3
		(PARTNER)	(YOU)	♦ 5 4
		SOUTH		♣ 10 9 5 2
		(DECLARER)		

WEST	NORTH	EAST	SOUTH
	1♦	Pass	1NT
Pass	3NT	Pass	Pass
Pass			

Partner leads the ♠Q against South's 3NT contract. Is there any possibility of defeating this contract? What cards will you need partner to hold? How do you plan to make sure that your side takes all of its tricks?

Solution 4.1

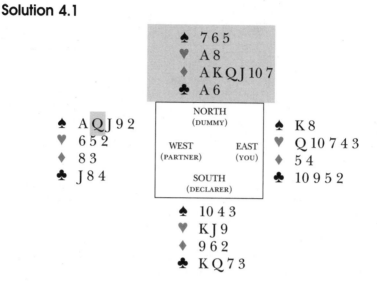

    Partner's lead of the ♠Q promises the ♠J but denies the ♠K. That's not news to you, since you're looking at the ♠K. But where's the ♠A? If declarer has it, there's no stopping the contract. Declarer will have at least one spade trick, one heart trick, six diamond tricks, and a club trick. The only hope to defeat the contract is for partner to hold the ♠A.

    That's possible, as on the actual hand, if partner is leading the top of an internal sequence. All you have to do now is make sure that your side takes the first five tricks. Suppose you play the ♠8 on the first trick. Partner will probably assume that the ♠8 is an encouraging card and that you hold the ♠K—especially when declarer doesn't win the first trick. Partner might now lead a low spade over to your ♠K, expecting you to lead back another spade so that your side can take all the tricks in the suit. That won't work out very well when you have no spade left to return. Declarer takes the rest of the tricks.

    Knowing you have the ♠K, partner could decide to play the ♠A at trick two, hoping you'll drop the ♠K underneath it even if you still have a low spade remaining. But why make things tough for partner? Play the ♠K on partner's ♠Q, and then return the ♠8. That will make sure there's no accident in taking your five tricks. If it were to turn out that declarer held the ♠A, no harm would be done by playing the ♠K on the first trick, since partner would still have the ♠J.

Hand 4.2

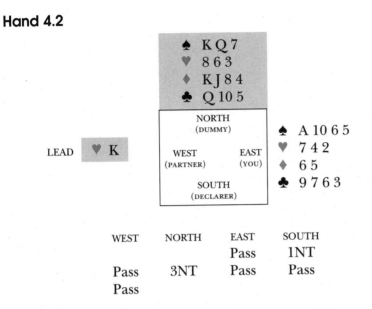

	WEST	NORTH	EAST	SOUTH
			Pass	1NT
	Pass	3NT	Pass	Pass
	Pass			

Partner's opening lead against the 3NT contract is the ♥K. Which card do you plan to play on the first trick? Suppose partner's ♥K wins the first trick and partner then leads the ♠8. How do you plan to defeat the contract?

Solution 4.2

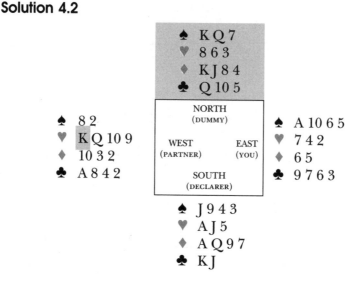

♠ K Q 7
♥ 8 6 3
♦ K J 8 4
♣ Q 10 5

NORTH
(DUMMY)

WEST
(PARTNER)

EAST
(YOU)

SOUTH
(DECLARER)

♠ 8 2
♥ K Q 10 9
♦ 10 3 2
♣ A 8 4 2

♠ A 10 6 5
♥ 7 4 2
♦ 6 5
♣ 9 7 6 3

♠ J 9 4 3
♥ A J 5
♦ A Q 9 7
♣ K J

Start by trying to visualize the type of holding from which partner
would lead the ♥K. Partner likely holds the ♥Q, but not the ♥A.
Partner may hold the ♥J, but could be leading the top of a broken
sequence and hold the ♥10 rather than the ♥J. Your first priority is
to let partner know what you think about the opening lead. Holding
no equal honor—the ♥A or ♥J—you should give a discouraging signal by playing the ♥2.

When partner shifts to the ♠8, use your imagination to help figure out what partner is up to. Holding something like ♥ K Q J x x,
partner could continue leading the suit despite your signal, since
partner wouldn't need any help to promote winners in the suit. Partner must have a holding—such as the one in the actual layout—
from which it would be dangerous to continue leading the suit after
your discouraging signal. Partner has led a spade hoping to find an
entry to your hand so that you can lead hearts from your side.

Having worked this out, hop up with the ♠A and lead back a heart.
This will establish two more heart winners for partner. Declarer now
has only eight tricks: one heart, four diamonds, and three spades—
after you've taken your ♠A. When declarer tries to promote a ninth
trick in the club suit, partner will win and take the established heart
winners. Your side ends up with one spade trick, three heart tricks,
and a club trick.

Hand 4.3

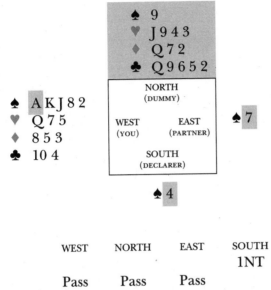

♠ 9
♥ J 9 4 3
♦ Q 7 2
♣ Q 9 6 5 2

NORTH
(DUMMY)

♠ A K J 8 2
♥ Q 7 5
♦ 8 5 3
♣ 10 4

WEST
(YOU)

EAST
(PARTNER)

♠ 7

SOUTH
(DECLARER)

♠ 4

WEST	NORTH	EAST	SOUTH
			1NT
Pass	Pass	Pass	

You elect to lead the ♠A, top of your broken sequence, against declarer's contract of 1NT. The singleton spade is played from dummy, partner plays the ♠7, and declarer the ♠4. What now?

Solution 4.3

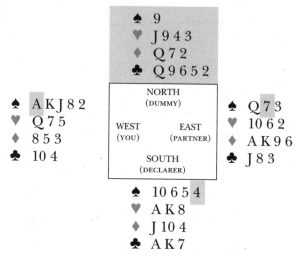

Partner's play of the ♠7 appears to be an encouraging signal. You can't see the ♠3, ♠4, or ♠5, so it's unlikely that the ♠7 is partner's lowest spade. The only reason partner would be encouraging you to lead another spade is if partner holds the ♠Q. You should play a low spade over to partner's ♠Q, so that partner can then return a spade and let you take the rest of the tricks in the suit.

On the actual hand, declarer is poised to take seven tricks if you don't get your tricks first. Declarer can take two heart tricks and five club tricks upon gaining the lead. It's important that the defenders don't lose their way. The first challenge is the spade suit. If you continue with a low spade at trick two, partner will indeed win the ♠Q and can return a spade so that your side gets the first five tricks. You can then lead a diamond over to partner's ♦A and ♦K to defeat the contract. How are you going to know to lead a diamond after taking your spade winners? On the last two spades, partner has another opportunity to use the attitude signal. Partner can either discard the ♦9, an encouraging signal in diamonds, or throw the ♥2 and ♣3, discouraging signals in those suits.

If you were to play the ♠K at trick two, you would no longer be able to untangle all your sure tricks. Similarly, if you were to switch to a heart or a club, declarer would be only too happy to take the tricks needed to make the contract.

Hand 4.4

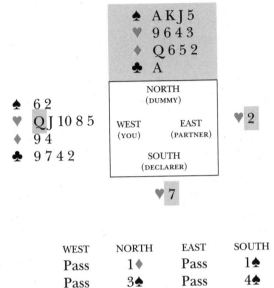

	♠ A K J 5	
	♥ 9 6 4 3	
	♦ Q 6 5 2	
	♣ A	

	NORTH (DUMMY)	
♠ 6 2		
♥ Q J 10 8 5	WEST EAST	♥ 2
♦ 9 4	(YOU) (PARTNER)	
♣ 9 7 4 2		
	SOUTH (DECLARER)	

♥ 7

WEST	NORTH	EAST	SOUTH
Pass	1♦	Pass	1♠
Pass	3♠	Pass	4♠
Pass	Pass	Pass	

You get off to the lead of the ♥Q against South's 4♠ contract. A low heart is played from dummy, partner plays the ♥2, and declarer plays the ♥7.

What's going on? Where are the ♥A and ♥K? What's your plan at trick two?

Solution 4.4

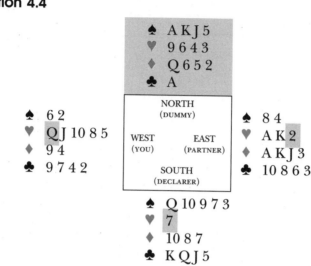

```
                        ♠ A K J 5
                        ♥ 9 6 4 3
                        ♦ Q 6 5 2
                        ♣ A
                     ┌─────────────────┐
      ♠ 6 2          │   NORTH         │        ♠ 8 4
      ♥ Q J 10 8 5   │   (DUMMY)       │        ♥ A K 2
      ♦ 9 4          │ WEST      EAST  │        ♦ A K J 3
      ♣ 9 7 4 2      │ (YOU)   (PARTNER)│       ♣ 10 8 6 3
                     │   SOUTH         │
                     │  (DECLARER)     │
                     └─────────────────┘
                        ♠ Q 10 9 7 3
                        ♥ 7
                        ♦ 10 8 7
                        ♣ K Q J 5
```

It looks as though your heart lead has worked out well, since you won the first trick, but now is not the time to sit back and relax. Start by asking yourself where the ♥A and ♥K are located. It would be unusual for declarer to hold both of them; otherwise, declarer would have likely won the first trick. It's possible that declarer holds the ♥A and partner holds the ♥K, although partner might have played the ♥K on your ♥Q to try to unblock the suit if that were the case. It's beginning to look as though partner may hold both the high hearts. If so, why did partner play the ♥2, a discouraging card?

Partner doesn't want you to lead another heart. The only explanation can be something like the actual layout. Partner is desperate to have you lead a diamond from your side, trapping dummy's ♦Q. If you switch to the ♦9, top of your doubleton, partner can win the next three diamond tricks to defeat the contract. If you lead another heart, declarer will ruff, draw trump, and eventually discard three of dummy's diamonds on club winners. Declarer will make an overtrick, losing only one heart and one diamond.

Why didn't partner overtake your ♥Q, play the ♦A and ♦K, and then lead another diamond for you to ruff? Partner doesn't know how many diamonds you hold. The correct defense might be to take two heart tricks and two diamond tricks. Once you lead the top card from your doubleton, partner knows the defense has three diamond tricks to take.

5

Working Together— Promoting Tricks

> " . . . from the highest to the humblest tasks, all
> are of equal honor; all have their part to play."
>
> — WINSTON CHURCHILL,
> *Speech to Canadian Senate,* [1941]

It's not too often that the defenders have enough sure tricks to defeat the contract right away. They usually need to develop additional winners, and one common method is through promotion. Working with partner to promote winners involves the same challenges as taking sure tricks. The defenders can't see each other's hand, but by following the guidelines and making good use of signals, the defenders can often prevail.

When making the opening lead, it's usually hard to know whether your side is about to take sure tricks in the suit or whether you need to develop winners in the suit through promotion, or perhaps length. Fortunately, the principles tend to be the same in each case.

Once the opening lead has been made and dummy comes down, the defenders are in a better position to decide how to go about taking or developing their tricks. Let's see how they work together when it turns out that they need to promote winners in a suit.

The Opening Lead Is a High Card

Suppose you have bid hearts during the auction, and partner is on lead against the opponents' contract. Partner dutifully leads your suit and this is what you see:

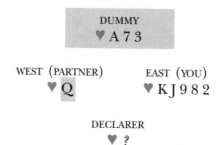

Partner leads the ♥Q, and declarer wins the trick with dummy's ♥A. You can tell that partner isn't leading the top of a sequence because you are staring at the ♥J. Partner is either leading a singleton heart, or the top of a doubleton. You can visualize the layout of the heart suit to be something like this:

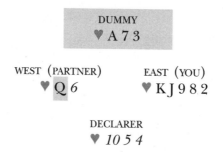

Partner's lead has helped you to promote winners in the suit and follows one of the basic principle behind promotion: play the high card from the short side first. It's the same principle used when taking sure tricks. When declarer plays the ♥A from dummy, play the ♥9, an encouraging signal. It's rather like a message of congratulations to partner, "Thanks for leading my suit."

Don't get too carried away with congratulations, however. Let's modify the situation slightly:

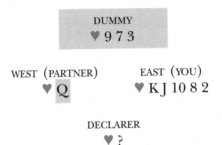

Partner has again led your suit, and your first instinct may be to send a message of appreciation by playing the ♥8, an encouraging card. Before doing this, you should visualize the likely layout of the suit, and one possibility might be:

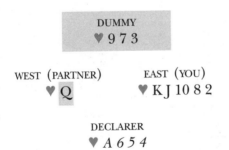

If you play the ♥8 on the first trick, declarer may choose to hold up and not play the ♥A. Your partner wins the trick, but has no hearts left to lead. Your hearts have not yet been promoted into winners. Instead, overtake partner's ♥Q with your ♥K. Now it doesn't matter whether or not declarer holds up playing the ♥A. You can continue leading the suit from your side.

Now let's suppose you haven't bid hearts during the auction but partner still leads the ♥Q:

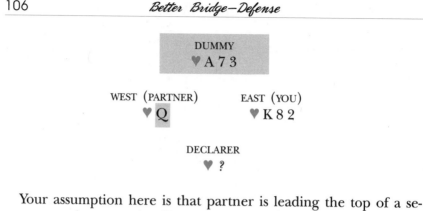

DUMMY
♥ A 7 3

WEST (PARTNER)   EAST (YOU)
♥ Q   ♥ K 8 2

DECLARER
♥ ?

Your assumption here is that partner is leading the top of a sequence, and you can visualize the layout of the heart suit to be something like this:

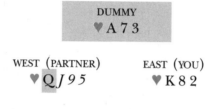

DUMMY
♥ A 7 3

WEST (PARTNER)   EAST (YOU)
♥ Q J 9 5   ♥ K 8 2

DECLARER
♥ 10 6 4

If declarer plays the ♥A from dummy, play the ♥8, an encouraging signal that lets partner know you have an equal honor. On regaining the lead, partner can lead a low heart to your ♥K, and your side can take all its promoted winners. Even if declarer doesn't play dummy's ♥A, you can play the ♥8, encouraging partner to lead the suit again.

Let's change the scenario a bit:

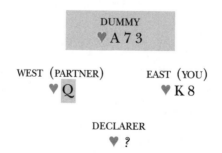

DUMMY
♥ A 7 3

WEST (PARTNER)   EAST (YOU)
♥ Q   ♥ K 8

DECLARER
♥ ?

Suppose declarer plays dummy's ♥A. If you play the ♥8 in this situation, the suit will become blocked. The remaining cards could look something like this:

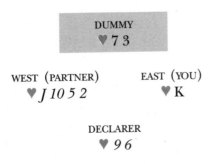

DUMMY
♥ 7 3

WEST (PARTNER)   EAST (YOU)
♥ J 10 5 2   ♥ K

DECLARER
♥ 9 6

Your side has promoted winners in the suit, but you can't take them. If either you or partner regains the lead, you'll be able to take a trick with the ♥K, but unless partner has another entry, that's all. Instead, play—unblock—your ♥K under dummy's ♥A. Now the remaining cards look like this:

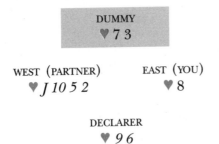

DUMMY
♥ 7 3

WEST (PARTNER)   EAST (YOU)
♥ J 10 5 2   ♥ 8

DECLARER
♥ 9 6

Whichever one of you regains the lead, you'll have no trouble taking the next four heart tricks. The situation would be similar if declarer played a low heart from dummy on the first trick. If you play the ♥8, the remaining cards look something like this:

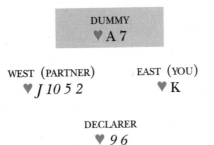

DUMMY
♥ A 7

WEST (PARTNER)   EAST (YOU)
♥ J 10 5 2   ♥ K

DECLARER
♥ 9 6

Partner can lead another heart, but declarer can duck this as well, letting you win the trick with the ♥K. You have no hearts left to continue leading the suit. Even if partner has an entry, declarer still has the ♥A left in the dummy.

Instead, overtake partner's ♥Q with your ♥K when declarer plays a low heart from dummy. Lead back your ♥8, and partner will be in a position to continue leading the suit to drive out dummy's ♥A.

Although unblocking plays are more frequently encountered against notrump contracts, they can be useful against suit contracts as well. Consider this hand:

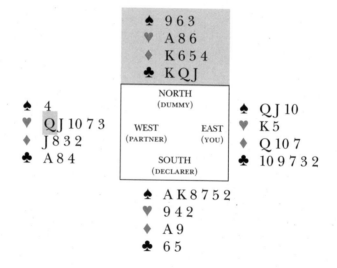

♠ 9 6 3
♥ A 8 6
♦ K 6 5 4
♣ K Q J

NORTH
(DUMMY)

♠ 4   ♠ Q J 10
♥ Q J 10 7 3   ♥ K 5
♦ J 8 3 2   ♦ Q 10 7
♣ A 8 4   ♣ 10 9 7 3 2

WEST   EAST
(PARTNER)   (YOU)

SOUTH
(DECLARER)

♠ A K 8 7 5 2
♥ 9 4 2
♦ A 9
♣ 6 5

Partner leads the ♥Q against North-South's 4♠ contract, and declarer plays the ♥A from dummy. You better get rid of your ♥K right now. Declarer will play two rounds of spades and get the bad news that there's a loser in the trump suit. Next, declarer leads a club to promote club winners in the dummy. Partner can win the ♣A and take two promoted heart winners to defeat the contract.

If you didn't unblock your ♥K on the first trick, declarer would make the contract. After winning the ♣A, partner could lead a heart to your ♥K, but there's no way to get back to partner's hand to take the last heart winner. Declarer would end up with five spade tricks, one heart trick, two diamond tricks, and two club tricks.

The Opening Lead Is a Low Card

When partner's opening lead is a low card, you generally do your best to try to win the trick, following the principle of third hand high. Here's a typical example:

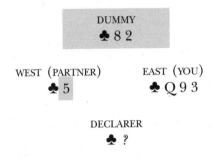

When partner leads the ♣5, and a low club is played from dummy, you would play the ♣Q. You can't be certain whether or not this will win the trick, but you're hoping it will do some good for your side. This might be the layout of the suit:

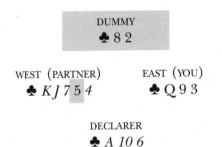

By playing the ♣Q, you force declarer to play the ♣A to win the trick. Partner's ♣K and ♣J are then promoted into winners. Partner lead the ♣5 not knowing how it was going to work out. If you had held the ♣A and ♣Q, your side might simply be taking its sure tricks. As it is, your side is promoting winners, by playing the high card from the short side first. It's interesting how the defenders can co-operate without actually seeing each other's cards.

Notice that you had to play your highest card in this situation. The ♣9 wouldn't have done the job.

Not Too High

It would nice if the principle of third hand high were a rule, rather than a guideline. It would save you from having to think about each situation. Fortunately, that's not the case—remember, bridge develops mental fitness. Each time you're in third position, you have to consider the circumstances before making your decision. Let's suppose these are the cards you see when partner leads the ♣5 against declarer's notrump contract:

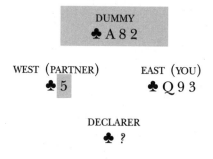

If a low card is played from dummy, you would play the ♣Q, third hand high. This is necessary if the layout is something like this:

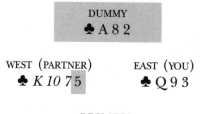

On the other hand, suppose the ♣A is played from dummy on the first trick. Now there's no need to play the ♣Q. Instead, play the ♣9, an encouraging signal in clubs. You must be prepared to adjust your play based on the card declarer chooses to play from dummy on the first trick. You may have to switch from playing third hand high to giving an attitude signal. Now consider this situation:

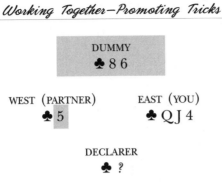

This is another case for third hand high, but how high is high? Your ♣Q and ♣J are equals. Either one of them will do the job. When this is the situation, the guideline is to **play the lower of equal honors**. To see why, let's go over to the other side of the table.

From the Other Side

Suppose you lead your fourth highest club against a notrump contract, and this is what you see on the first trick:

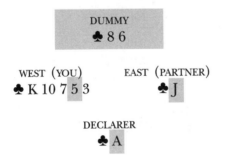

That promotes your ♣K into a winner, but if you regain the lead for your side, how do you plan to continue? You need to visualize the layout of the hidden clubs. Since the most important outstanding club is the ♣Q, your first task is to figure out whether it lies in declarer's hand or partner's hand. A little deductive reasoning will soon provide the answer. Holding the ♣Q as well as the ♣A, declarer would have won the first trick with the ♣Q, keeping the ♣A as a second winner in the suit. Partner must hold the ♣Q, and the layout you can visualize is something like this:

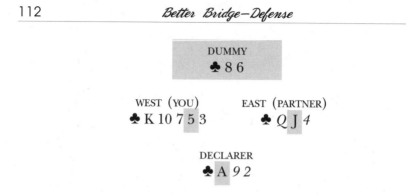

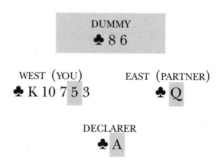

Since that's the case, your next play should be a low club over to partner's ♣Q, so partner can lead back a club to the rest of your winners.

Now let's suppose the play to the first trick goes a little differently:

Again, your ♣K has been promoted into a winner, but what do you plan to do if you regain the lead? The key missing card is the ♣J. Does partner hold that card, or is it in declarer's hand? With or without the ♣J, declarer would have to play the ♣A to win the first trick.

The secret here is that you have an agreement on which honor partner would play as third hand when holding equal honors, such as the ♣ Q J, or ♣ Q J 10. Although the basic guideline is third hand high, partner only plays as high a card as necessary to try to win the trick. The standard agreement is that **third hand plays the lowest of equal honors**. Holding the ♣ Q J, partner would play the ♣J, lower of the two equal honors. With the ♣ Q J 10, partner would play the ♣10, lowest of the three touching high cards. This is the exact opposite of leading from equal honors, where you lead the highest of your touching cards.

In the above layout, partner's play of the ♣Q denies possession of the ♣J, since partner would play the ♣J with touching honors. You now know that declarer must hold that card and can visualize the original layout to be something like this:

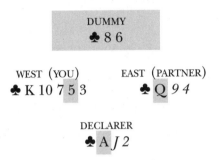

DUMMY
♣ 8 6

WEST (YOU)   EAST (PARTNER)
♣ K 10 7 5 3   ♣ Q 9 4

DECLARER
♣ A J 2

You won't be able to take all your winners by leading a low card over to partner. You'll have to decide how best to continue. If you can see that declarer will make the contract unless you can immediately take your club winners, you'll have to play the ♣K and hope that declarer started with only a doubleton ♣ A J, and that the ♣J will now fall under your ♣K. If you're not in such a hurry, you can wait until partner wins a trick, so that partner can lead through declarer. That will work well if the remaining cards look something like this:

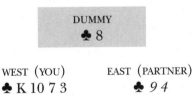

DUMMY
♣ 8

WEST (YOU)   EAST (PARTNER)
♣ K 10 7 3   ♣ 9 4

DECLARER
♣ J 2

When partner leads a club, declarer's ♣J is trapped, and your side gets all four club tricks. The important point is that you know where the ♣J is located once partner plays the ♣Q on the first trick.

Let's return for a moment to the earlier layout in which partner held both the ♣Q and ♣J:

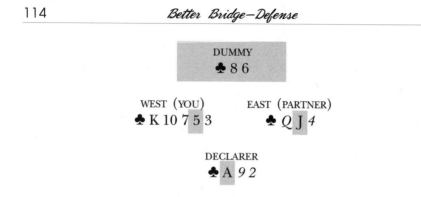

Here partner played the lower of the touching high cards, the ♣J, and when declarer won the ♣A, you were able to deduce the location of the ♣Q.

Equal Honors

Let's again move across the table and put you back in the position of third hand. You will need to be careful about what constitutes an equal honor. Suppose this is the situation:

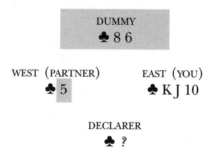

Partner leads the ♣5 against declarer's notrump contract, and the ♣6 is played from dummy. Which card do you play? Although the ♣10 is the lower of your touching high cards, you should still play the ♣K, third hand high. The complete layout might be something like this:

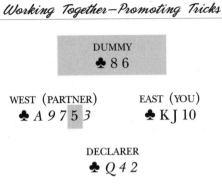

If you play the ♣10, declarer will be only too pleased to win the first trick with the ♣Q. By playing the ♣K on the first trick, you prevent declarer from getting a trick in the suit, since you can next return the ♣J, trapping declarer's ♣Q.

Of course, it wouldn't have made much difference which club you played if this were the actual layout:

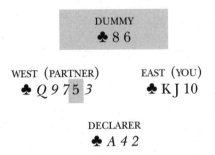

Now all your club honors are essentially equal, and your ♣10 will be sufficient to drive out declarer's ♣A. Unless you can tell whether partner holds the ♣A or ♣Q, however, you simply play your highest card. It's only when your highest cards in the suit are touching that you play the lower of your equals.

Before choosing the card to play as third hand, take a close look at the cards that are in the dummy. Consider this situation:

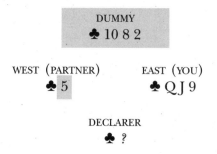

DUMMY
♣ 10 8 2

WEST (PARTNER)   EAST (YOU)
♣ 5   ♣ Q J 9

DECLARER
♣ ?

If declarer plays the ♣10 from dummy, you will need to play the ♣J, the lower-ranking of your two touching cards. But suppose declarer plays a low club from the dummy. Now you should play your ♣9. Because of the appearance of the ♣10 in dummy, your ♣9 has essentially become an equal. If declarer holds the ♣A or ♣K, your ♣9 is just as effective as the ♣ Q or ♣J in driving out declarer's high card. This might be the complete layout, for example:

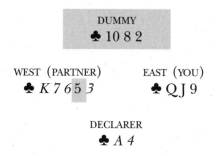

DUMMY
♣ 10 8 2

WEST (PARTNER)   EAST (YOU)
♣ K 7 6 5 3   ♣ Q J 9

DECLARER
♣ A 4

When your ♣9 forces out declarer's ♣A, partner will be able to visualize that you hold both the ♣Q and ♣J; otherwise, declarer would have won the first trick with a lower card than the ♣A.

If we go back across the table, you can see how this principle often allows you to visualize the complete layout of every card in the suit after only one trick has been played. For example:

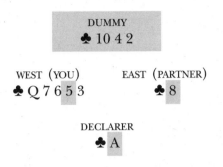

You lead the ♣5, the ♣2 is played from dummy, partner plays the
♣8, and declarer wins the trick with the ♣A. Do you have a picture
of the complete layout of the suit? You should be able to place all
the unseen cards: the ♣K, ♣J, and ♣9.

First of all, partner can't hold the ♣K. Partner couldn't see your
♣Q or declarer's ♣A, so partner would have played the ♣K—third
hand high—holding that card. Also, declarer can't hold either the
♣J or ♣9, since declarer would have won the first trick more cheaply
holding one of those cards. The entire layout of the suit must be:

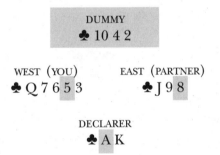

It's amazing how those hidden cards suddenly pop into view.

Although the defenders' agreement to play the lower of equal
honors when playing third hand high will often pinpoint the location of all the hidden high cards, there are times when there's room
for doubt. Consider this situation:

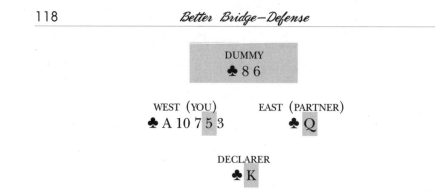

You lead fourth highest against a notrump contract, partner plays the ♣Q, and declarer wins the trick with the ♣K. Where's the ♣J? Declarer must hold that card because partner would have played the ♣J holding both the ♣Q and ♣J.

But suppose the play to the first trick goes in this manner:

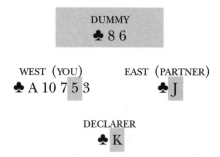

Which player holds the ♣Q? At first glance, it might seem that partner holds that card, since declarer played the ♣K to the first trick. Declarer, however, is under no obligation to play the lowest card which will win the trick. Declarer could be making a deceptive play by winning with the ♣K, rather than the ♣Q, when this is the actual layout:

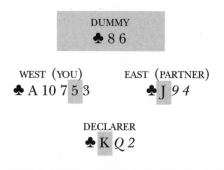

You'll be disappointed if you later lead a low club, hoping partner holds the ♣Q. On the other hand, the full layout of the suit could be like this:

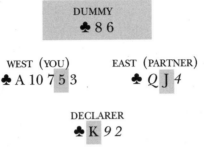

DUMMY
♣ 8 6

WEST (YOU)   EAST (PARTNER)
♣ A 10 7 5 3   ♣ Q J 4

DECLARER
♣ K 9 2

You have no way of knowing for sure whether or not declarer holds the ♣Q, and you'll have to rely on other clues to help you out. You may be able to tell from the auction—perhaps partner has supported clubs—or you may be able to tell from the subsequent play—partner may be able to provide some helpful signals.

Even though you won't always know exactly where the missing high cards are located, you will some of the time—and that's better than nothing. Let's see an example in an actual hand. The auction doesn't give much information:

WEST	NORTH	EAST	SOUTH
			1NT
Pass	3NT	Pass	Pass
Pass			

You lead your fourth best heart, and you see this on the first trick:

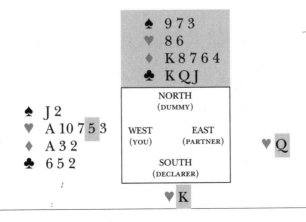

♠ 9 7 3
♥ 8 6
♦ K 8 7 6 4
♣ K Q J

NORTH
(DUMMY)

♠ J 2
♥ A 10 7 5 3   WEST   EAST
♦ A 3 2   (YOU)   (PARTNER)   ♥ Q
♣ 6 5 2

SOUTH
(DECLARER)

♥ K

A low heart is played from dummy, partner plays the ♥Q, and declarer wins the trick with the ♥K. Declarer now leads the ♦J. Have you decided whether or not to play your ♦A? After all, there's two conflicting guidelines here: "cover an honor with an honor" and "second hand low." Your choice shouldn't have anything to do with that. You have enough clues to guide you along the right path.

Partner's play to the first trick has told you that declarer holds the ♥J. Unless declarer started with a doubleton heart, there's no need to hop up with the ♦A to lead the ♥A. It's better to play a low diamond and hope that your partner can gain the lead to play a heart through declarer's ♥J. It looks as though declarer is about to take a diamond finesse, and partner may hold the ♦Q. That will be just the entry you need to partner's hand. Even if declarer holds the ♦Q, it's highly unlikely that declarer will be able to take nine tricks if you don't play your ♦A on this trick. You can wait to take your ♦A, and perhaps partner's signals will help you in the meantime.

Here's the complete hand:

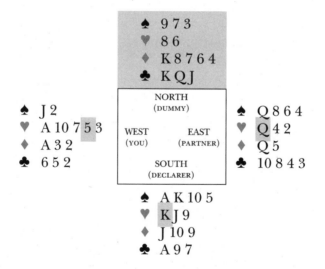

When you play a low diamond, declarer will take the finesse and lose to partner's ♦Q. Partner will return a heart, trapping declarer's ♥J, and letting you take the next four heart tricks. You'll also get a trick with the ♦A to defeat the contract two tricks. If you were to play the ♦A on the first trick and try to take your heart tricks, declarer would make the contract.

You could also defeat the contract if the complete hand were something like this:

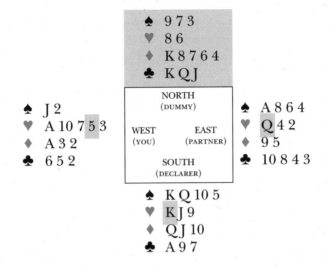

♠ 9 7 3
♥ 8 6
♦ K 8 7 6 4
♣ K Q J

NORTH
(DUMMY)

♠ J 2
♥ A 10 7 5 3
♦ A 3 2
♣ 6 5 2

WEST
(YOU)

EAST
(PARTNER)

♠ A 8 6 4
♥ Q 4 2
♦ 9 5
♣ 10 8 4 3

SOUTH
(DECLARER)

♠ K Q 10 5
♥ K J 9
♦ Q J 10
♣ A 9 7

The ♦J would win the trick, and declarer would lead another diamond. You could hold up again, and wait to take your ♦A on the third round of the suit. On this round of diamonds, partner could discard the ♠8, an encouraging signal in that suit. Now you'd know where partner's entry was located. You could lead a spade to partner's ♠A, and partner could return a heart to defeat the contract.

Promoting Winners
When Declarer Leads a Suit

Sometimes declarer leads a suit in which you have an opportunity to promote winners. Guidelines such as second hand low and cover an honor with an honor will often help you out, but you'll need to assess each situation to decide which one applies.

Splitting Honors

Consider this situation in which declarer leads a low spade toward dummy:

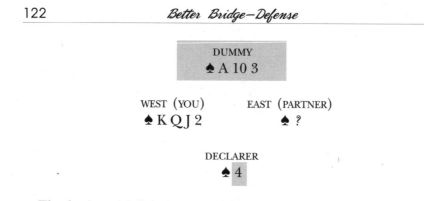

DUMMY
♠ A 10 3

WEST (YOU)   EAST (PARTNER)
♠ K Q J 2   ♠ ?

DECLARER
♠ 4

The basic guideline is second hand low, but that's probably not such a good idea in this case. If you play your ♠2, it's possible that declarer might choose to play dummy's ♠10. Partner doesn't have a spade higher than the ♠10, so declarer will end up winning two tricks in the suit. Instead, play one of your spade honors to drive out dummy's ♠A and promote your remaining high spades into winners.

This is referred to as *splitting your honors.* You usually play the lowest of equal honors, the ♠J in the above layout. This is similar to playing the lowest of touching honors when you play third hand high. It's the opposite of leading the top of touching honors.

Splitting honors requires some thought. You usually split honors only when you can see that there's a good possibility of promoting a trick for your side—or at least preventing declarer from getting an extra trick. Consider this situation:

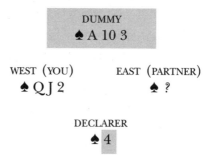

DUMMY
♠ A 10 3

WEST (YOU)   EAST (PARTNER)
♠ Q J 2   ♠ ?

DECLARER
♠ 4

It may well be best to play the ♠J if this is the complete layout that you visualize:

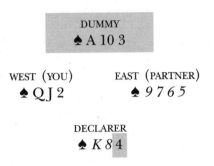

If you play the ♠2, declarer might insert dummy's ♠10 and win three tricks in the suit. By playing the ♠J, you drive out dummy's ♠A and restrict declarer to two winners. Playing the ♠J might not work out so well, however, if the actual situation is something like this:

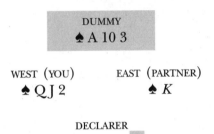

You'll end up with only one trick in the suit when you were entitled to two. Usually, you'll be able to tell whether or not this is a likely layout. If declarer has bid spades during the auction, for example, this becomes more of a possibility.

Avoid splitting your honors in this type of situation:

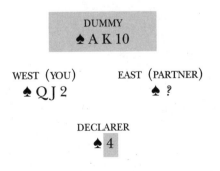

Here you can see that there's nothing to promote by splitting your honors. If you play the ♠J, declarer can win the trick with dummy's ♠K, then cross back over and lead another low spade. Your ♠Q will now be trapped by dummy's remaining ♠ A 10. It's usually best to play a low spade initially. Declarer may not be planning to play dummy's ♠10 on the first round, and may choose to win the first trick with the ♠K. Now you may be in a position to promote a winner in the suit later on during the play by driving out dummy's remaining high spade.

Deciding whether or not to split your honors can be even more challenging when a low card is led from the dummy. Consider this situation:

DUMMY
♠ 8 6 4

WEST (PARTNER)   EAST (YOU)
♠ ?   ♠ K Q 7 2

DECLARER
♠ ?

If declarer leads a low spade from dummy, should you split your honors or play second hand low? It's impossible to tell unless you have some clues from the bidding or play so far. It would be a good idea to play the ♠Q and promote your ♠K into a trick if this is the complete layout:

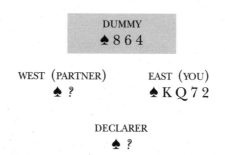

DUMMY
♠ 8 6 4

WEST (PARTNER)   EAST (YOU)
♠ 10 9 5 3   ♠ K Q 7 2

DECLARER
♠ A J

It wouldn't be so successful if this is what the suit looks like:

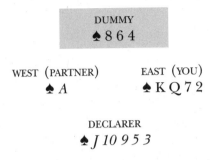

Declarer will often have a holding somewhere between these two extremes:

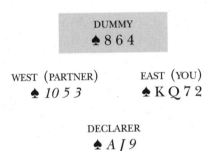

If this is the situation, it's still difficult to tell which card you should play. A lot depends on what declarer is planning to do. If your side only needs one trick from this suit to defeat the contract, play the ♠Q to promote the ♠K as a winner. If you need two tricks, play low. Declarer may play the ♠A or the ♠9. In either case, your side gets two tricks. If declarer guesses to play the ♠J . . . too bad.

Unless you're reasonably certain that it's correct to split your honors, you're usually better off to follow the old adage of second hand low, leaving declarer to guess which high cards you hold.

Covering Honors

When declarer leads a high card and you hold a higher-ranking card, you have to decide whether to play second hand low or to cover declarer's high card with your own. Here's a typical situation:

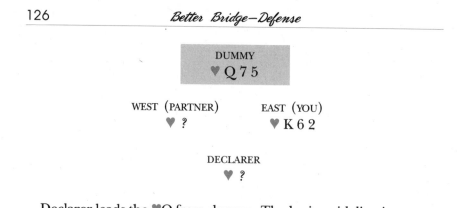

Declarer leads the ♥Q from dummy. The basic guideline is to **cover an honor with an honor**. If you play the ♥K, declarer will have to play the ♥A to win the trick and will have used up two high cards in exchange for one of yours. That's not a bad idea, since all the remaining cards in the suit will be promoted several notches in importance now that the ♥A, ♥K, and ♥Q are gone. It only benefits your side, however, when it's your side's cards that have been promoted. It won't do you much good to cover, for example, if this is the complete layout:

```
                   DUMMY
                  ♥ Q 7 5

   WEST (PARTNER)          EAST (YOU)
       ♥ 4 3                ♥ K 6 2

                  DECLARER
                 ♥ A J 10 9 8
```

Once you cover, all of declarer's remaining cards have been promoted into winners. Of course, it probably won't matter much, since declarer can repeat the finesse against your ♥K if you don't cover. On the other hand, you definitely want to cover if this is the situation:

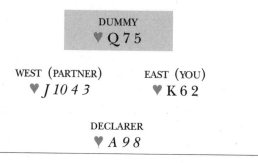

```
                   DUMMY
                  ♥ Q 7 5

   WEST (PARTNER)          EAST (YOU)
     ♥ J 10 4 3             ♥ K 6 2

                  DECLARER
                   ♥ A 9 8
```

If you don't cover, the ♥Q will win the trick, and declarer will get two tricks from the suit.

Without seeing the hidden hands, how can you judge whether or not to cover? There's often no way to know, and that's where the guideline comes in handy. After, all, it didn't do any harm to cover in the first layout above—it just didn't do any good.

Don't follow the guideline as a reflex. If you have reason to believe that there's nothing to be gained by covering, then don't cover. If declarer has bid hearts more than once during the auction, for example, it would be unwise to cover in case this is the actual layout:

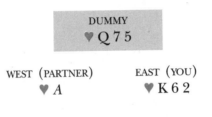

DUMMY
♥ Q 7 5

WEST (PARTNER)   EAST (YOU)
♥ A   ♥ K 6 2

DECLARER
♥ J 10 9 8 4 3

Great will be the crash if you do cover!

One of the more challenging situations arises when there are two or more touching honors in the dummy. For example:

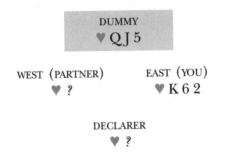

DUMMY
♥ Q J 5

WEST (PARTNER)   EAST (YOU)
♥ ?   ♥ K 6 2

DECLARER
♥ ?

Do you cover the ♥Q, or wait until the ♥J is led? The guideline here is to **wait to cover the last touching honor**. If the ♥Q is led on the first round of the suit, you don't cover. If the ♥J is then led, you do cover. To understand why, you need to visualize the possible layouts of the suit. Here's one scenario in which it makes a difference which honor you cover:

DUMMY
♥ Q J 5

WEST (PARTNER)　　　　EAST (YOU)
♥ A 10 9 4　　　　　　♥ K 6 2

DECLARER
♠ 8 7 3

If you cover the first honor, you'll win the trick, but the remaining cards will look like this:

DUMMY
♥ J 5

WEST (PARTNER)　　　　EAST (YOU)
♥ A 10 9　　　　　　♥ 2

DECLARER
♥ 8 7

Declarer can now get a trick from the suit by leading toward dummy's ♥J. If instead you don't cover the first honor, partner wins the trick, and the remaining cards look like this:

DUMMY
♥ J 5

WEST (PARTNER)　　　　EAST (YOU)
♥ 10 9 4　　　　　　♥ K 6

DECLARER
♥ 8 7

Partner can now lead the ♥10, and dummy's ♥J is trapped. Declarer doesn't take any tricks in the suit.

Here's another possible layout in which it makes a difference which honor you cover:

DUMMY
♥ Q J 5

WEST (PARTNER)   EAST (YOU)
♥ *10 7 4 3*   ♥ K 6 2

DECLARER
♥ *A 9 8*

If you cover the first honor, declarer wins the ♥A, leaving these cards:

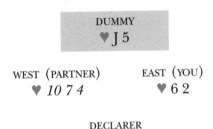

DUMMY
♥ J 5

WEST (PARTNER)   EAST (YOU)
♥ *10 7 4*   ♥ *6 2*

DECLARER
♥ *9 8*

Declarer can now lead the ♥9 and partner's ♥10 is trapped. If partner covers the ♥9, dummy's ♥J wins the trick, and declarer wins another trick with the ♥8. If partner doesn't cover the ♥9, declarer plays a low heart from dummy and wins the trick. Again, declarer gets three tricks from the suit.

If you don't cover the first honor, the following layout is left after declarer wins the first trick:

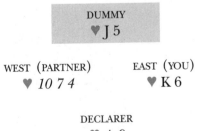

DUMMY
♥ J 5

WEST (PARTNER)   EAST (YOU)
♥ *10 7 4*   ♥ K 6

DECLARER
♥ *A 9*

Now declarer can take only one more trick in the suit. If declarer leads the ♥5 from dummy, you play the ♥6, and declarer must play the ♥A to win the trick. If declarer leads the ♥J from dummy, you cover, since it's the last of the touching honors from dummy. Declarer must play the ♥A to win the trick, and partner's ♥10 is promoted into the highest card.

Knowing when to cover honors requires a lot of practice. Try to visualize the layout each time to see if there's anything to gain by covering. If you think there could be something to gain, then cover; otherwise, play low.

Summary

When trying to promote winners, use the same guidelines as when taking sure tricks:

- High card from the short side first.
- Third hand high.
- High cards encourage, low cards discourage.

These guidelines are no substitute for considering each situation on its own merit. Try visualizing the layout of the unseen cards, and use that knowledge to address those situations that require special care:

- Avoid blocking suits.
- Play the lower of equal honors when playing third hand high.

When playing second hand to a trick:

- Split your honors when necessary to prevent declarer from winning a trick too cheaply.
- Cover an honor with an honor when you can potentially promote a winner for your side.
- Cover the last of touching honors.

Practice Hands

Hand 5.1

```
                    ♠ 9 5 2
                    ♥ A 5 4
                    ♦ K Q J 9 7 4
                    ♣ K
           ┌─────────────────────┐
           │      NORTH          │    ♠ K 7
           │     (DUMMY)         │    ♥ Q J 9 6 2
 LEAD  ♠ Q │  WEST      EAST     │    ♦ 6 3
           │ (PARTNER)  (YOU)    │    ♣ J 8 7 3
           │                     │
           │      SOUTH          │
           │    (DECLARER)       │
           └─────────────────────┘
```

WEST	NORTH	EAST	SOUTH
	1♦	Pass	2♣
Pass	2♦	Pass	3NT
Pass	Pass	Pass	

Partner leads the ♠Q against South's 3NT contract. What sort of picture do you have of the spade layout? Where are the ♠A, ♠J, and ♠10. How do you intend to help defeat the contract?

Solution 5.1

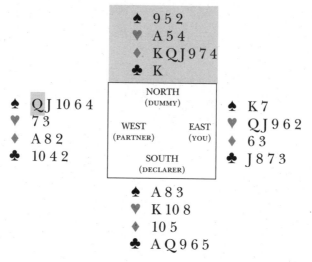

♠ 9 5 2
♥ A 5 4
♦ K Q J 9 7 4
♣ K

NORTH
(DUMMY)

♠ Q J 10 6 4
♥ 7 3
♦ A 8 2
♣ 10 4 2

WEST
(PARTNER)

EAST
(YOU)

♠ K 7
♥ Q J 9 6 2
♦ 6 3
♣ J 8 7 3

SOUTH
(DECLARER)

♠ A 8 3
♥ K 10 8
♦ 10 5
♣ A Q 9 6 5

Partner's lead of the ♠Q is likely the top of a three-card sequence headed by the ♠ Q J 10. Partner can't be leading from a broken sequence headed by ♠ Q J 9 because you can see the ♠9 in the dummy. Partner is unlikely to be leading from an interior sequence headed by ♠ A Q J because South has bid notrump and is likely to have at least one high card in spades. If partner held only a two-card sequence headed by ♠ Q J, partner would have led fourth highest.

You must be careful not to block the spade suit by playing the ♠7 on the first trick. If you do, declarer can make the contract in two ways. Declarer could win the first trick and lead diamonds to drive out partner's ♦A. Partner can lead a spade to your ♠K, but that's all for the defense. Declarer takes the rest of the tricks. Alternatively, declarer could let your partner's ♠Q win the first trick and could let your ♠K win the second trick when partner led another spade. You wouldn't have any spades left to lead. Whatever you led, declarer would win and drive out the ♦A. Since declarer would still have the ♠A, that would be the last trick for the defense.

Instead, play the ♠K on partner's ♠Q. Declarer can no longer make the contract. If declarer wins the first trick and leads diamonds, partner wins and takes four spade tricks. If declarer lets you win the first trick, you lead back the ♠7 to partner who continues to lead spades to drive out declarer's ♠A. When declarer tries to promote winners in diamonds, partner takes the ♦A and the rest of the established spade winners.

Hand 5.2

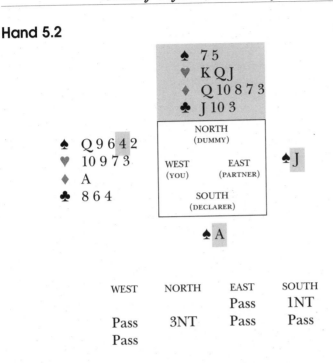

	♠ 7 5	
	♥ K Q J	
	♦ Q 10 8 7 3	
	♣ J 10 3	

| | NORTH | |
| | (DUMMY) | |

♠ Q 9 6 4 2
♥ 10 9 7 3
♦ A
♣ 8 6 4

| WEST | EAST |
| (YOU) | (PARTNER) |

♠ J

| | SOUTH | |
| | (DECLARER) | |

♠ A

WEST	NORTH	EAST	SOUTH
		Pass	1NT
Pass	3NT	Pass	Pass
Pass			

Your opening lead against the 3NT contract is the ♠4, fourth from longest and strongest. The ♠5 is played from dummy, partner plays the ♠J, and declarer wins the trick with the ♠A. What's the layout of the spade suit?

Declarer now leads a low diamond toward dummy, and you win the trick with the ♦A as both dummy and partner follow with low diamonds. Is it a good idea to lead another spade?

Solution 5.2

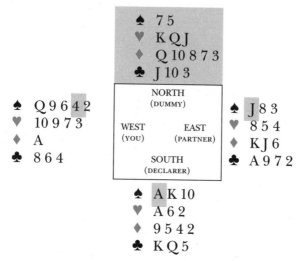

Partner's play of the ♠J to the first trick let's you know that the spade layout is similar to that in the diagram. Partner would have played the ♠K—third hand high—holding that card. Partner would have played the ♠10—lower of equals—holding both the ♠J and ♠10. So, declarer must hold both the ♠K and ♠10.

When you win the ♦A, there's no point in leading another spade. You'll be leading into the jaws of declarer's ♠ K 10. Declarer will end up with three spade tricks, and you'll end up with none, because even if you can eventually establish your last two spades as winners, you have no entry with which to take them. Instead, you'll have to wait until partner can lead spades.

Ideally, you would like to find an entry to partner's hand, so that partner can lead a spade through declarer. On the actual hand, it doesn't much matter whether you lead a heart or a club—as long as you don't lead another spade. Declarer can't make the contract without letting your partner gain the lead in both diamonds and clubs. As long as your partner leads back a spade after winning a trick, the defense will prevail. Declarer can't prevent you from getting a trick with the ♠Q, to go along with three diamond tricks and the ♣A.

Hand 5.3

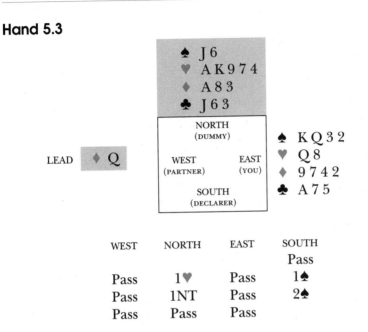

♠ J 6
♥ A K 9 7 4
♦ A 8 3
♣ J 6 3

NORTH
(DUMMY)

LEAD ♦ Q

WEST
(PARTNER)

EAST
(YOU)

♠ K Q 3 2
♥ Q 8
♦ 9 7 4 2
♣ A 7 5

SOUTH
(DECLARER)

WEST	NORTH	EAST	SOUTH
			Pass
Pass	1♥	Pass	1♠
Pass	1NT	Pass	2♠
Pass	Pass	Pass	

Partner leads the ♦Q against South's partscore contract, and declarer wins the first trick in dummy with the ♦A. Where's the ♦K? How many spades do you think are in the South hand?

What do you plan to play if declarer leads the ♠J from dummy at trick two? What if declarer leads the ♣J?

Solution 5.3

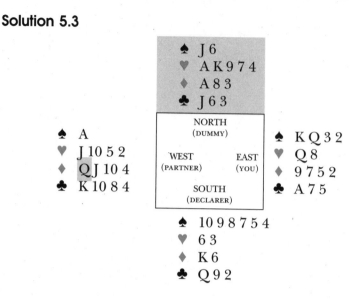

Partner's lead of the ♦Q shows the ♦J but denies the ♦K. Declarer must have the ♦K. South has bid spades twice during the auction without any support from partner. South should have at least a five-card suit and probably a six-card suit.

If declarer leads the ♠J from dummy, play second hand low. Since declarer has at least five spades, partner has at most two and could easily have a singleton or void. There's nothing to promote in partner's hand by covering, and nothing to be gained by splitting your honors. In fact, as you can see from the actual hand, you'll lose a trick if you play one of your spade honors on the first trick, since partner's ♠A will fall on the same trick. If you play second hand low, your side will eventually get three trump tricks.

On the other hand, if the ♣J is led from dummy, you should cover with your ♣A. You don't know anything about declarer's club suit, so you should follow the principle of covering an honor with an honor. If you do, declarer will end up losing three club tricks, since partner's ♣K and ♣10 will trap declarer's ♣Q. If you don't cover, partner will win the trick with the ♣K, but declarer can later lead a club from dummy toward the ♣Q and will get a trick whether or not you play your ♣A.

The hand can be defeated only if your side ends up with three spade winners and three club winners. To do that, you have to make careful use of your high cards.

Hand 5.4

```
                          ♠ A 6
                          ♥ 10 7 4
                          ♦ J 4
                          ♣ AKQJ92
                          NORTH
                          (DUMMY)
  ♠ Q 10 4
  ♥ K 6 5 3 2      WEST          EAST        ♥ 9
  ♦ A 9 5 2        (YOU)      (PARTNER)
  ♣ 10
                          SOUTH
                          (DECLARER)

                          ♥ A
```

WEST	NORTH	EAST	SOUTH
Pass	1♣	Pass	1♦
Pass	3♣	Pass	3NT
Pass	Pass	Pass	

Against the opponents' 3NT contract, you start off with the ♥3. The ♥4 is played from dummy, partner plays the ♥9, and declarer wins the first trick with the ♥A.

What is the layout of the heart suit around the table? Which card do you play when declarer leads the ♦3 toward dummy at trick two?

Solution 5.4

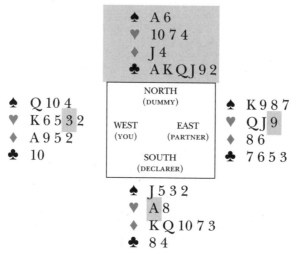

Partner must hold the ♥Q and ♥J; otherwise, declarer would have won the first trick with one of those cards. Declarer must hold the ♥8; otherwise partner would have played it to the first trick as the lower of equals. The heart layout should be that shown in the actual hand.

When declarer plays a low diamond toward dummy at trick two, rise immediately with the ♦A. Since you know the exact layout of the heart suit, this is no time for second hand low. You continue by leading a low heart to partner's ♥J. When partner wins this trick and leads back the ♥Q, overtake with the ♥K, and take the rest of your heart winners. You get one diamond trick and four heart tricks to defeat the contract.

Don't let declarer sneak through a diamond trick. After getting a diamond trick, declarer can take the ♠A and six club tricks to go along with the ♥A. That's enough for the contract. Leading a low diamond at trick two is a clever play by declarer, but it can't fool you once you know how the heart suit lies.

Working Together—
With Long Suits

"Little strokes, fell great oaks."

— Benjamin Franklin,
Poor Richard's Almanac, [1750]

Defending gives you the chance to show your resourcefulness. You won't always be able to defeat the contract by taking your sure tricks or by promoting winners using your high cards. Declarer's side usually has most of the high cards, so you have to look for other ways to develop tricks. The tried and true formula is to go after one of your side's long suits. That's why you tend to lead a suit bid by your side during the auction, or fourth highest from your own long suit if you have no other information.

There's power in the long suits. By repeatedly leading the suit, you hope to force out all of declarer's cards in the suit, eventually establishing your remaining cards as winners through length. It's often a race to see which side can develop their winners first, and you have the advantage of the opening lead. If you can develop some winners and regain the lead, there's nothing declarer can do to stop you from taking your winners in a notrump contract. Developing a long suit is less effective against a suit contract, unless declarer eventually runs out of trumps.

When developing winners through length, you have the same challenges that face declarer. You must be careful to use your entries wisely, so that you can eventually take your established tricks. Let's see how the defenders work together to overcome any obstacles.

Giving Up the Lead

To develop tricks through length, you have to be willing to give up tricks to the opponents. Each time you give up the lead, you'll need to regain it, so that you can lead the suit again. You can't afford to waste the power of the high cards in other the suits. Consider this hand from which you, as West, have to lead after the auction has gone:

WEST	NORTH	EAST	SOUTH
	1♦	Pass	1NT
Pass	3NT	Pass	Pass
Pass			

♠ A 8 3
♥ 8 6 5 2
♦ A K 4
♣ A 8 3

You start with four sure tricks, but that's not enough to defeat the 3NT contract. Where is your fifth defensive trick? You have 15 high card points, and the opponents need about 26 points to undertake a game contract. It's unlikely that partner holds even a single high card. Your only hope is that the partnership has some length in hearts, and you start off by leading that suit. Let's see how that works out:

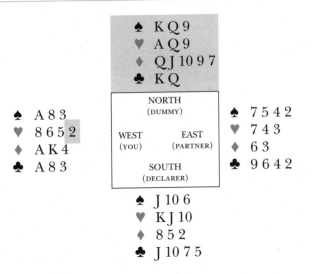

♠ K Q 9
♥ A Q 9
♦ Q J 10 9 7
♣ K Q

NORTH
(DUMMY)

♠ A 8 3
♥ 8 6 5 2
♦ A K 4
♣ A 8 3

WEST
(YOU)

EAST
(PARTNER)

♠ 7 5 4 2
♥ 7 4 3
♦ 6 3
♣ 9 6 4 2

SOUTH
(DECLARER)

♠ J 10 6
♥ K J 10
♦ 8 5 2
♣ J 10 7 5

A heart is the only lead that gives your side a chance. Declarer has only three sure tricks and must go about promoting winners in the other suits. After winning the first heart trick, suppose declarer leads the ♣K from dummy, you win and lead a second round of hearts. Declarer wins and leads a diamond. You win and lead a third round of hearts. There's nothing declarer can do. Declarer still doesn't have nine tricks established, and when declarer leads another diamond or a spade, you can win and take the setting trick with your established heart.

The first thing to notice is that you didn't need any strength in the heart suit to establish a trick. You were a little lucky that the opponents' six hearts were divided exactly 3–3, but partner could have held more than three hearts which would have improved your chances of establishing a trick.

The second thing to notice is that you couldn't afford to lead a high card before leading a heart.* Suppose you led one of your high diamonds so that you could see dummy before deciding what to do. When you now switch to a heart, it's too late. Declarer can lead a second round of diamonds, driving out your remaining high card in that suit. You lead another heart, and declarer leads a club

---

*The contract can be made if you lead the ♣A before leading a heart. You can defeat the contract if you lead the ♠A and immediately switch to hearts, but that would also be fatal if declarer's clubs and spades were exchanged.

to drive out your ♣A. Declarer still has a heart left and will make the contract with three heart tricks, three diamond tricks, and three club tricks.

Finally, you must be careful not to let declarer sneak through a diamond trick. If declarer were to win the first heart and lead a diamond toward dummy, you have to win a diamond trick immediately to lead another heart. If you don't, declarer will win a diamond trick and then drive out your ♣A and ♠A. Declarer will win the race, getting two spade tricks, three heart tricks, one diamond trick, and three club tricks. It's certainly a race, and you want to be first at the finish line.

Anyway, that's the basic idea. You want to establish your long suit while you still have high cards in the other suits to use as entries. The situation is more challenging when the high cards are divided between the defenders' hands. Consider this situation. You're defending as East after the bidding has gone:

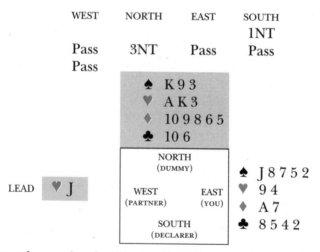

WEST	NORTH	EAST	SOUTH
			1NT
Pass	3NT	Pass	Pass
Pass			

♠ K 9 3
♥ A K 3
♦ 10 9 8 6 5
♣ 10 6

NORTH
(DUMMY)

LEAD   ♥ J

WEST   EAST
(PARTNER)   (YOU)

SOUTH
(DECLARER)

♠ J 8 7 5 2
♥ 9 4
♦ A 7
♣ 8 5 4 2

Partner's opening lead is the ♥J. Declarer wins the first trick with dummy's ♥K and leads a low diamond. In this situation, if you aren't sure about what to do, you could follow the old guideline of second hand low. Before automatically doing that, however, you should take a moment to consider the clues available.

Partner's lead of the ♥J tells you that declarer holds the ♥Q. The ♥A and ♥K were in dummy, and partner would have led the ♥Q holding a sequence such as ♥ Q J 10. Nonetheless, partner is likely to have some length in the suit—perhaps five or six cards—and your side may be able to develop some winners in the suit through length. Here's your opportunity to help out by winning this trick with the ♦A and leading a second round of hearts.

Let's see how that works out on the actual hand:

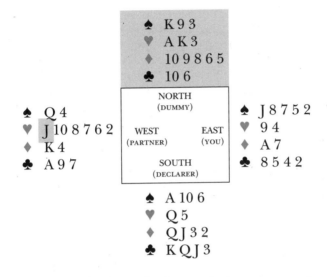

If you win the ♦A and lead a heart, declarer can no longer make the hand. Declarer wins the heart trick with the ♥Q and leads another round of diamonds to promote three winners in that suit. But partner wins the ♦K and leads another round of hearts. Declarer has only eight tricks and will have to lead a club to promote a ninth trick. Partner wins with the ♣A and takes three heart tricks to defeat the contract by two tricks.

If you had played low on the first diamond trick, partner would win the trick with the ♦K and could lead a second round of hearts. Declarer will win this and lead another diamond, driving out your ♦A. You have no hearts left to lead, so you can't help partner to establish the suit. Whatever you return, declarer can drive out partner's ♣A and will end up making an overtrick: two spades, three hearts, three diamonds, and two clubs.

You had to use your entry while you still had a heart left to lead. This is a lot easier to see when looking at the combined hands. That's how you'd want to handle your entries when establishing the heart suit—keeping the ♦K and ♣A with the length. Still, if you can visualize what's likely to happen, you can achieve the same result without actually seeing partner's hand.

Ducking

Sometimes, the only entry to the winners you develop through length lies in the long suit itself. If that's the case, you must be careful of the order in which you take your tricks. Sometimes, this happens without any extra effort. Consider this suit:

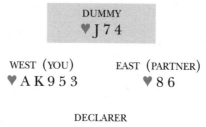

DUMMY
♥ J 7 4

WEST (YOU)   EAST (PARTNER)
♥ A K 9 5 3   ♥ 8 6

DECLARER
♥ Q 10 2

When leading this suit against a notrump contract, you would start with the ♥5—fourth highest—because you don't have a three-card sequence. Declarer would win the first trick, but now your side is perfectly poised to take the next four tricks in the suit because these are the remaining cards:

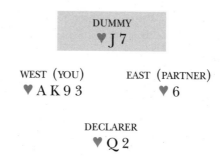

DUMMY
♥ J 7

WEST (YOU)   EAST (PARTNER)
♥ A K 9 3   ♥ 6

DECLARER
♥ Q 2

If you regain the lead, you can take your four heart tricks by playing the ♥A and ♥K, and then taking your two remaining winners which have been established through length. If partner is the one to regain the lead, partner still has the ♥6 left as a link card to your winners. Essentially, you couldn't establish the suit without giving up a trick to the opponents, and you did this on the first round of the suit.

Now let's look at a similar situation in the context of a hand. The auction has gone:

WEST	NORTH	EAST	SOUTH
	1♥	Pass	2♣
Pass	2♦	Pass	2NT
Pass	3NT	Pass	Pass
Pass			

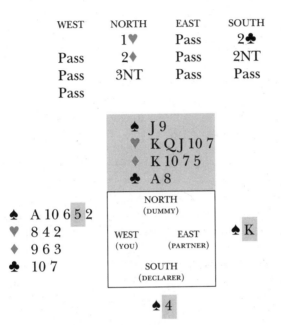

With the opponents bidding three suits, it's not surprising that you lead the fourth suit, especially when that turns out to be your long suit anyway. You lead the ♠5, declarer plays the ♠9, and partner wins the first trick with the ♠K, as declarer follows suit with the ♠4. Partner now returns the ♠7, declarer plays the ♠8, and it's up to you.

The first thing to consider is which player holds the ♠Q? Partner would play the lower of equal honors when playing third hand high, so partner's play of the ♠K denies possession of the ♠Q. Since declarer holds that card, you're going have to give up a trick in spades if you want to establish the suit.

If you take your ♠A and then lead the suit again, you will establish your winners but be left with no entry with which to reach them. Instead, the time to give up a spade trick is now. Let declarer win the second spade trick, and hold on to your ♠A as an entry to your winners. Here are the four hands:

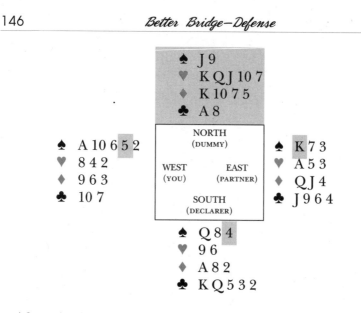

After winning the second spade trick, declarer has no choice but to eventually try and promote the extra winners needed for the contract in the heart suit. Partner will win the ♥A and still has the ♠3 to return to your carefully preserved ♠A. Now you're in the right hand at the right time to take your two established spade winners. In all, you get four spade tricks and the ♥A to defeat the contract.

If you had won the second spade trick, partner would have no way to reach your hand after winning the ♥A. Declarer would end up with ten tricks, rather than eight.

Letting the opponents win a trick you could have won is called *ducking*. If you have to lose a trick to the opponents, it's usually better to do it sooner rather than later.

Let's try a hand from the other side of the table. This time you're East, and the auction goes:

WEST	NORTH	EAST	SOUTH
		1♦	1NT
Pass	3NT	Pass	Pass
Pass			

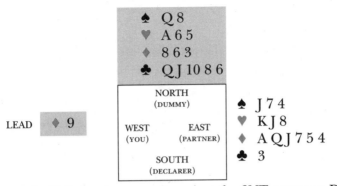

Partner dutifully leads your suit against the 3NT contract. Declarer plays a low diamond from dummy, and you play third hand high, winning the first trick with your ♦A. Now what? Oops, it's too late. Here's the complete hand:

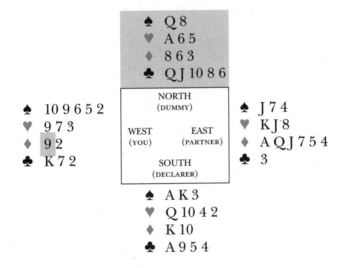

If you take the first trick with the ♦A and lead back the ♦Q to drive out declarer's ♦K, you'll establish all your remaining diamonds as winners but there's no way to reach them. Declarer will have to lose a trick to partner's ♣K, but partner won't have a diamond left to lead over to your hand. Declarer will end up with three spade tricks, one heart trick, one diamond trick, and four club tricks—enough for the contract.

This isn't the time to be playing third hand high. Instead, play your ♦J on the first trick. This will force declarer to win the trick with the ♦K. Now when partner gets in with the ♣K, partner will still have a diamond left to lead. You'll get five diamond tricks to go along with the ♣K and end up defeating the contract by two tricks.

You can tell from the auction and partner's opening lead of the ♦9 that declarer holds the ♦K. Since declarer is entitled to a diamond trick, it's best to take your losses early and give up the trick while partner still has another diamond. It's the same principle as ducking to preserve an entry.

Summary

When developing tricks through length, you have to be willing to give up tricks to the opponents in order to establish winners in your long suit. Use the following guidelines:

- Keep your high cards in other suits as entries to regain the lead.
- Keep an entry on the same side as the long suit.
- Duck to preserve an entry in your long suit.

Practice Hands

Hand 6.1

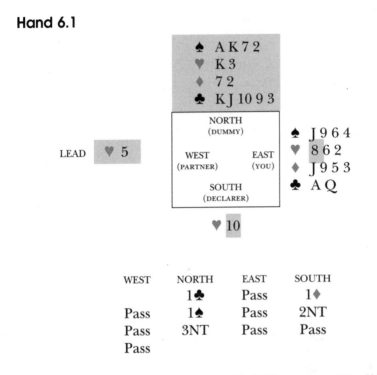

	WEST	NORTH	EAST	SOUTH
		1♣	Pass	1♦
	Pass	1♠	Pass	2NT
	Pass	3NT	Pass	Pass
	Pass			

Partner leads the ♥5 against South's 3NT contract. The ♥3 is played from dummy, you play the ♥8—third hand high—and declarer wins the first trick with the ♥10.

Declarer now leads the ♣2, partner plays the ♣4, and the ♣J is played from dummy. You win the trick with the ♣Q and have to decide what to do.

Solution 6.1

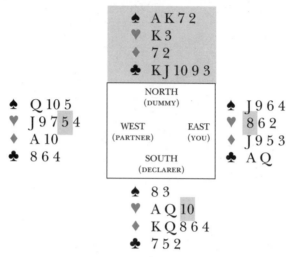

Although the play to the first heart trick was not very inspiring and declarer presumably still has some strength left in the heart suit, there's no reason to panic. Simply return partner's suit. Declarer will win this trick and lead another club to drive out your ♣A. Lead another heart.

Even though declarer has considerable strength in the heart suit, you will eventually drive out all of declarer's hearts. After establishing three winners in clubs, declarer still needs to promote one trick in diamonds to make the contract. Partner gets to win a trick with the ♦A and take the two established heart tricks to defeat the contract.

There's nothing spectacular about this hand. The opening lead is from partner's longest suit. You play third hand high to the first trick. When you get the lead, you return partner's suit. When you get the lead a second time, you return partner's suit once more. Slow and steady wins the race on this hand.

Hand 6.2

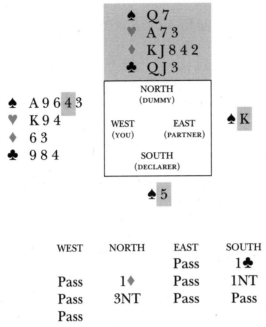

WEST	NORTH	EAST	SOUTH
		Pass	1♣
Pass	1♦	Pass	1NT
Pass	3NT	Pass	Pass
Pass			

You lead the ♠4 from your long suit against North-South's 3NT contract. The ♠7 is played from dummy, partner plays the ♠K, and declarer plays the ♠5.

Partner now leads back the ♠8, and declarer plays the ♠J. What's going on in the spade suit? How do you plan to defeat the contract?

Solution 6.2

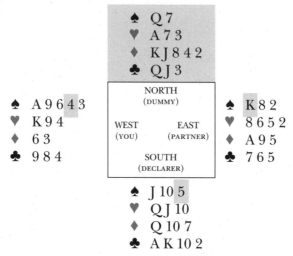

After winning the first trick with the ♠K, partner returns the ♠8. Partner would lead back the top card, the ♠10, if partner held both the ♠10 and ♠8. Partner would lead back a low card, the ♠2, if partner's remaining cards were ♠ 10 8 2. So, partner doesn't hold the ♠10 despite declarer's play of the ♠J on the second trick.

Although it's enticing to capture both dummy's ♠Q and declarer's ♠J with your ♠A, you must resist temptation. You need the ♠A as an entry to your long suit, since you have no other sure entry. Declarer is entitled to one spade trick, and it's best to take your losses early. Let declarer win this trick, and hope that either you or partner can regain the lead.

On the actual hand, declarer can't make the contract without promoting some winners in the diamond suit. Partner can win the ♦A and will still have the ♠2 as a link card over to your carefully preserved ♠A. Now that all the other spades are gone, you can take your two established spade winners to defeat the contract.

If you were deceived by declarer's play of the ♠J into winning the second trick, you could no longer defeat the contract. You could lead another spade to establish the suit, but partner would have no way to reach your hand after winning a trick with the ♦A.

Hand 6.3

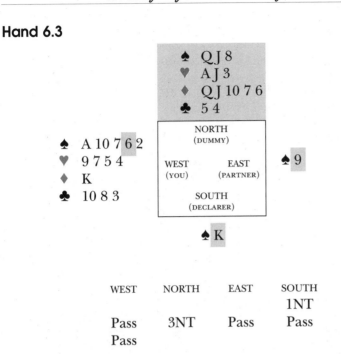

♠ QJ8
♥ AJ3
♦ QJ 10 7 6
♣ 54

NORTH
(DUMMY)

♠ A 10 7 6 2
♥ 9 7 5 4
♦ K
♣ 10 8 3

WEST
(YOU)

EAST
(PARTNER)

♠ 9

SOUTH
(DECLARER)

♠ K

WEST	NORTH	EAST	SOUTH
			1NT
Pass	3NT	Pass	Pass
Pass			

You lead the ♠6, fourth from longest and strongest, against declarer's 3NT contract. The ♠8 is played from dummy, partner plays the ♠9, and declarer wins the trick with the ♠K.

Declarer leads a low diamond toward dummy, and your ♦K wins the trick. What now?

Solution 6.3

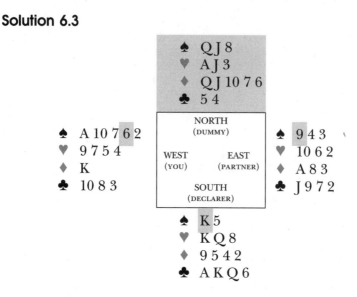

Your spade lead hasn't exactly struck gold in partner's hand, but there's still a chance. From the way declarer is playing diamonds, it looks as though declarer is trying to promote some winners in the suit and partner holds the ♦A—holding the ♦A, declarer would probably have tried a finesse. Your side will likely get a second opportunity to regain the lead before declarer has enough tricks to make the contract.

Declarer has shown a balanced hand and must have started with at least two spades. But unless declarer started with four spades, you can still develop two winners in spades by giving up another trick in the suit. If you play your ♠A and then another spade to remove dummy's remaining cards in the suit, you will also remove partner's remaining spades. When partner gets the lead with the ♦A, partner will have no spades left to lead.

The solution is to lead another low spade after winning the ♦K, giving up a second trick in the suit while retaining the ♠A as an entry. You'll have to hope partner, rather than declarer, holds three cards in spades. On the actual hand, this defeats the contract. After winning the ♦A, partner has a spade left to lead over to your ♠A. Now that all the other spades are gone, you can take the fourth and fifth tricks for the defenders with your last two spades.

Hand 6.4

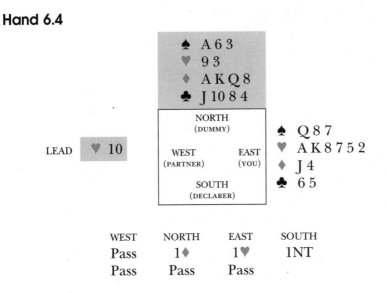

♠ A 6 3
♥ 9 3
♦ A K Q 8
♣ J 10 8 4

NORTH
(DUMMY)

LEAD ♥ 10

WEST
(PARTNER)

EAST
(YOU)

SOUTH
(DECLARER)

♠ Q 8 7
♥ A K 8 7 5 2
♦ J 4
♣ 6 5

WEST	NORTH	EAST	SOUTH
Pass	1♦	1♥	1NT
Pass	Pass	Pass	

Partner leads the ♥10 against South's 1NT contract, and A low heart is played from dummy. How do you visualize the layout of the heart suit? How do you plan to defeat the contract?

Solution 6.4

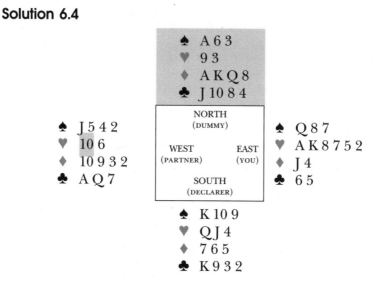

	♠ A 6 3	
	♥ 9 3	
	♦ A K Q 8	
	♣ J 10 8 4	

NORTH (DUMMY)

♠ J 5 4 2		♠ Q 8 7
♥ 10 6	WEST (PARTNER) EAST (YOU)	♥ A K 8 7 5 2
♦ 10 9 3 2		♦ J 4
♣ A Q 7	SOUTH (DECLARER)	♣ 6 5

	♠ K 10 9	
	♥ Q J 4	
	♦ 7 6 5	
	♣ K 9 3 2	

Partner has led your suit against the notrump contract. Since partner would lead the top of touching honors, or low from a three-card suit, the ♥10 looks like a singleton or the top of a doubleton. Declarer holds the ♥Q and ♥J, and at least one more heart. You're going to have to let declarer win a heart trick in order to establish the suit, and there's no time like the present. Duck the first round of hearts, playing the ♥8 as an encouraging card. Declarer will win the first trick but doesn't have enough sure tricks to make the contract. Declarer will probably play the ♦A, ♦K, and ♦Q, hoping the defenders' diamonds divide 3–3. When this doesn't materialize, declarer will lead a club, hoping to develop an extra trick from that suit.

Partner will win a club trick and must then decide what to do. Partner was probably a little surprised when you didn't play a heart honor on the first trick but should figure out what's going on. Partner knows you overcalled the suit, and you also played an encouraging card on the first trick, so partner will probably lead the ♥6. That's just the card you want to see. You take the next five heart tricks, and together with partner's two club tricks, that's enough to defeat the contract. You may even defeat the contract an extra trick if declarer took the three top diamonds before playing a club. Partner's ♦10 will now be a winner. If you were to win the first heart trick, partner would have no hearts left after you establish the suit. Declarer would wind up making an overtrick when partner can find no entry to your hand after winning a club trick.

Working Together—
Taking Finesses

"To know is nothing at all; to imagine is everything."

— ANATOLE FRANCE,
The Crime of Sylvestre Bonnard,
[1881]

The art of finessing doesn't lie solely in declarer's domain. The defenders can take advantage of the finesse and must often do so in order to defeat a contract. The success or failure of each finesse depends on the location of the high cards. The defenders need to combine knowledge with imagination if they are to make effective use of this technique.

The Defensive Finesse

The defenders take finesses in exactly the same way as declarer. The basic idea is to lead toward the card you hope will win a trick when the opponents hold a higher-ranking card. You can also lead a high

card to trap one of declarer's high cards when you can afford to
have it covered. Let's look at examples of both situations.

NORTH (DUMMY)
♠ A Q J 3

WEST (YOU)   EAST (PARTNER)
♠ 6 5 4   ♠ K 10 8 2

SOUTH (DECLARER)
♠ 9 7

If the defenders want to take a trick from this suit, you have to
lead a spade from your side. Essentially, you're leading a low card
toward the card you hope will take a trick, partner's ♠K. This is also
the basis for the defensive guideline of leading through strength—
dummy's high cards—and up to weakness—declarer's low cards. If
your partner has to lead the suit, you won't get a trick because partner will be leading into dummy's strength.

It's also interesting to look at this suit from declarer's perspective.
Declarer has a finessing position in spades. Declarer may well lead a
low card toward dummy, hoping that you hold the ♠K. Declarer plans
to finesse dummy's ♠Q or ♠J. An unsuccessful finesse by declarer is
the same as a successful finesse by the defenders, and vice-versa.

Do you need to lead the suit for partner? Not if declarer is planning to take the finesse anyway. But there are some hands where
declarer plans to make the contract by developing other suits. If
your side needs to get one trick from the spade suit before declarer
has established enough tricks to make the contract, you'll have to
lead spades when you have the opportunity. It's often a race to see
which side will be first to develop enough winners.

Here's an example where you can afford to lead a high card to
trap one of the opponents' high cards:

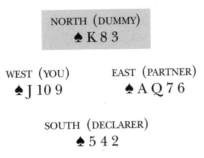

NORTH (DUMMY)
♠ K 8 3

WEST (YOU)   EAST (PARTNER)
♠ J 10 9   ♠ A Q 7 6

SOUTH (DECLARER)
♠ 5 4 2

When you lead the ♠J, dummy's ♠K is trapped. If declarer doesn't play the ♠K, partner let's your ♠J win the trick—probably playing the ♠7 as an encouraging card—and you can lead the ♠10 to repeat the finesse. If declarer covers the ♠J with dummy's ♠K, partner wins the trick with the ♠A, and your side can again take all the tricks in the suit.

In successfully taking a finesse against dummy's ♠K in the above layout, you start by following the basic guideline of leading the top of a sequence. Partner simply plays as high as necessary to ensure that your side wins the trick.

You can only lead a high card if you can afford to have it covered. Let's take away the ♠10 from your hand and give it to declarer:

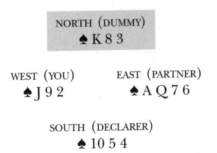

NORTH (DUMMY)
♠ K 8 3

WEST (YOU)   EAST (PARTNER)
♠ J 9 2   ♠ A Q 7 6

SOUTH (DECLARER)
♠ 10 5 4

If you lead the ♠J in this situation, declarer can cover with dummy's ♠K, forcing partner to win the trick with the ♠A. Partner can take a second trick with the ♠Q, but now declarer has the highest-ranking card in the suit, the ♠10.

What do you do in this situation? It depends how many tricks you need. If you only need two, it doesn't much matter. If you need all the tricks from this suit, you'll need a little help from declarer. You would start by leading a low spade—your standard lead from this

suit when you don't have a sequence. Declarer might play dummy's
♠K on the first round. After all, declarer doesn't know which defender holds the ♠A. If that happens, your side can take all the tricks
in the suit right away. If declarer plays a low spade from dummy on
the first trick, partner can win the trick with the ♠Q, but can't lead
another spade without giving declarer a trick with dummy's ♠K. You'll
have to sit back and wait until declarer has to lead the suit. If declarer later leads a low spade toward dummy's ♠K, partner can win
the ♠A and return a spade to your ♠J. It's all a bit complicated, but
the situation would be the same if you were declarer trying to take
all the tricks from this suit.

Most of the time, the challenge will come in recognizing the opportunity for a defensive finesse. Consider this hand. The auction goes:

WEST	NORTH	EAST	SOUTH
	1♦	Pass	1♥
Pass	2♥	Pass	4♥
Pass	Pass	Pass	Pass

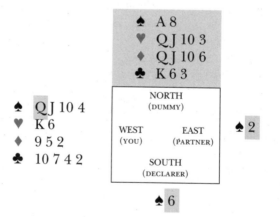

You lead the ♠Q against the 4♥ contract, and the first trick is won
by dummy's ♠A, as partner plays the ♠2 and declarer the ♠6. Declarer now leads one of the high hearts from dummy. Partner plays
the ♥5, declarer plays the ♥2, and you win the trick with the ♥K.
Now what?

It looks safe enough to lead another spade, but before making
any play, you should take the time to visualize what the hidden hands

look like and how you might defeat the contract. First, where's the
♠K? Either declarer or partner could have that card, but partner's
♠2 on the first trick was a discouraging signal. Partner probably
doesn't hold the ♠K. Even if partner does hold the ♠K, partner's ♠2
is a signal suggesting that you don't lead the suit again.

Where's the ♥A? Partner could hold that card, but it looks as
though declarer won the first trick in dummy in order to take a finesse in the heart suit, hoping your partner held the ♥K. So, where
are your tricks coming from if you are to defeat the contract? You'll
need partner to have some strength in the minor suits. If partner
holds the ♦A or ♦K, it won't do much good to lead diamonds from
your side. If partner holds some high cards in clubs, however, it may
be necessary for you to lead through dummy's strength, the ♣K, to
help partner out. Based on that reasoning, you should lead a club.
Here's the entire hand:

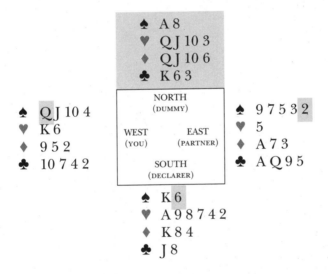

	♠ A 8	
	♥ Q J 10 3	
	♦ Q J 10 6	
	♣ K 6 3	

	NORTH (DUMMY)	
♠ Q J 10 4		♠ 9 7 5 3 2
♥ K 6	WEST (YOU)　　EAST (PARTNER)	♥ 5
♦ 9 5 2		♦ A 7 3
♣ 10 7 4 2	SOUTH (DECLARER)	♣ A Q 9 5

	♠ K 6	
	♥ A 9 8 7 4 2	
	♦ K 8 4	
	♣ J 8	

When you lead a club, declarer can no longer make the hand.
Partner has dummy's ♣K trapped and will win two tricks in the suit.
Partner will also get a trick with the ♦A to defeat the contract.

If you don't lead a club after winning the ♥K, declarer will make
the contract by driving out partner's ♦A after drawing your last trump.
Partner can't lead clubs without giving up a trick to dummy's ♣K,
but if partner doesn't lead a club, declarer has enough tricks: two
spades, five hearts, and the three established diamond winners.

The defenders can defeat the contract with the help of a finesse, but only if they recognize the opportunity. It's easier to see from partner's side, but partner can do nothing more than give you a discouraging signal in spades and hope you figure out what to do from there.

Trapping Hidden Cards

The defenders can't see each other's cards. It's interesting that this doesn't always put them at a disadvantage. Often the defenders will know long before declarer whether a finesse is destined for success or failure. They may also be in a position to ensure success no matter which side of the table declarer's high cards are located.

For example, suppose partner leads the ♥Q and this is what you see:

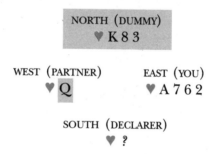

Right away you can see that dummy's ♥K is trapped, since you can visualize the complete layout:

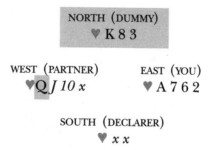

Declarer can't be sure whether or not the ♥K will win a trick because your partner could be leading from an interior sequence, such as ♥ A Q J 10. You know something that declarer doesn't.

You also know where the ♥K is located if this is the situation:

NORTH (DUMMY)
♥ 9 8 3

WEST (PARTNER)   EAST (YOU)
♥ Q   ♥ A 7 6 2

SOUTH (DECLARER)
♥ ?

Declarer must hold the ♥K, and your finesse is destined to lose. If
you were defending against a suit contract, you would usually play
your ♥A—third hand high—in case this is the layout:

NORTH (DUMMY)
♥ 9 8 3

WEST (PARTNER)   EAST (YOU)
♥Q J 10 5 4   ♥ A 7 6 2

SOUTH (DECLARER)
♥ K

With this combination of cards, you would actually do better as a
defender than as declarer. As a declarer, you would probably take
the finesse and lose to South's singleton ♥K. As a defender, you
can't go wrong once partner leads the ♥Q.

In addition to the king, there are other high cards that declarer
can't hide from the defenders. Consider this layout.

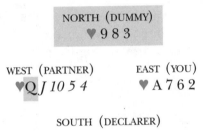

NORTH
♥ ?

WEST (PARTNER)   EAST (YOU)
♥ A J 10 9   ♥ K 7 2

SOUTH (DECLARER)
♥ ?

If you were declarer in a notrump contract and wanted to take all four tricks from this suit, you would have to guess which opponent held the ♥Q. As a defender, you don't have to guess! Partner merely leads the ♥J, top of the interior sequence, and lets nature take its course. For example, suppose the ♥Q comes down in the dummy:

NORTH (DUMMY)
♥ Q 8 4

WEST (PARTNER)   EAST (YOU)
♥ J   ♥ K 7 2

SOUTH (DECLARER)
♥ ?

Dummy's ♥Q is trapped. You can see partner's ♥J, so if declarer plays a low heart from dummy, you don't need to play the ♥K. Instead, you can make an encouraging signal with the ♥7, and partner's ♥J will win the trick. If the ♥Q is played from dummy, you cover with the ♥K, and again your side wins the trick.

Notice that you don't actually know that the ♥A is in partner's hand and that partner is leading from an interior sequence. For all you know, declarer has the ♥A and partner is leading the top of a three-card sequence or a broken sequence. Other than the ♥J, the only card you know partner holds is the ♥10. Nonetheless, it makes no difference to your play. If declarer plays low from dummy, you hold on to the ♥K, expecting partner's ♥J to drive out declarer's ♥A; if declarer plays the ♥Q, you cover with the ♥K, expecting to drive out declarer's ♥A and promote partner's ♥10 into a winner.

Let's move the ♥Q from the dummy into declarer's hand. This is how things look:

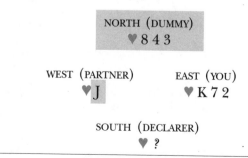

NORTH (DUMMY)
♥ 8 4 3

WEST (PARTNER)   EAST (YOU)
♥ J   ♥ K 7 2

SOUTH (DECLARER)
♥ ?

You can't see the ♥Q in the dummy and you know partner doesn't have it, since partner leads the top of touching cards. That places the ♥Q in declarer's hand. When a low heart is played from dummy, you play the ♥K, third hand high, to prevent declarer from winning a trick with the ♥Q. You can visualize that partner may have led from an interior sequence and are hoping the complete layout is something like this:

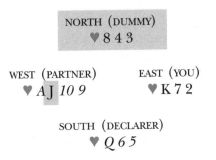

NORTH (DUMMY)
♥ 8 4 3

WEST (PARTNER)   EAST (YOU)
♥ A J *10 9*   ♥ K 7 2

SOUTH (DECLARER)
♥ Q 6 5

Once the ♥K wins the first trick, you can return the ♥7—top of your remaining doubleton—and declarer's ♥Q is trapped. Declarer can't hide the location of the ♥Q once the ♥J is led, and the defenders can always take all their tricks in the suit—without a guess!

You can't be 100% sure of the location of the ♥A when partner leads the ♥J, since this could be the layout:

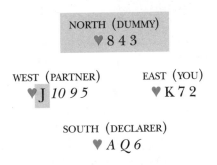

NORTH (DUMMY)
♥ 8 4 3

WEST (PARTNER)   EAST (YOU)
♥ J *10 9 5*   ♥ K 7 2

SOUTH (DECLARER)
♥ A Q 6

But playing the ♥K won't do any harm, if this is the situation, and you will still know where the ♥Q lies when declarer captures the ♥K with the ♥A.

Here's another situation in which both partners can quickly figure out the location of the unseen high cards:

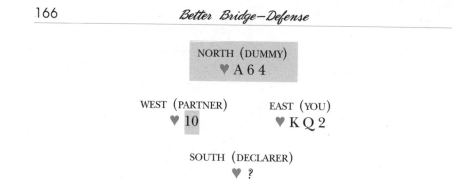

Partner leads the ♥10, and declarer plays a low heart from dummy. You know that declarer holds the ♥J because partner leads the top of touching cards. You'll need to play the ♥Q to win the first trick, since the full layout must be something like this:

NORTH (DUMMY)
♥ A 6 4

WEST (PARTNER)   EAST (YOU)
♥ 10 *9 x x*   ♥ K Q 2

SOUTH (DECLARER)
♥ *J x x*

When you win the first trick with the ♥Q, partner will also know the location of all the high cards. Partner will know that you also hold the ♥K, otherwise declarer would have won the first trick. Partner will know that declarer holds the ♥J because you play the lower of your equal honors as third hand.

Knowing this is the layout, you don't want to lead a second round of hearts from your side.* Instead, you want to wait until partner gains the lead and can lead another heart through dummy's ♥A to establish a trick with your ♥K. Partner knows the situation, and will understand why you didn't continue leading hearts after winning the first trick with the ♥Q. Essentially, the defense is taking a repeated finesse—leading twice toward the ♥ K Q 2.

---

*Against a notrump contract, you will sometimes have no choice but to continue leading hearts from your side. You would lead back the ♥K, hoping that declarer started with a doubleton heart, ♥ J x, so that your ♥K will capture declarer's ♥J while driving out dummy's ♥A at the same time.

Here's a hand where the defenders must cooperate to take their finesses:

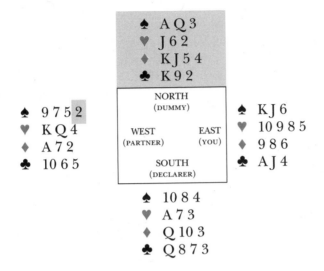

```
                    ♠ A Q 3
                    ♥ J 6 2
                    ♦ K J 5 4
                    ♣ K 9 2
                ┌─────────────────┐
                │     NORTH       │
   ♠ 9 7 5 2    │    (DUMMY)      │    ♠ K J 6
   ♥ K Q 4      │                 │    ♥ 10 9 8 5
   ♦ A 7 2      │ WEST      EAST  │    ♦ 9 8 6
   ♣ 10 6 5     │(PARTNER)  (YOU) │    ♣ A J 4
                │                 │
                │     SOUTH       │
                │   (DECLARER)    │
                └─────────────────┘
                    ♠ 10 8 4
                    ♥ A 7 3
                    ♦ Q 10 3
                    ♣ Q 8 7 3
```

South is playing in a contract of 1NT and partner gets off to the lead of the ♠2. Declarer has no idea where the missing high cards in spades are located and will probably play a low spade from dummy, hoping your partner holds the ♠K, ♠J, or both. You win the trick with the ♠J. You don't want to lead a spade back into the jaws of dummy's remaining ♠ A Q, so you lead a heart. You don't know the complete layout of the heart suit, but you're following the general principle of leading through declarer's strength up to the weakness in dummy. Declarer will probably play a low heart on this trick also, and partner will win the trick with the ♥Q.

Partner knows that you have the ♠K, since your ♠J won the first trick. So partner leads another spade. Declarer still doesn't know which of you holds the ♠K and will probably play dummy's ♠Q. Declarer is taking a finesse at the same time that your side is taking a finesse. As you knew ahead of time, declarer's finesse isn't going to work, and you'll win this trick with the ♠K. You could return your last spade to establish the rest of partner's suit, but you might also lead back a heart, through declarer, to help partner in that suit.

If you lead back a heart, declarer is helpless. If declarer plays a low heart, partner will win the ♥K and can lead another spade, or another heart, to establish a winner for your side through length.

Even if declarer plays the ♥A, partner's ♥K is now established as a winner. When declarer drives out partner's ♦A, the defense can come to enough winners to defeat the contract.

The defenders have to be careful about leading both spades and hearts from the right side. The defense would not be successful if partner leads the ♥K originally, or if you lead spades from your side. Neither defender has a picture of the complete hand at the start, but as the play progresses, the layout of each suit becomes clearer to both defenders.

A Challenge for Third Hand

Although you can usually place the missing high cards when partner leads an honor, the situation is a little different when partner leads a low card, especially when a high card appears in the dummy. Sometimes, it's not too difficult to decide which card to play as third hand. For example:

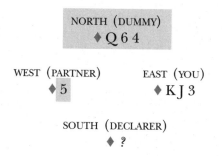

NORTH (DUMMY)
♦ Q 6 4

WEST (PARTNER)   EAST (YOU)
♦ 5   ♦ K J 3

SOUTH (DECLARER)
♦ ?

Partner leads the ♦5 against declarer's contract, and this is what you see in dummy. If declarer calls for dummy's ♦Q, you play the ♦K, trying to win the trick. If declarer plays a low diamond from dummy, you insert the ♦J. With the ♦Q in dummy, your ♦K and ♦J have essentially become equals, and your ♦J is all that is required for third hand high. You can visualize two possibilities. First, partner may hold the ♦A:

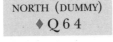

NORTH (DUMMY)
♦ Q 6 4

WEST (PARTNER)   EAST (YOU)
♦ *A 9 7 5 2*   ♦ K J 3

SOUTH (DECLARER)
♦ *10 8*

If that's the case, your ♦J will win the trick. You can then take a trick with the ♦K and lead the ♦3 back to partner's winners. The second possibility is that declarer holds the ♦A:

NORTH (DUMMY)
♦ Q 6 4

WEST (PARTNER)   EAST (YOU)
♦ *10 9 7 5 2*   ♦ K J 3

SOUTH (DECLARER)
♦ *A 8*

Your ♦J will force declarer to play the ♦A to win the trick, elevating your ♦K into a winner. Dummy's ♦Q won't get a trick if the suit is led by declarer, or if partner gains the lead and leads the ♦10. Your ♦K is still there to capture dummy's ♦Q.

The second layout is more likely if you're defending against a suit contract, since partner will rarely lead a low card when holding the ♦A. Against a notrump contract, either layout is a reasonable possibility.

Now let's make the situation more challenging:

NORTH (DUMMY)
♦ Q 6 4

WEST (PARTNER)   EAST (YOU)
♦ 5   ♦ K 10 3

SOUTH (DECLARER)
♦ ?

This won't be difficult if the ♦Q is played from dummy, since you'll simply cover with the ♦K to try to win the trick. But what if a low diamond is played from dummy? To decide which card to play, you have to visualize the possible layouts. There are four possible placements of the missing high cards.

First, partner could hold both the ♦A and ♦J:

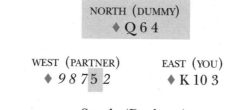

NORTH (DUMMY)
♦ Q 6 4

WEST (PARTNER)   EAST (YOU)
♦ A J 7 5 2   ♦ K 10 3

SOUTH (DECLARER)
♦ 9 8

Playing the ♦10 is best, since it will win the trick. You can then win a trick with the ♦K and lead back your ♦3 to partner's winners. If you play the ♦K, you'll win the trick, but you can no longer prevent declarer from getting a trick with dummy's ♦Q.

Second, declarer could hold both the ♦A and ♦J:

NORTH (DUMMY)
♦ Q 6 4

WEST (PARTNER)   EAST (YOU)
♦ 9 8 7 5 2   ♦ K 10 3

South (Declarer)
♦ A J

It would be best to play the ♦10. Declarer would win with the ♦J and could get a second trick with the ♦A, but that's all. If you were to play the ♦K, declarer would win the ♦A and subsequently get tricks with both the ♦J and ♦Q.

In the third possible layout, partner holds the ♦J and declarer holds the ♦A:

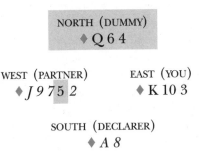

NORTH (DUMMY)
♦ Q 6 4

WEST (PARTNER)   EAST (YOU)
♦ J 9 75 2   ♦ K 10 3

SOUTH (DECLARER)
♦ A 8

Again it is best to play the ♦10. Declarer can win the trick with the ♦A, but that's all. Your ♦K still has dummy's ♦Q trapped. If you were to play the ♦K on the first trick, declarer would get a trick with the ♦A and a second trick with dummy's ♦Q.

In the final layout, partner holds the ♦A and declarer holds the ♦J:

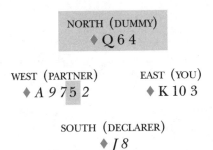

NORTH (DUMMY)
♦ Q 6 4

WEST (PARTNER)   EAST (YOU)
♦ A 9 75 2   ♦ K 10 3

SOUTH (DECLARER)
♦ J 8

If this is the situation, playing the ♦K would win the first trick, while playing the ♦10 would let declarer win the first trick. Although this would seem like a good argument for playing the ♦K, that's not really true. Against a suit contract, this layout is highly unlikely, since partner would not usually lead a low card when holding the ♦A. Against a notrump contract, even if you play the ♦K, your side will still have to let declarer win one trick in the suit before you can establish all your winners. By playing the ♦10 on the first trick, you're merely giving declarer a trick sooner, rather than later.

By visualizing all the possible layouts, you can work out that it's best to play the ♦10 in this situation. It will gain in the first three cases, and break even in the fourth.

Trying to visualize all the possible layouts is the best way to decide exactly how high to play as third hand, but there are so many variations that it's sometimes easier to fall back on the following guideline:

- When you have a higher honor than dummy, try to save your high card until the high card is played from dummy by inserting a lower-ranking card that could possibly win the trick.

This is easier to understand by going through a couple of examples. Consider this layout where partner is on lead against a notrump contract:

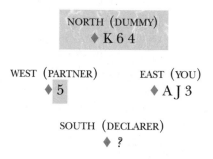

NORTH (DUMMY)
♦ K 6 4

WEST (PARTNER)   EAST (YOU)
♦ 5   ♦ A J 3

SOUTH (DECLARER)
♦ ?

If the ♦K is played from dummy, you would win the trick with the ♦A. If a low diamond is played from dummy, insert the ♦J—a card which could win the trick if partner has the ♦Q—and hold on to the ♦A to capture dummy's ♦K. Even if declarer holds the ♦Q, playing the ♦J won't do any harm:

NORTH (DUMMY)
♦ K 6 4

WEST (PARTNER)   EAST (YOU)
♦ 10 8 7 5 2   ♦ A J 3

SOUTH (DECLARER)
♦ Q 9

Declarer is always entitled to one trick from this suit, but if you play the ♦A on the first round, declarer will get two tricks, the ♦K and ♦Q. By playing the ♦J, declarer wins the first trick with the ♦Q, but that's all. Your ♦A remains to capture dummy's ♦K. Here's another situation:

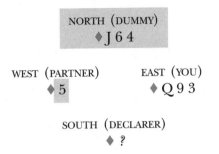

NORTH (DUMMY)
♦J 6 4

WEST (PARTNER)   EAST (YOU)
♦5   ♦Q 9 3

SOUTH (DECLARER)
♦ ?

If a low diamond is played from dummy, insert the ♦9, keeping dummy's ♦J trapped. The ♦9 could conceivably win the trick:

NORTH (DUMMY)
♦J 6 4

WEST (PARTNER)   EAST (YOU)
♦ A K 10 5 2   ♦ Q 9 3

SOUTH (DECLARER)
♦ 8 7

A more likely layout is something like this:

NORTH (DUMMY)
♦J 6 4

WEST (PARTNER)   EAST (YOU)
♦ K 10 7 5 2   ♦ Q 9 3

SOUTH (DECLARER)
♦ A 8

Your ♦9 will be sufficient to drive out declarer's ♦A. If you were to play the ♦Q, declarer could win with the ♦A and later lead toward dummy's ♦J for a second trick in the suit.

The concept of keeping dummy's high card trapped also applies when partner is leading your suit. For example, suppose you have bid diamonds during the auction and this is the layout you see when partner leads your suit:

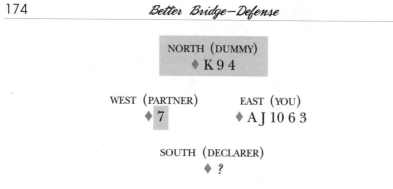

NORTH (DUMMY)
♦ K 9 4

WEST (PARTNER)   EAST (YOU)
♦ 7   ♦ A J 10 6 3

SOUTH (DECLARER)
♦ ?

If a low diamond is played from dummy, play the ♦10, keeping dummy's ♦K trapped. The full layout is probably something like this:

NORTH (DUMMY)
♦ K 9 4

WEST (PARTNER)   EAST (YOU)
♦ 7 2   ♦ A J 10 6 3

SOUTH (DECLARER)
♦ Q 8 5

If you were to play the ♦A on the first trick, declarer would later get tricks with both the ♦K and ♦Q. By inserting the ♦10 on the first round, declarer can win with the ♦Q but can't get a second trick from dummy's ♦K. Hopefully, partner can regain the lead to play the ♦2 through dummy so that you can get all your winners.

Here's a full hand to illustrate the concept of keeping dummy's high card trapped. The auction goes like this:

WEST	NORTH	EAST	SOUTH
			1♥
Pass	3♥	Pass	4♥
Pass	Pass	Pass	

Partner leads the ♠2, and the dummy comes down.

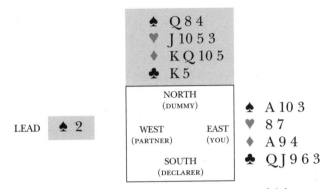

LEAD ♠ 2

Declarer plays a low spade from dummy, and it's up to you. You could win the first trick for sure by playing the ♠A, but it's also possible that the ♠10 will win the trick if partner has both the ♠K and ♠J. Even if partner doesn't hold both those cards, you'd like to keep your ♠A to capture dummy's high card. Since you can't tell where all the defensive tricks are coming from, you follow the guideline and insert the ♠10. Declarer wins this first trick with the ♠K. This is a bit of a disappointment, but the hand isn't over yet. This is the complete layout:

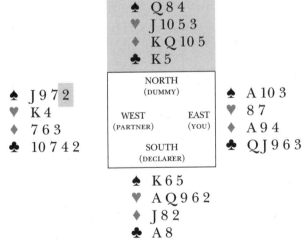

After winning the ♠K, declarer plays a club to dummy's ♣K and leads the ♥J. Declarer tries the heart finesse, but it loses to partner's ♥K. It's all up to partner now. Although partner doesn't know for certain that you hold the ♠A, there's little hope if you don't. Partner can lead back the ♠J, and dummy's ♠Q is trapped. If declarer plays a

low spade, partner's ♠J wins the trick; if declarer covers, you win the
♠A and lead back the ♠3 to partner's ♠9. The defense gets two spade
tricks, a heart trick, and a diamond trick—enough to defeat the contract.

If you had played the ♠A on the first trick, the defense would be
over quickly. Declarer would also lose a heart trick and a diamond
trick, but that would be all.

Rule of Eleven

When partner leads the fourth highest card from a suit, the implica-
tion is that partner has exactly three cards higher than the one that
was led. By looking at the cards in the dummy and your own hand,
you can sometimes visualize exactly which cards partner holds. For
example, suppose partner leads the ♣6 against declarer's notrump
contract and this is what you see:

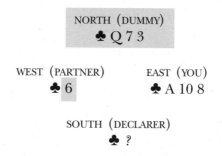

NORTH (DUMMY)
♣ Q 7 3

WEST (PARTNER)   EAST (YOU)
♣ 6   ♣ A 10 8

SOUTH (DECLARER)
♣ ?

You can see all the clubs higher than the ♣6 except for the ♣K,
♣J, and ♣9. Those must be the three cards partner holds to make
the ♣6 the fourth highest card in partner's hand. You can visualize
the complete layout as something like this:

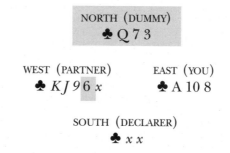

NORTH (DUMMY)
♣ Q 7 3

WEST (PARTNER)   EAST (YOU)
♣ K J 9 6 x   ♣ A 10 8

SOUTH (DECLARER)
♣ x x

You're not quite sure about those little x's, but the rest of the cards pop into view. If declarer plays a low club from dummy, you can confidently play the ♣8 and win the trick.

This news that declarer has no higher card than partner's ♣6 can also be obtained by applying what is referred to as the *rule of eleven.** When the lead is the fourth highest card in a suit, the rule of eleven states:

- Subtract the pips on the card led from eleven. The result is the number of cards in the other three hands that are higher than the one led.

When partner leads the ♣6 in the above layout, you can subtract the six "pips" from eleven, leaving you with five cards in the other three hands that are higher than the ♣6. Since you can see two higher cards in the dummy and have three higher cards in your own hand, there's none left for declarer.

The rule of eleven doesn't appear to be a particularly useful observation, since you could tell that declarer had no higher card by visualizing partner's holding in the suit. It becomes more useful, however, when you can't see all the higher cards. Suppose these are the cards you see when partner leads the ♣6:

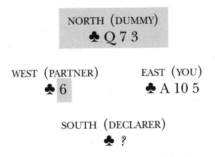

NORTH (DUMMY)
♣ Q 7 3

WEST (PARTNER)   EAST (YOU)
♣ 6   ♣ A 10 5

SOUTH (DECLARER)
♣ ?

Subtracting six from eleven lets you know that there are five cards higher than the ♣6 among dummy's hand, your hand, and declarer's

---

*The rule of eleven is often credited to Robert Foster of Scotland, a famous authority on card games, who described it in a letter to a friend in 1890 and published it in his *Whist Manual.* An Oxford scholar, E. Benecke, independently made the same discovery around the same time.

hand. This time you can see only four of them: the ♣Q, ♣7, ♣A, and ♣10. That leaves exactly one higher card in declarer's hand. You don't know which card—it could be the ♣K, ♣J, ♣9, or ♣8—but you do know that declarer has only one of those cards. Suppose you play the ♣10 on the first trick and declarer wins this with the ♣J. You would know declarer has no higher clubs left. You could confidently play your ♣A and a low club to partner's known ♣K, when you re-gained the lead.

Let's try another layout:

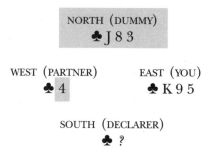

Subtracting the four pips on partner's card from eleven gives you a total of seven higher cards in the other three hands. There are two in dummy and three in your hand. That leaves two for declarer. The complete layout could be something like this:

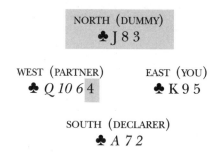

You can't know for sure the exact cards declarer holds, but you do know that declarer has two cards higher than the ♣4. In this ex-ample, the knowledge doesn't help you decide which card to play on the first trick if a low club is played from dummy. You'll have to fall back on the guideline of trying to keep a card higher than dummy's honor, in which case, you would play the ♣9. After all, the

♣9 might win the first trick if partner's three cards higher than the ♣4 were the ♣A, ♣Q, and ♣10. On the above layout, the ♣9 wouldn't win the trick, but would force declarer to play the ♣A to win the trick.

Sometimes, however, the rule of eleven does let you know exactly what to do. Consider this layout where partner leads the ♣7 against declarer's notrump contract:

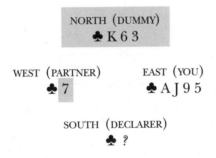

If a low club is played from dummy, you can play the ♣5, letting partner's ♣7 win the trick! Subtracting seven from eleven leaves four, and you can see all four cards higher than the ♣7 between your hand and the dummy. That leaves no higher card in declarer's hand. The complete layout of the suit must be something like this:

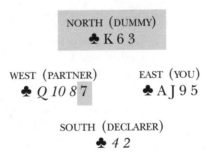

If you automatically play the ♣J—or the ♣9—on the first round, you would win the trick, but now you couldn't lead the suit again from your side without giving a trick to dummy's ♣K. By letting partner's ♣7 win the first trick, partner can lead another club, trapping dummy's ♣K.

Here's an example of putting the rule to work on a full hand. The auction proceeds:

WEST	NORTH	EAST	SOUTH
			1♦
Pass	1♥	Pass	2NT
Pass	3NT	Pass	Pass
Pass			

Partner leads the ♠5, and the dummy comes down.

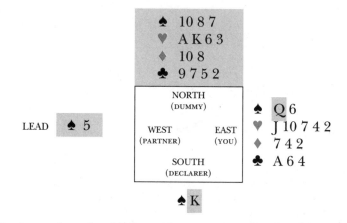

Declarer plays the ♠7 from dummy, you play the ♠Q—third hand high—and declarer wins the trick with the ♠K. Declarer now leads a low heart to dummy's ♥K and plays a low club from dummy. Were you ready for this? Is it time for second hand low?

When partner leads the ♠5, you can apply the rule of eleven which lets you know there are six higher cards in the other three hands. You can see three in dummy and two in your hand, leaving one for declarer. When declarer's ♠K captures your ♠Q on the first trick, you know that is declarer's only spade higher than the ♠5. Partner must have the rest of the high spades, so the suit is established. When a low club is led from dummy, there's no time to waste. Take the ♣A, and lead your remaining spade to partner's winners. Here's the complete hand:

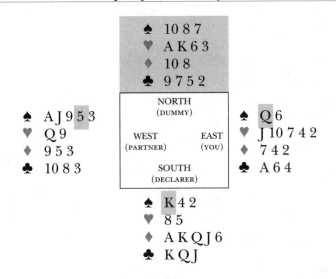

♠ 10 8 7
♥ A K 6 3
♦ 10 8
♣ 9 7 5 2

NORTH
(DUMMY)

♠ A J 9 5 3
♥ Q 9
♦ 9 5 3
♣ 10 8 3

WEST
(PARTNER)

EAST
(YOU)

♠ Q 6
♥ J 10 7 4 2
♦ 7 4 2
♣ A 6 4

SOUTH
(DECLARER)

♠ K 4 2
♥ 8 5
♦ A K Q J 6
♣ K Q J

If you play a low club, declarer wins a club trick and quickly ends up with nine winners: the first spade trick, two heart tricks, five diamond tricks, and the club trick. If you jump up with the ♣A and lead a spade, your side wins the race. Partner takes four spade winners to go along with your ♣A.

The rule of eleven is a shorthand method to help you visualize the layout of the cards once partner leads fourth highest from a four-card or longer suit. You can always work out a possible layout that includes the three higher cards in partner's hand, but the rule can save you the effort.

Avoiding Confusion

Here's a situation that could prove awkward for the partnership. You're sitting to the left of declarer. Your side still needs several tricks to defeat the contract, part way through the play partner leads a spade for the first time in this layout:

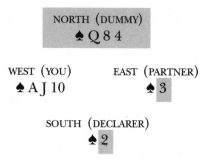

Declarer plays the ♠2, and you have to decide which card to play. Playing the ♠A is best if this is the complete layout of the suit:

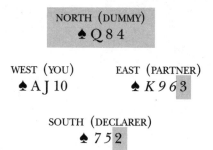

You win the trick with the ♠A and lead back the ♠J, trapping dummy's ♠Q. Declarer doesn't get any tricks in the suit. On the other hand, this might be the layout of the spade suit:

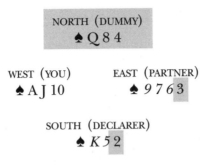

NORTH (DUMMY)
♠ Q 8 4

WEST (YOU)   EAST (PARTNER)
♠ A J 10   ♠ 9 7 6 3

SOUTH (DECLARER)
♠ K 5 2

If you play the ♠A, declarer will get tricks with both the ♠K and the ♠Q. It would be best to play the ♠10 on the first round, letting declarer win a trick with dummy's ♠Q. Now you have declarer's ♠K trapped next partner regains the lead. Declarer is restricted to one trick in the suit.

Since you can't see declarer's cards, how are you to know whether or not to play your ♠A? Sometimes, the auction may give you a clue as to whether or not declarer holds a high card in the suit. More often than not, however, you're faced with a dilemma. The solution is for the partnership to have the following agreement:

- When leading a new suit in the middle of the hand, lead a low card to indicate some strength in the suit; otherwise lead a high card.

Let's return to the first possible layout:

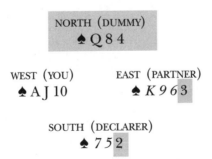

NORTH (DUMMY)
♠ Q 8 4

WEST (YOU)   EAST (PARTNER)
♠ A J 10   ♠ K 9 6 3

SOUTH (DECLARER)
♠ 7 5 2

When this is the situation and partner decides to lead a spade, partner would lead the ♠3, a low spade, showing some strength in the suit. You would now know to win the ♠A and return the ♠J, trapping dummy's ♠Q with partner's "known" ♠K.

Now look at the second possible layout:

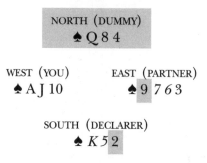

NORTH (DUMMY)
♠ Q 8 4

WEST (YOU)   EAST (PARTNER)
♠ A J 10   ♠ 9 7 6 3

SOUTH (DECLARER)
♠ K 5 2

With no high card in the suit, partner would lead the ♠9 or ♠7, a high card. You would know to play the ♠10 on the first round of the suit, keeping declarer's ♠K trapped.

Here's another example:

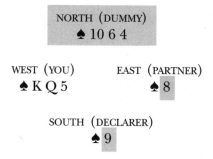

NORTH (DUMMY)
♠ 10 6 4

WEST (YOU)   EAST (PARTNER)
♠ K Q 5   ♠ 8

SOUTH (DECLARER)
♠ 9

In the middle of the hand, partner leads the ♠8, declarer plays the ♠9, and you win the trick with the ♠Q. Is it safe to lead back a spade? Probably not. Partner's ♠8 looks like a high card, so you can envision the layout of the suit to be something like this:

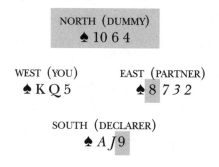

NORTH (DUMMY)
♠ 10 6 4

WEST (YOU)   EAST (PARTNER)
♠ K Q 5   ♠ 8 7 3 2

SOUTH (DECLARER)
♠ A J 9

Partner is helping you out by leading through declarer's strength up to the weakness on dummy. You will have to wait until partner regains the lead and can lead another spade through declarer, repeating the defensive finesse. Holding the ♠A, or possibly even the ♠J, partner would lead back a low spade, expressing interest in having you continue the suit from your side.

Letting Declarer Guess

When declarer is taking a finesse, the defenders are also taking a finesse, in a sense. As a defender, you try to avoid making declarer's task any easier. For example, suppose declarer leads a low heart toward dummy in this situation:

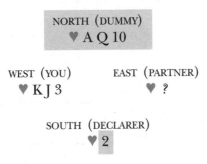

NORTH (DUMMY)
♥ A Q 10

WEST (YOU)   EAST (PARTNER)
♥ K J 3   ♥ ?

SOUTH (DECLARER)
♥ 2

You can see that a finesse of either dummy's ♥Q or ♥10 will be successful—since you hold both the ♥K and ♥J—but you shouldn't help declarer by playing the ♥K to force dummy to play the ♥A. You shouldn't even play the ♥J to make sure declarer doesn't finesse dummy's ♥10. Play second hand low, the ♥3. You don't know declarer's intention. Declarer might have a singleton heart and be planning to play dummy's ♥A. Declarer might be afraid of letting your partner get the lead and decide to play the ♥A. Declarer might choose to finesse dummy's ♥Q, rather than the ♥10, allowing you to promote a winner later on. Declarer may not have read all the books in this series and may never have heard about finesses.

Here's another situation for which you must be prepared in order to avoid helping declarer:

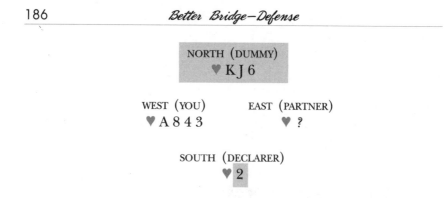

NORTH (DUMMY)
♥ K J 6

WEST (YOU)   EAST (PARTNER)
♥ A 8 4 3   ♥ ?

SOUTH (DECLARER)
♥ 2

When declarer leads a low heart toward dummy, unless you can clearly see that you can defeat the contract by taking a trick with the ♥A, it's usually best to play a low heart. If declarer holds the ♥Q, it won't make much difference. Declarer will win the trick with one of dummy's high cards, and you'll get your ♥A later. What you might visualize, however, is something like this:

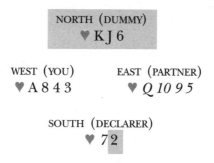

NORTH (DUMMY)
♥ K J 6

WEST (YOU)   EAST (PARTNER)
♥ A 8 4 3   ♥ Q 10 9 5

SOUTH (DECLARER)
♥ 7 2

When you play a low card, declarer has to guess which card to play from the dummy to get a winner from this suit. If declarer decides to finesse dummy's ♥J, hoping you have the ♥Q, partner will win the trick, and you'll get a trick with your ♥A. If you were to play your ♥A right away—or think about it for too long—declarer would no longer have to guess in order to get a trick.

If you look at this last layout from another point of view, your side is trying to get tricks with the help of a finesse. It's as though you're leading a low heart toward partner's hand, hoping to get a trick with the ♥Q. It's all in the outlook as to which side is actually taking the finesse.

As a guideline, you should usually play low whenever declarer leads a low card toward dummy and there is an apparent hole in dummy's suit. Look at this layout:

NORTH (DUMMY)
♥ Q 10 6

WEST (YOU)   EAST (PARTNER)
♥ K 8 4   ♥ 5

SOUTH (DECLARER)
♥ A

Declarer plays a low heart from dummy and wins the trick with the ♥A as both you and partner follow with low hearts. Are you ready when declarer now leads a low heart toward dummy? Play low smoothly, leaving declarer to guess. You can visualize that the layout is something like this:

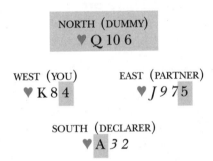

NORTH (DUMMY)
♥ Q 10 6

WEST (YOU)   EAST (PARTNER)
♥ K 8 4   ♥ *J 9 7 5*

SOUTH (DECLARER)
♥ A *3 2*

If you play a low heart, declarer is going to have to decide whether to play the ♥10 or ♥Q from dummy in order to win a second trick in the suit. Declarer is bound to go wrong some of the time. You can be fairly certain that partner holds the ♥J in this situation. If declarer held the ♥J, declarer probably would have taken a finesse by leading a high card from dummy, hoping your partner held the ♥K.

Try your luck defending this next hand after the auction goes:

WEST	NORTH	EAST	SOUTH
	1NT	Pass	4♠
Pass	Pass	Pass	

You lead the ♣K against this auction, and this is what you see on the first trick:

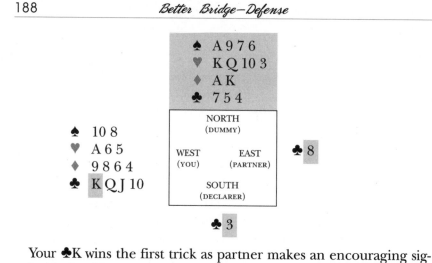

Your ♣K wins the first trick as partner makes an encouraging signal with the ♣8. You lead another club which also wins the trick, but when you lead a third round, declarer trumps. Declarer then plays the ♠K and ♠Q to draw your trump as partner discards a low diamond on the second round of trumps. Now declarer leads a low heart toward dummy.

Hopefully, you were well prepared to play a low heart. Your side already has two tricks, but you aren't going to get any more tricks from spades, diamonds, or clubs. Your only hope is the heart suit. You need two tricks. You and I can both see that declarer won't have to lose two heart tricks because the ♥K and ♥Q are nicely placed in the dummy. But declarer doesn't know which defender holds the ♥A.

Suppose declarer plays dummy's ♥Q, which wins the trick. Declarer crosses back by playing a spade and leads another heart toward dummy. Are you prepared to play low again? You're hoping the complete hand looks something like this:

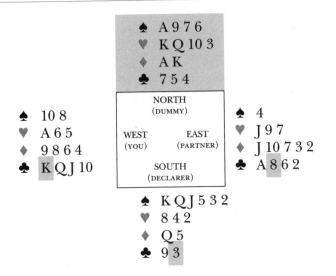

♠ A 9 7 6
♥ K Q 10 3
♦ A K
♣ 7 5 4

NORTH
(DUMMY)

♠ 10 8
♥ A 6 5
♦ 9 8 6 4
♣ K Q J 10

WEST
(YOU)

EAST
(PARTNER)

♠ 4
♥ J 9 7
♦ J 10 7 3 2
♣ A 8 6 2

SOUTH
(DECLARER)

♠ K Q J 5 3 2
♥ 8 4 2
♦ Q 5
♣ 9 3

Having already lost two club tricks, declarer has a problem when you play a low heart on the second round of the suit. If you hold the ♥A, the winning decision is to play dummy's ♥K. But if you hold the ♥J and your partner holds the ♥A, the winning decision is to finesse dummy's ♥10. Declarer may look at you suspiciously when you follow with a low heart on the second round of the suit, but declarer can't be sure whether it's you or partner who didn't play the ♥A on the first trick in the suit. If you play low hearts innocently both times, declarer may play dummy's ♥10. Partner will win the trick with the ♥J, and lead a heart over to your ♥A to defeat the contract. You have just defeated an unbeatable contract!

Summary

The defenders need to work together to recognize the opportunities for finesses and to successfully bring them about. They follow the same basic principles as declarer: leading toward the card they hope will win a trick; leading a high card only if they can afford to have it covered. Keep the following guidelines in mind:

- Try to visualize the layout of the unseen high cards.
- Lead through dummy's or declarer's strength to help partner win tricks with high cards.
- When partner's opening lead is a low card and you have a higher honor than dummy, try to save your high card until the high card is played from dummy by inserting a lower-ranking card that could possibly win the trick.
- When partner leads fourth highest, subtract the pips on the card led from eleven. The result is the number of cards in the other three hands that are higher than the one led.
- When leading a new suit in the middle of the hand, lead a low card to indicate some strength in the suit; otherwise lead a high card.
- When declarer leads toward a suit containing a hole, play low if possible to give declarer an opportunity to guess incorrectly which high card to play.

Practice Hands

Hand 7.1

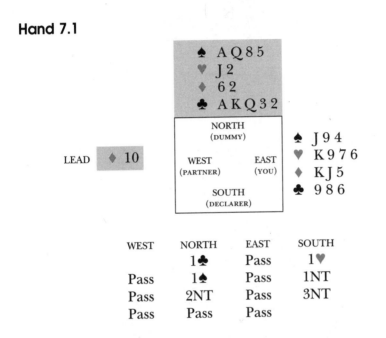

♠ A Q 8 5
♥ J 2
♦ 6 2
♣ A K Q 3 2

NORTH
(DUMMY)

LEAD ♦ 10

WEST
(PARTNER)

EAST
(YOU)

SOUTH
(DECLARER)

♠ J 9 4
♥ K 9 7 6
♦ K J 5
♣ 9 8 6

WEST	NORTH	EAST	SOUTH
	1♣	Pass	1♥
Pass	1♠	Pass	1NT
Pass	2NT	Pass	3NT
Pass	Pass	Pass	

After the opponents struggle into 3NT, partner leads the ♦10. What do you think partner's diamond suit looks like? How do you plan to defend?

Solution 7.1

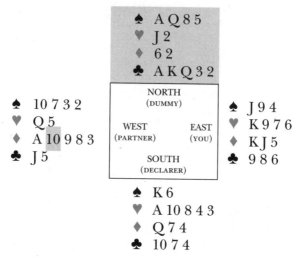

Partner's lead of the ♦10 shows the next lower card, the ♦9, but denies the next higher card, the ♦J—which isn't surprising, since you hold that card. Partner could be leading the top of a three-card sequence such as ♦ 10 9 8 x x, the top of a broken sequence such as ♦ 10 9 7 x x, or the top of an interior sequence such as ♦ A 10 9 x x or ♦ Q 10 9 x x. You don't know for certain whether declarer holds the ♦A, ♦Q, or both.

Whichever combination partner is leading from, it can't do any harm for you to play the ♦K on the first trick—third hand high. If declarer wins this with the ♦A, you can still hope partner holds the ♦Q, or that you will be able to drive out that card out later on. On the actual hand, your ♦K wins the first trick. Declarer could still have the ♦A and be holding up, but you don't care. You lead back the ♦J, top of your remaining doubleton. This traps declarer's ♦Q, and your side takes the first five tricks.

If you didn't play the ♦K on the first trick, declarer would win the trick with the ♦Q and take three spade tricks, a heart trick, and five club tricks, to end up with an overtrick. Partner's lead of the ♦10 helps to trap the ♦Q wherever it is located. If it had shown up in the dummy, you would also known what to do.

Hand 7.2

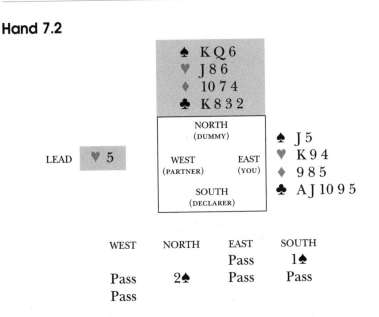

♠ K Q 6
♥ J 8 6
♦ 10 7 4
♣ K 8 3 2

NORTH
(DUMMY)

LEAD ♥ 5

WEST
(PARTNER)

EAST
(YOU)

SOUTH
(DECLARER)

♠ J 5
♥ K 9 4
♦ 9 8 5
♣ A J 10 9 5

WEST	NORTH	EAST	SOUTH
		Pass	1♠
Pass	2♠	Pass	Pass
Pass			

Partner's opening lead against the opponents' partscore contract of 2♠ is the ♥5.

Assuming partner's lead is fourth highest, how do you visualize the layout of the heart suit? Which card do you plan to play if a low heart is played from dummy on the first trick?

If you later have an opportunity to lead diamonds, which diamond will you lead?

If partner had led the ♣7 initially, which club would you play if a low club were played from dummy?

Solution 7.2

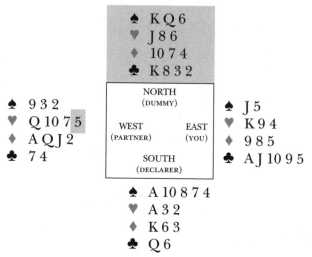

```
                    ♠ K Q 6
                    ♥ J 8 6
                    ♦ 10 7 4
                    ♣ K 8 3 2
                 ┌──────────────┐
                 │    NORTH     │
    ♠ 9 3 2      │   (DUMMY)    │      ♠ J 5
    ♥ Q 10 7 5   │ WEST   EAST  │      ♥ K 9 4
    ♦ A Q J 2    │(PARTNER)(YOU)│      ♦ 9 8 5
    ♣ 7 4        │    SOUTH     │      ♣ A J 10 9 5
                 │  (DECLARER)  │
                 └──────────────┘
                    ♠ A 10 8 7 4
                    ♥ A 3 2
                    ♦ K 6 3
                    ♣ Q 6
```

If the ♥5 is partner's fourth highest, the rule of eleven states there are 11 – 5 = 6 higher cards in the other hands. You can see three in dummy and two in your hand, leaving declarer with exactly one higher card. Since you're defending a suit contract, it's unlikely partner has led a low card when holding the ♥A, so that's probably declarer's one card higher than the ♥5. You could use this reasoning to play the ♥9 on the first trick, since it will be high enough to force out declarer's ♥A. You'd also play the ♥9 rather than the ♥K following the guideline of trying to keep a higher honor than the one in dummy. If you were to play the ♥K on the first trick, declarer could win the ♥A and subsequently lead a heart toward dummy's ♥J to establish a second trick in the suit.

When you later get the lead, plan to lead a diamond through declarer's assumed strength and up to the weakness in dummy. Lead the ♦9, your highest diamond, to warn partner you have no strength in the suit. On the actual hand, diamonds must be led from your side so partner can take a finesse against declarer's ♦K. If declarer plays a low diamond, partner will win the trick with the ♦J and wait for diamonds to be led again.

If partner leads the ♣7 at the beginning of the hand or in the middle of the hand, play the ♣9 when a low club is played from dummy. Declarer can win the trick with the ♣Q, but won't get a second club trick because dummy's ♣K is trapped. With careful defense, your side gets two heart tricks, three diamond tricks, and one club trick.

Hand 7.3

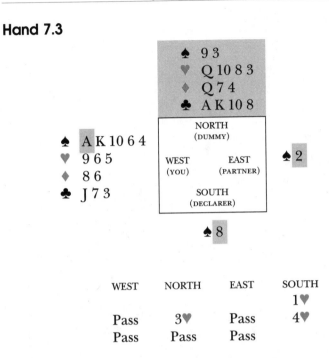

WEST	NORTH	EAST	SOUTH
			1♥
Pass	3♥	Pass	4♥
Pass	Pass	Pass	

You lead the ♠A against South's contract of 4♥. The ♠3 is played from dummy, partner contributes the ♠2, and declarer plays the ♠8. What now?

Solution 7.3

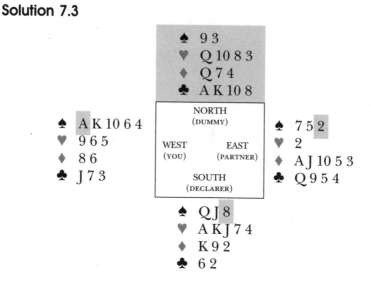

♠ 9 3
♥ Q 10 8 3
♦ Q 7 4
♣ A K 10 8

NORTH
(DUMMY)

WEST
(YOU)

EAST
(PARTNER)

SOUTH
(DECLARER)

♠ A K 10 6 4
♥ 9 6 5
♦ 8 6
♣ J 7 3

♠ 7 5 2
♥ 2
♦ A J 10 5 3
♣ Q 9 5 4

♠ Q J 8
♥ A K J 7 4
♦ K 9 2
♣ 6 2

Partner's low spade is a discouraging signal. On the actual hand, if you lead another spade, you will establish declarer's ♠Q as a winner. Declarer can use this to discard one of dummy's diamonds and will end up losing only one diamond trick.

Warned by partner's signal, you should shift your attention to the other suits. If your side has tricks coming from the heart suit or club suit, partner won't need any help from you. But if partner has some strength in diamonds, partner may need some help in trapping the opponents' high cards. After winning the first trick, lead the ♦8, top of your doubleton.

Now it's up to partner. Your ♦8 looks like a high card, so partner can visualize that declarer holds the ♦K. When a low diamond is played from dummy, partner should insert the ♦10, letting declarer win the trick but keeping dummy's ♦Q trapped.

After winning the ♦K, declarer will draw trump a lead a spade to drive out your ♠K. Now you have the opportunity to lead your ♦6, competing the finesse. Dummy's ♦Q is trapped, and partner wins two diamond tricks to defeat the contract. Cooperation and visualization are required from both partners to defeat this contract.

Hand 7.4

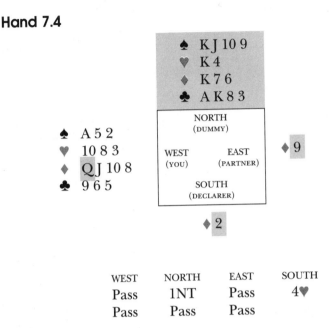

	♠ KJ10 9
	♥ K4
	♦ K76
	♣ AK83

NORTH (DUMMY)

♠ A52
♥ 108 3
♦ QJ 10 8
♣ 9 6 5

WEST (YOU)   EAST (PARTNER)

♦ 9

SOUTH (DECLARER)

♦ 2

WEST	NORTH	EAST	SOUTH
Pass	1NT	Pass	4♥
Pass	Pass	Pass	

You lead the ♦Q against South's 4♥ contract. A low diamond is played from dummy, partner plays the ♦9, and declarer plays the ♦2.

Jumping to the conclusion that partner holds the ♦A, you continue by leading the ♦J, which also wins the trick. Unfortunately, when you lead a third round of diamonds, declarer ruffs and draws trump. Declarer has to play three rounds of hearts to draw all your trump after partner discards on the second round of the suit.

Now declarer leads a low spade. Were you ready for this? Would it make any difference if the third round of diamonds had not been trumped by declarer?

Solution 7.4

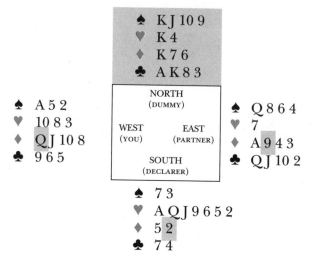

♠ K J 10 9
♥ K 4
♦ K 7 6
♣ A K 8 3

NORTH
(DUMMY)

♠ A 5 2
♥ 10 8 3
♦ Q J 10 8
♣ 9 6 5

WEST
(YOU)

EAST
(PARTNER)

♠ Q 8 6 4
♥ 7
♦ A 9 4 3
♣ Q J 10 2

SOUTH
(DECLARER)

♠ 7 3
♥ A Q J 9 6 5 2
♦ 5 2
♣ 7 4

By leading the ♦Q, you manage to trap dummy's ♦K—a successful finesse for the defense. You get two tricks from the suit before declarer is able to ruff and draw your trump. When partner discards on the second round of trump, you can draw the conclusion that declarer started with a seven-card heart suit. That gives declarer seven heart winners plus dummy's ♣A and ♣K. Declarer needs only one more trick to make the contract.

When declarer leads a low spade toward dummy, your instinct might be to play the ♠A, to prevent declarer from winning an immediate trick with dummy's ♠K. That wouldn't stop declarer from making the contract, since declarer will still get a trick with the ♠K. Your only hope is that partner holds the ♠Q and declarer may miss-guess the situation. If you play a low spade, declarer might play dummy's ♠J—or ♠10 or ♠9. Partner will win the trick with the ♠Q, and you still get a trick with the ♠A. You have to be prepared to play a low spade once you see the hole in dummy's suit. If you have to think a long time before playing a low spade, declarer will likely come to the correct conclusion that you hold the ♠A.

If the first three rounds of diamonds all won tricks for your side, you would need only one more trick to defeat the contract. If declarer subsequently led a low spade toward dummy, this wouldn't be the time to play low. You could see that playing the ♠A would defeat the contract, and you shouldn't give declarer any chance to get a tenth trick.

8

Working Together—
Using the Trump Suit

"Tell the truth or trump—but get the trick."

— MARK TWAIN,
Pudd'nhead Wilson,
[1894]

When the auction is over and the opponents have been able to select the trump suit, there may be a bit of disappointment. After all, having control of which suit is trump can be a big advantage. Declarer can use the trump suit to stop your side from getting winners with your high cards, to ruff losing cards in the dummy, to help establish suits, and to use as communication back and forth between hands—on with the next hand!

Not so fast. This is no time to sit back. You can turn the trump suit into an advantage for your side. You may be able to use your side's trump to ruff declarer's winners; you may be able to prevent declarer from using the trump suit to ruff losers; or you may be able to run declarer out of trumps and take over control of the hand. Let's look at some of the opportunities for the defenders in a trump contract. You're still in the game!

Getting A Ruff

The opponents reach 4♠ with the following auction:

WEST	NORTH	EAST	SOUTH
	Pass	Pass	1♠
Pass	2♠	Pass	4♠
Pass	Pass	Pass	

Partner leads the ♦A, and this is what you see when the dummy comes down:

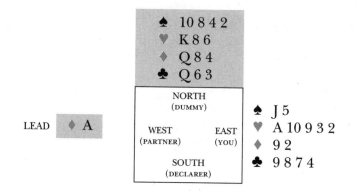

Partner's lead of the ♦A is likely the top of touching high cards from a diamond suit headed by the ace-king. That should be two tricks for your side, and your ♥A should provide another. Where is your side's fourth trick coming from? Partner could have a winner in spades or clubs, but there may be no need to rely on that.

With only two diamonds in your hand, you can trump the third round if partner continues to lead the suit. How can you persuade partner to keep leading the suit? Time to use the attitude signal. On the first round of diamonds, play the ♦9, an encouraging card. When partner plays the ♦K, you'll follow with the ♦2. Looking at the ♦Q in dummy, partner might wonder why you're encouraging a diamond continuation, but since you could have played the ♦2 on the first trick if you preferred another suit, partner should lead a third round of diamonds. You can trump this and play the ♥A to defeat the contract. Here's the complete hand:

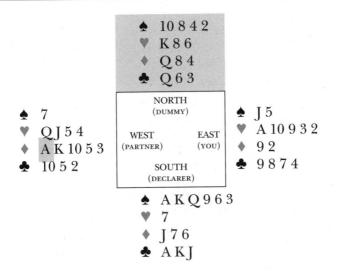

If partner had led any other suit after winning the first two diamond tricks, declarer would draw trump upon gaining the lead, and you would never get your ruff. This is a fairly straightforward hand, hardly worth a glance. Let's change the hand a little bit:

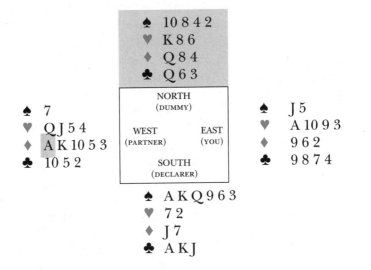

With the same hand as before, partner would again lead the ♦A. If partner were to continue leading diamonds, declarer could make the contract by discarding a heart on dummy's ♦Q. You would send partner a discouraging signal, however, by playing the ♦2 on the first round. Even if partner guesses wrong and switches to a club, you'll play a low club, giving another discouraging signal. After winning a trick with the ♦K, partner can now try leading the ♥Q, and your side will be able to take two heart tricks.

Let's return to the original situation and make a small modification to the dummy:

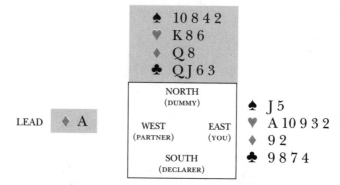

Dummy now has only two diamonds and will be able to trump the third round of diamonds. That's all right. Since you have a higher trump than dummy, you should still encourage partner to keep leading diamonds. When dummy trumps the third round, you can *overruff* with your higher-ranking trump to win the trick.

Be careful about automatically encouraging partner to continue leading a suit when you have a doubleton. Suppose this is the situation:

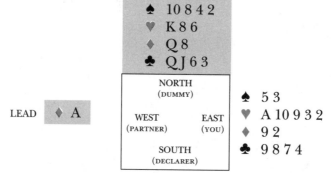

If you play the ♦9 followed by the ♦2, partner will assume you want another diamond led. If partner leads another diamond, however, declarer can ruff with dummy's ♠8 or ♠10, and you won't be able to overruff. It's better to give partner a discouraging signal with the ♦2. This could be the complete hand:

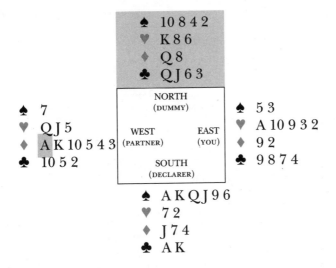

If partner were to lead a third round of diamonds, declarer could play a high trump from dummy to win the trick, then draw your trump. Declarer could then play the ♣A and ♣K, cross to dummy with a trump, and discard the two small hearts on dummy's extra club winners to make an overtrick. If you make a discouraging signal, partner may switch to the ♥Q, trapping dummy's ♥K. Your side could take two heart tricks and two diamond tricks to defeat the contract.

You also need to be careful in this situation:

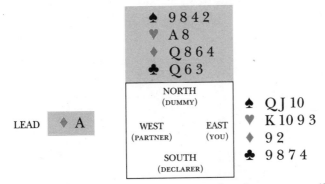

If you send partner an encouraging signal, partner will continue leading diamonds to give you a ruff. That would not be a success on this hand, if the full layout were something like this:

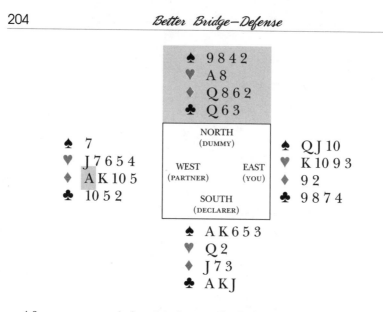

After you trump the third round of diamonds, declarer takes the rest of the tricks. Whatever you return, declarer draws the rest of the trump and eventually discards a heart on dummy's established ♦Q. You never get a trick with your ♥K.

Since you'll always get a trump trick through promotion—once the ♠A and ♠K are played—there's no need to get a ruff. Instead, make a discouraging signal in diamonds. Hopefully, partner will switch to a heart, through dummy's ♥A to your ♥K. Now declarer can't prevent your side from getting a spade trick, a heart trick, and two diamond tricks.

On some hands, you may need to wake partner up to the fact that you want a ruff. Consider this situation after the auction has gone:

WEST	NORTH	EAST	SOUTH
	1♦	Pass	1♠
Pass	2♠	Pass	Pass
Pass			

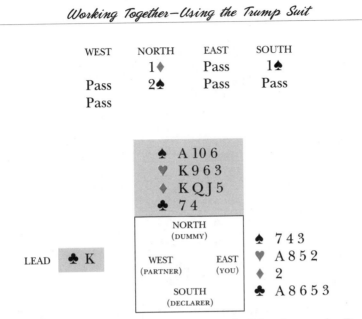

♠ A 10 6
♥ K 9 6 3
♦ K Q J 5
♣ 7 4

NORTH
(DUMMY)

LEAD　♣ K

WEST
(PARTNER)

EAST
(YOU)

SOUTH
(DECLARER)

♠ 7 4 3
♥ A 8 5 2
♦ 2
♣ A 8 6 5 3

Partner leads the ♣K, and you have to decide what to do. Partner's lead looks like the top of touching high cards, but with only two clubs in the dummy, it seems your side is going to take only two tricks in that suit. You have a trick with the ♥A, but it doesn't look as though there's much hope unless partner holds the ♦A. If that's the case, you may be able to put your low trumps to work.

How are you going to persuade partner to lead a diamond? If you play the ♣3 as a discouraging signal, partner is likely to assume that you have some strength in hearts and may shift to that suit. The best way to let partner know what you want is to overtake the ♣K with your ♣A and lead back your singleton diamond.

Partner might be a little surprised at this sudden turn of events, but it should set off an alarm that's something is going on when you lead into the strength in the dummy. Partner's first though might be that you hold a singleton ♣A, but that's unlikely, since South might have bid clubs with such a long suit. Instead, partner should follow your line of defense and lead back a diamond for you to ruff. Since partner still has the ♣Q left, you can lead back a low club to partner and get a second ruff. Together with your ♥A, that's enough to defeat the contract. Here's the complete hand:

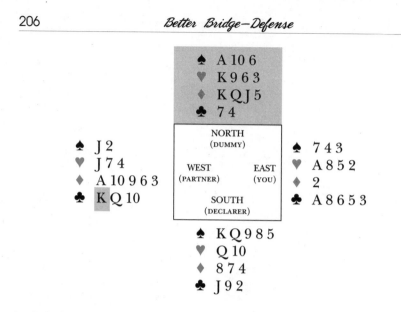

It takes good cooperation from both partners to recognize the opportunity for a ruff and to then bring it about successfully.

Suit Preference

Entries play an important role when you're trying to get a ruff. It's not enough to lead your short suit. You must be able to cross over to partner's hand before all your trump are drawn, so that partner can lead back the suit to give you a ruff. Consider this situation after the auction has gone:

WEST	NORTH	EAST	SOUTH
	1NT	Pass	4♠
Pass	Pass	Pass	

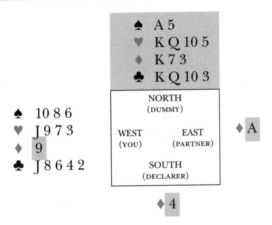

With no potential high card tricks in your hand, you decide to lead your singleton diamond. This works out well when partner wins the first trick with the ♦A and leads back a diamond for you to trump. So far, so good. Your side has two tricks, but you need two more to defeat the contract. It would be nice if you could get back over to partner's hand, so that partner could lead another diamond for you to ruff.

Partner might have the ♥A, or partner might have the ♣A. Which suit should you lead? It's very unlikely partner has both aces, since the opponents have bid to the game level and partner has already turned up with the ♦A. If you guess wrong, declarer will win the trick and draw your trump. It will be too late to get your second ruff.

With no hints from the auction, it appears to be a pure guess. In this situation, however, partner can tell you which suit to lead! Partner can't say anything out loud—that's not part of the game—but partner can send the message using the diamond suit itself. Thinking ahead, partner can foresee the dilemma you'll have after trumping the diamond. You won't have any diamonds left, and you'll not want to lead a trump if you desire another ruff. That leaves only two suits to choose between: hearts and clubs. The way the defenders communicate under these circumstances is to give a *suit preference signal* using the card that is led back:

- A high-ranking card asks for the higher-ranking of the two suits; a low-ranking card asks for the lower-ranking of the two suits.

On the actual hand, if partner returns the ♦2—a low-ranking diamond—partner is suggesting that you lead back a club—the lower-
ranking of the two suits. The complete hand might look like this:

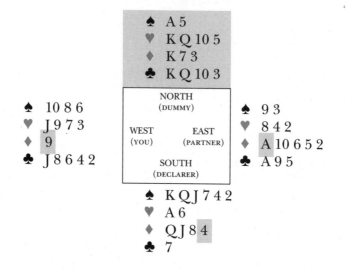

After trumping the diamond, you lead back a club. Partner wins
the trick with the ♣A and leads another diamond for you to ruff. If
you had led back a heart, declarer would win, draw your trump, and
take the rest of the tricks—discarding the ♣7 on one of dummy's
heart winners.

If partner had led back the ♦10, a high-ranking diamond, you
would lead back the higher-ranking of the two suits, hearts. The
complete hand might be this:

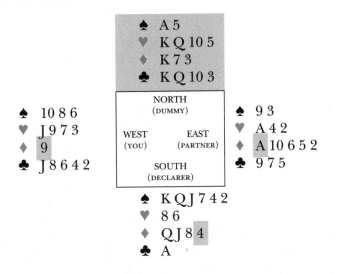

♠ A 5
♥ K Q 10 5
♦ K 7 3
♣ K Q 10 3

NORTH
(DUMMY)

♠ 10 8 6
♥ J 9 7 3
♦ 9
♣ J 8 6 4 2

WEST
(YOU)

EAST
(PARTNER)

♠ 9 3
♥ A 4 2
♦ A 10 6 5 2
♣ 9 7 5

SOUTH
(DECLARER)

♠ K Q J 7 4 2
♥ 8 6
♦ Q J 8 4
♣ A

When you lead back a heart, partner wins and gives you another diamond ruff. No guess—no problem.

What if partner held neither the ♥A nor the ♣A and didn't care which suit you led back? Then partner could return a middle-ranking diamond, the ♦5 or ♦6, showing no preference for either suit.

Although suit preference works spectacularly well on hands like those above, things won't always be as clear cut. Both partners must be aware that the situation calls for a suit preference signal, rather than an attitude or count signal. If you don't hold a very low-ranking or high-ranking card in the suit in which you are trying to give a suit preference signal, partner may find the message difficult to read.

Suit preference signals can be given in a variety of ways. Let's look at an example from the other side of the table. The auction goes:

WEST	NORTH	EAST	SOUTH
	1♥	Pass	1♠
Pass	4♠	Pass	Pass
Pass			

Partner leads the ♥3 against South's 4♠ contract, and this is what you see:

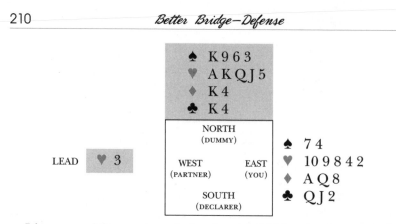

It's unusual for partner to lead a suit bid by the opponent's, and once you look at the hearts in dummy and your own hand, it's clear that partner is leading a singleton. Partner was hoping you could win the first trick with the ♥A and lead one back for a ruff. Unfortunately, that's not going to happen. Your first instinct might be to play a low heart on this trick as an attitude signal to tell partner that you don't have anything useful in hearts.

Consider what's going to happen. Partner may regain the lead and will want to know which suit to lead next. You have a clear preference for diamonds, the higher-ranking of the two suits in which partner will be interested—clubs and diamonds. How can you tell partner that you prefer diamonds to clubs? You may get an opportunity later on to give an attitude signal in one or both of the suits, but by then, it may be too late. You have an opportunity right now—on the first heart trick—to tell partner which suit you prefer.

Looking at the dummy. Partner already knows your attitude toward the heart suit. There's no point in using an attitude signal in this situation. Instead, play the ♥10, the highest-ranking heart you can afford. Since partner knows you can't be interested in hearts, this is a suit preference signal for diamonds, the higher-ranking of the other two suits. Here's the complete hand.

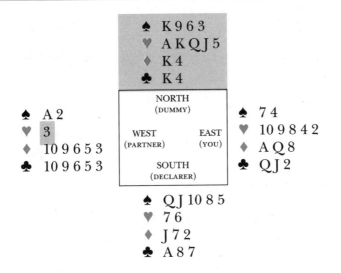

After winning the first heart trick, declarer leads a trump, and partner wins the trick with the ♠A. Partner has seen your suit preference signal for diamonds and leads a diamond, trapping dummy's ♦K. You can take your two diamond tricks and lead a heart for partner to trump. The contract is defeated.

If you had played a low heart on the first trick, partner might interpret that as a suit preference signal for clubs, the lower-ranking suit. If partner leads back a club, declarer will quickly draw trump and make the contract with at least one overtrick.

Ruffing Declarer's Winners

There are times when it's advantageous to have partner trump a trick even when declarer can overruff. One reason is to get rid of one of declarer's winners. Consider the following situation. You lead the ♦A after the auction has gone:

WEST	NORTH	EAST	SOUTH
	1NT	Pass	3♥
Pass	4♥	Pass	Pass
Pass			

```
                    ♠ A 9 7 2
                    ♥ K 9 4
                    ♦ Q J 9
                    ♣ K Q J
                  ┌─────────────┐
                  │ NORTH       │
  ♠ J 10 6        │ (DUMMY)     │
  ♥ 8 2           │             │  ♦ 7
  ♦ A K 10 8 6 3  │ WEST   EAST │
  ♣ 8 4           │ (YOU) (PARTNER)│
                  │             │
                  │ SOUTH       │
                  │ (DECLARER)  │
                  └─────────────┘
                      ♦ 4
```

Partner plays the ♦7 on the first trick, and declarer plays the ♦4. Partner could be making an encouraging signal with a doubleton diamond, or partner may even have a singleton diamond. You continue with the ♦K, hoping that partner has a singleton, but partner plays the ♦2 and declarer follow suit with the ♦5. Since there's only thirteen cards in the suit, neither partner nor declarer have any diamonds left at this point.

There doesn't seem to much point in leading another diamond. If partner trumps the diamond, declarer can play a higher trump to win the trick. You will, however, get rid of one of declarer's winners. There doesn't appear to be a better choice. If partner wanted you to shift to another suit right away, partner could have made a discouraging signal in diamonds. So, lead another diamond, and here's the full hand.

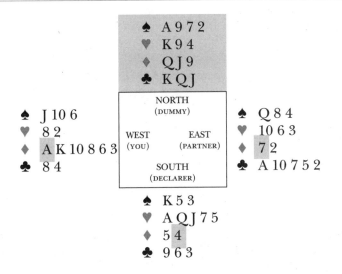

When you lead the third round of diamonds, partner trumps and declarer overtrumps. Partner might not be too pleased at first, but declarer can no longer make the contract. Declarer lost the first two diamond tricks. Declarer will eventually have to lose a spade trick as well as the ♣A. If you had not made partner trump declarer's winner, declarer would have made the contract by discarding a low spade on dummy's established ♦Q.

Trump Promotion

Like magicians, the defenders can sometimes promote winners from the trump suit out of thin air. Suppose that spades are trump and this is the layout of the suit:

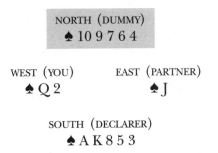

It hardly looks as though your side is entitled to a trump trick, since declarer can simply play the ♠A and ♠K to draw all your side's trump. That's only if declarer has the lead, however. If your side has the lead, there may be an opportunity to promote your ♠Q into a winner. Consider this hand. North-South have reached a contract of 4♠:

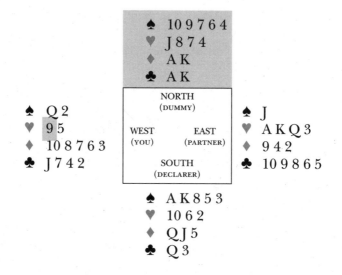

With very little in terms of high cards, you decide to lead your doubleton heart and strike gold in partner's hand. Partner takes the first three tricks with the ♥A, ♥K, and ♥Q. That appears to be all the tricks the defenders are going to take, but look what happens if partner now leads the ♥3. Although dummy's ♥J is a winner and declarer has no more hearts, there's nothing that declarer can do to avoid defeat.

If declarer doesn't trump, or trumps with a low spade, you can immediately win the trick by ruffing with the ♠Q. If declarer trumps with the ♠A or ♠K, you discard, and the ♠Q has suddenly been promoted into the second highest card in the suit. After declarer plays the remaining high spade, your ♠Q becomes a winner. The defense has promoted a trump winner.

This effect can be even more spectacular if the hand is changed around a little:

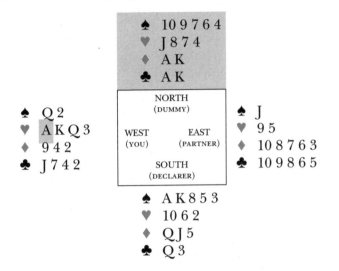

	♠ 109764	
	♥ J874	
	♦ AK	
	♣ AK	

NORTH (DUMMY)

♠ Q2		♠ J
♥ AKQ3	WEST (YOU) EAST (PARTNER)	♥ 95
♦ 942		♦ 108763
♣ J742	SOUTH (DECLARER)	♣ 109865

	♠ AK853	
	♥ 1062	
	♦ QJ5	
	♣ Q3	

This time, you take the first three tricks with the ♥A, ♥K, and ♥Q. With nothing else to do, you lead your last heart, the ♥J is played from dummy, and partner ruffs with the ♠J. There's nothing declarer can do. If declarer doesn't overruff, the contract is already defeated. If declarer does overruff with a high spade, your ♠Q has again been promoted into the setting trick.

This type of trump promotion by the defenders is often referred to as an *uppercut*. It's as though the ♠J is a blow to declarer's seemingly invincible trump suit.

Trump Echo

At times it's important to know exactly how many trumps your partner holds. You may have to decide between trying to give partner a ruff or trying to take winners in another suit. Consider the following hand after the auction proceeds:

WEST	NORTH	EAST	SOUTH
	1♣	Pass	1♥
Pass	2♥	Pass	4♥
Pass	Pass	Pass	

Partner leads the ♣7 against South's 4♥ contract, and this is what you see:

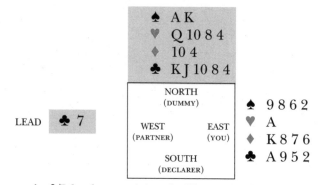

Partner's ♣7 looks suspiciously like a singleton, so after winning the first trick with the ♣A, you plan to lead back a club for partner to trump. You have to decide which club to lead back, since partner will assume you're giving a suit preference signal. You don't have a sure entry in diamonds, but you prefer diamonds to spades, so you lead back the ♣2.

Partner trumps this and leads a low diamond. You play third hand high, the ♦K, and declarer wins this trick with the ♦A. Declarer leads a low heart to dummy's ♥Q, and you win the ♥A. That's the third trick for the defense. There's two possibilities for defeating the contract. If partner has a trump left, you can lead another club for partner to ruff. If partner doesn't have a trump left, you can lead a diamond and hope that partner has the ♦Q. Which is it to be?

Predicaments like this are a challenge to resolve unless the partnership uses the *trump echo*. The standard agreement in this situation is that:

- With three trump, play a high trump followed by a low trump—a trump echo; with a doubleton trump, play the low trump followed by the higher trump.

This is the exact opposite of the count signal in any other suit—where high-low shows an even number and low-high shows an odd number—but that's the way it is. It does allow the partnership to resolve the above dilemma. If, for example, partner trumped the first club with the ♥7 and then played the ♥3 when declarer led a trump, partner is showing three hearts by "echoing." You can lead back another club for partner to ruff. The complete hand might be:

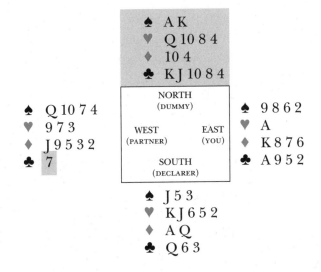

Partner ruffs the club with the ♥9, partner's third trump, and the contract is defeated. If partner had played the ♥3 followed by the ♥7, you would lead back a diamond, hoping the complete hand looked something like this:

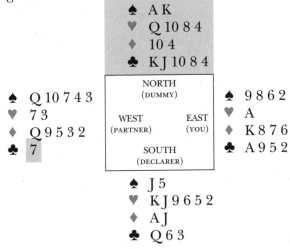

Here partner takes the setting trick with the ♦Q. If you led back another club, partner could only discard, and the contract would be made with an overtrick.

The trump echo is useful in this situation, and some partnerships use it all the time—whether or not they are trying to get a ruff—to let partner know how many trump are in the hidden hands. The latter practice has some drawbacks, as it often gives more useful information to declarer than to partner, but each partnership can adopt its own style. It's one more way of helping partner to accurately visualize those unseen cards.

The Forcing Game

Another defensive ploy in a suit contract is to try to run declarer out of trumps. If you can do that, and regain the lead, you'll be in a position to take any winners you have left. Consider this hand:

♠ 10 8 6 5
♥ A 9 4 2
♦ K Q J 9
♣ 6

You're on lead after the auction has been:

WEST	NORTH	EAST	SOUTH
	1NT	Pass	3♥
Pass	4♥	Pass	Pass
Pass			

It might be tempting to lead your singleton club against this contract. If partner can win a trick and give you a ruff, you'll only need to find one more trick to go along with your ♥A. When you have some length in the trump suit, however, it's usually a better idea to try to establish some winners. Once all the trump are gone, your winners may prove too much for declarer to handle. On this type of hand, the ♦K will usually prove to be the more effective lead. To see why, let's take a look at the complete hand.

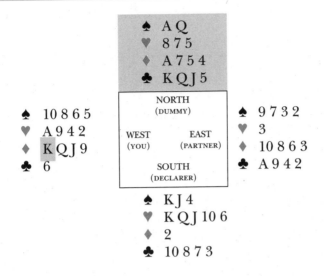

♠ A Q
♥ 8 7 5
♦ A 7 5 4
♣ K Q J 5

NORTH
(DUMMY)

♠ 10 8 6 5
♥ A 9 4 2
♦ K Q J 9
♣ 6

WEST
(YOU)

EAST
(PARTNER)

♠ 9 7 3 2
♥ 3
♦ 10 8 6 3
♣ A 9 4 2

SOUTH
(DECLARER)

♠ K J 4
♥ K Q J 10 6
♦ 2
♣ 10 8 7 3

If you lead a club, the hand will be over quickly. You are lucky enough to find partner with the ♣A, and partner will return a club for you to ruff. When you now lead the ♦K, declarer wins with dummy's ♦A and leads a trump to drive out your ♥A. That's the last trick for your side. If you lead another diamond, declarer ruffs and draws the rest of your trump. Declarer has the rest of the tricks.

If you lead the ♦K originally, the outcome is quite different. Declarer wins the first trick with dummy's ♦A and leads a trump. You win the ♥A, and lead another high diamond. Declarer has to trump this to win the trick and now has only three hearts left. If declarer draws all three of your remaining trump, declarer will be left with no hearts. When declarer now leads a club to drive out the ♣A, partner can win and lead another diamond. With no trump left, your side takes two diamond tricks to defeat the contract.

Even if declarer doesn't draw all your trump after finding out that the trump are divided badly, partner can still lead a diamond upon winning the ♣A, and declarer cannot prevent you from getting tricks with both your low trumps.

Defending in this manner is called a *forcing defense*. You keep forcing declarer to ruff until declarer runs out of trump.

Leading Trump

Although the defenders want to take advantage of the trump suit whenever possible, it can be equally effective to prevent declarer from making the best use of the trump suit. A common technique is to use dummy's trump to ruff losing cards from declarer's hand. The defenders should be on the lookout for this and try to thwart declarer's plans. Here's an example after the auction has gone:

WEST	NORTH	EAST	SOUTH
		Pass	1♠
Pass	2♠	Pass	Pass
Pass			

Your partner leads the ♦2 against declarer's 2♠ contract, and this is what you see:

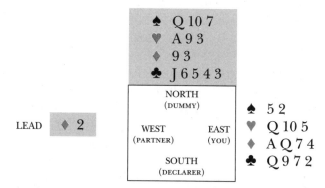

Try to picture your partner's holding in the diamond suit. It looks as though partner has led fourth highest from a four-card suit, and partner may well hold the ♦K, leaving declarer with three diamonds. That's the good news. The bad news is that there are only two diamonds in the dummy. Once you take your two diamond tricks, declarer will be able to ruff a diamond in the dummy.

To prevent this from happening, after winning the ♦A lead a trump. You want to try to get rid of all of dummy's trump before declarer can make use of them. Here's the complete hand:

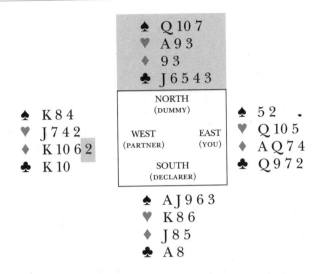

♠ Q 10 7
♥ A 9 3
♦ 9 3
♣ J 6 5 4 3

NORTH
(DUMMY)

♠ K 8 4
♥ J 7 4 2
♦ K 10 6 2
♣ K 10

WEST
(PARTNER)

EAST
(YOU)

♠ 5 2
♥ Q 10 5
♦ A Q 7 4
♣ Q 9 7 2

SOUTH
(DECLARER)

♠ A J 9 6 3
♥ K 8 6
♦ J 8 5
♣ A 8

If you shift to a spade, declarer is powerless. If declarer takes the finesse, partner wins the ♠K, and seeing what's on your mind, leads another trump. Declarer can lead another diamond, but partner wins and leads a third round of trump, removing the last spade from dummy. If declarer rises with the ♠A on the first round of trump, partner's ♠K becomes a winner, and partner can lead two rounds of trumps upon regaining the lead in diamonds.

Declarer ends up losing a spade trick, a heart trick, three diamond tricks, and a club trick. The defenders perform their assignment once more.

Summary

In a suit contract, the defenders can sometimes take advantage of the trump suit to accomplish their goal of defeating the contract. When defending against a trump suit, keep the following points in mind:

- Look for opportunities to ruff declarer's winning tricks or to help partner ruff declarer's winners.
- Suit preference signals can be used to tell partner which suit to lead in ruffing situations: a high-ranking card asks for the higher-ranking of the two suits; a low-ranking card asks for the lower-ranking of the two suits.
- When necessary, a defender can show partner how many trump cards are held: with three trump, play a high trump followed by a low trump—a trump echo; with a doubleton trump, play the low trump followed by the higher trump.
- Look for opportunities to promote winners in the trump suit when there doesn't appear to be any other source of tricks.
- Holding length in the trump suit, look for opportunities to run declarer out of trump.
- Lead trump when it looks as though declarer is planning to trump losers in the dummy.

Practice Hands

Hand 8.1

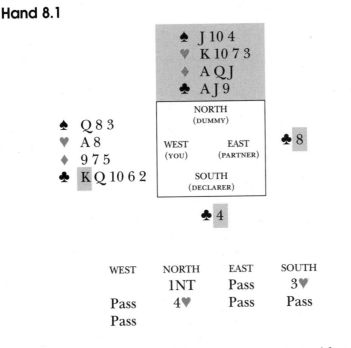

♠ J 10 4
♥ K 10 7 3
♦ A Q J
♣ A J 9

NORTH
(DUMMY)

♠ Q 8 3
♥ A 8
♦ 9 7 5
♣ K Q 10 6 2

WEST
(YOU)

EAST
(PARTNER)

♣ 8

SOUTH
(DECLARER)

♣ 4

WEST	NORTH	EAST	SOUTH
	1NT	Pass	3♥
Pass	4♥	Pass	Pass
Pass			

Against the opponents' 4♥ contract, you start with a lead of the ♣K. Declarer wins the trick with dummy's ♣A as partner plays the ♣8 and declarer the ♣4.

Declarer now plays a low heart from dummy. Partner plays the ♥2, and declarer plays the ♥Q. After winning a trick with the ♥A, you have several options: you could lead a spade to try and develop winners in that suit; you could lead a diamond through dummy's strength, hoping partner has the ♦K; you could take your club winner. How do you plan to continue?

Solution 8.1

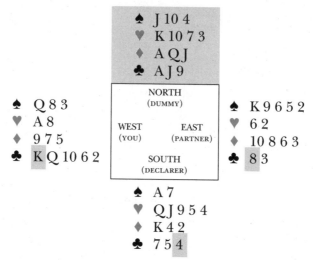

Your lead of the ♣K has promoted your ♣Q into a winner, but if you take a trick with it, dummy's ♣J will be established. Partner's ♣8 is an encouraging signal in clubs, however, and it gives you a clue about what to do next.

After winning a trick with the ♥A, you continue leading clubs. When you play the ♣Q, partner follows with the ♣3, confirming that the ♣8 was the start of an encouraging signal. Follow partner's suggestion, and lead another club. Partner will trump this for the third defensive trick. Eventually, your side will come to a spade trick and the contract will be defeated. If you had led anything else after winning the ♥A, declarer would draw your partner's last trump and end up making the contract.

You should lead a high club for partner to ruff, letting partner know that you prefer spades to diamonds. That way, partner will feel secure leading back a spade after receiving the ruff. On the actual hand, it doesn't make much difference, since you'll still defeat the contract if partner leads back a diamond. It's good practice, however, to always be thinking ahead about what you want partner to do upon gaining the lead.

Hand 8.2

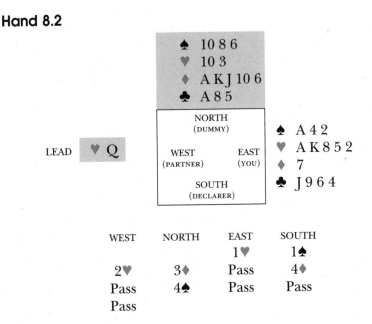

	WEST	NORTH	EAST	SOUTH
			1♥	1♠
	2♥	3♦	Pass	4♦
	Pass	4♠	Pass	Pass
	Pass			

After supporting your suit, partner leads the ♥Q. What do you think partner's heart holding looks like? Which card do you expect to find in partner's hand?

Where are your defensive tricks going to come from? Which card should you play to the first trick? To the second trick?

Solution 8.2

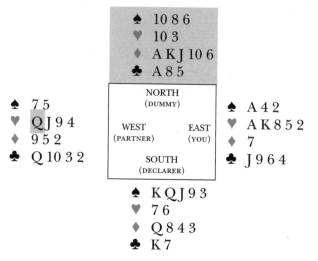

Having supported your suit, partner's lead of the ♥Q should be the top of touching high cards. Partner likely started with ♥ QJ x or ♥ QJ x x, so you expect to find the ♥J in partner's hand. You can count on two heart tricks—provided declarer doesn't have a single-ton or a void—and one spade trick. It's doubtful that your side can get a club trick, although partner might hold something useful in clubs.

A better possibility is to get a diamond ruff. You have a singleton, and you also have the ♠A to prevent declarer from drawing trump before you have an opportunity to get your ruff. Unfortunately, part-ner is unlikely to switch to a diamond if you let partner win the first trick. Even if you play a discouraging spade, partner is more likely to switch to a club than a diamond.

No problem. You know what needs to be done, so you should overtake partner's ♥Q with your ♥K and lead back your singleton diamond. Partner will be a little surprised, but should be able to figure out what's going on. When declarer leads a trump, you win a trick with the ♠A. Now comes the clever part. Since you have worked out that partner holds the ♥J, you can lead a low heart over to partner's ♥J. Again, partner will be a little surprised to win this trick, but hopefully not too astonished to return a diamond for you to ruff. It takes a bit of imagination to defeat this contract, but all the clues you need are there to guide you along.

Hand 8.3

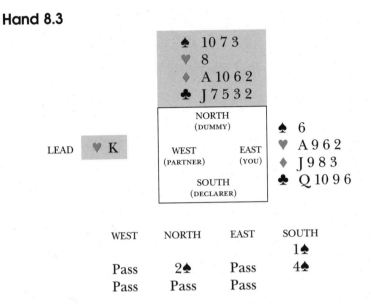

♠ 10 7 3
♥ 8
♦ A 10 6 2
♣ J 7 5 3 2

NORTH
(DUMMY)

LEAD   ♥ K

WEST
(PARTNER)

EAST
(YOU)

SOUTH
(DECLARER)

♠ 6
♥ A 9 6 2
♦ J 9 8 3
♣ Q 10 9 6

WEST	NORTH	EAST	SOUTH
			1♠
Pass	2♠	Pass	4♠
Pass	Pass	Pass	

Partner leads the ♥K against South's contract of 4♠. What might partner's heart holding look like? What will declarer probably be planning to do? What do you plan to do?

Solution 8.3

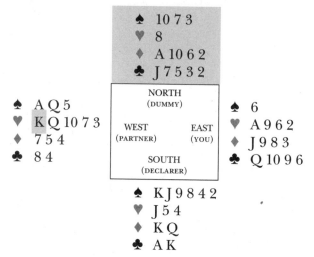

                        ♠ 10 7 3
                        ♥ 8
                        ♦ A 10 6 2
                        ♣ J 7 5 3 2

                        NORTH
                        (DUMMY)

♠ A Q 5   ♠ 6
♥ K Q 10 7 3   WEST   EAST   ♥ A 9 6 2
♦ 7 5 4   (PARTNER)   (YOU)   ♦ J 9 8 3
♣ 8 4   ♣ Q 10 9 6

                        SOUTH
                        (DECLARER)

                        ♠ K J 9 8 4 2
                        ♥ J 5 4
                        ♦ K Q
                        ♣ A K

It looks as though partner is leading the top of touching high cards, so partner has a heart suit headed by the ♥K and ♥Q. Although you hold the ♥A, your side won't be able to take any more than one heart trick as long as there are spades in the dummy.

Declarer probably has some low hearts and is planning to trump them in the dummy. To prevent this, your side needs to lead trump right away. It's better to lead trump from your side of the table, through declarer's strength and up to the weakness in dummy. Overtake partner's ♥K with your ♥A, and lead a spade.

Looking at the complete hand, a spade lead from your side dooms the contract. Partner has declarer's ♠K trapped. Partner can win two spade tricks and then lead a third round, getting rid of all of dummy's trump. Declarer is left with two heart losers to get rid of, and there's no way to do that. Declarer can't even take three diamond winners because there is no longer an entry to dummy outside of the diamond suit itself. With careful defense from this point on, the contract will be defeated two tricks.

If you did not overtake and lead a trump, declarer would make the contract. Spades cannot effectively be led from partner's side of the table, and after winning tricks with the ♦K and ♦Q, declarer will be able to trump one heart loser in the dummy and discard the other on the ♦A.

Hand 8.4

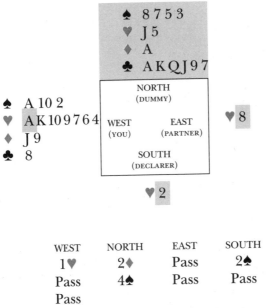

	WEST	NORTH	EAST	SOUTH
	1♥	2♦	Pass	2♠
	Pass	4♠	Pass	Pass
	Pass			

The opponents reach 4♠, and your opening lead is the ♥A. A low heart is played from dummy, partner plays the ♥8, and declarer the ♥2. When you continue with the ♥K, partner plays the ♥3, and declarer the ♥Q.

That's two tricks for the defense, and you can see one more from the ♠A. Where might your fourth defensive trick come from? What's the minimum partner must hold to enable you to defeat the contract. What do you plan to do at trick three?

Solution 8.4

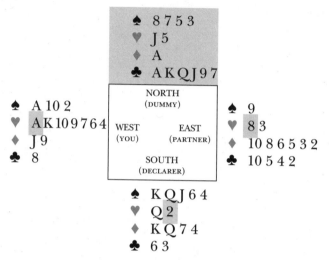

After winning the first two tricks in the heart suit, the only place left from which your side is likely to get tricks is the trump suit. Partner is unlikely to hold any high cards in the spade suit, but as little as the ♠9 will be sufficient if partner cooperates.

Even though none of the other players has any hearts left, lead another heart. If partner can ruff this with the ♠9, your ♠10 will get promoted into a second trump winner. Look at the complete layout. Partner's ♠9 forces declarer to overruff with the ♠J. Declarer can play the ♠K to drive out your ♠A, and can take a trick with the ♠Q, but now your ♠10 has been promoted into a winner.

The defensive uppercut does the job. Partner could have held a higher spade, such as the ♠J or ♠Q, but the ♠9 is all you need—and makes the defense that much more spectacular!

9

Finding the Right Discard

"When in doubt, win the trick."

— EDMUND HOYLE,
Twenty-four Rules for Learners

One of the challenges for a defender is to find the right discards when declarer or partner is taking winners in a suit. You need to know which cards to keep and which to throw away.

It's a two-sided process. When deciding which cards to keep, you try to visualize the hidden cards, based on the auction, partner's signals, and the way the play has gone so far. When deciding what to discard, you need to consider the message that you want to send to partner. Let's look at some examples.

Holding the Right Cards

Before choosing a discard, consider which suits you need to keep. Sometimes, it will be obvious. More often than not, you'll have to think about the situation.

231

Guarding Against Dummy's Length

As a general guideline, try to hold on to the same length in a suit as there is in the dummy or in declarer's hand. It's a little easier when the length is in the dummy, since you can see the cards. Consider this example.

WEST	NORTH	EAST	SOUTH
	1♦	Pass	1NT
Pass	3NT	Pass	Pass
Pass			

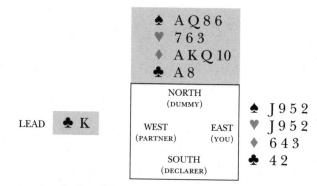

♠ A Q 8 6
♥ 7 6 3
♦ A K Q 10
♣ A 8

NORTH
(DUMMY)

WEST
(PARTNER)

EAST
(YOU)

SOUTH
(DECLARER)

LEAD ♣ K

♠ J 9 5 2
♥ J 9 5 2
♦ 6 4 3
♣ 4 2

Partner leads the ♣K against the 3NT contract, and declarer plays the ♣8 from dummy, letting partner win the trick. Partner leads another club, and dummy wins the ♣A as you follow with your last club. Declarer now plays four rounds of diamonds. You can follow suit to the first three rounds, but must find a discard on the fourth round. You have the same holding in both spades and hearts, but the guideline suggests that you discard a heart, rather than a spade, so that you keep the same length as dummy in the spade suit.

You might be thinking, "What if declarer holds four hearts?" After all, you also want to try to keep the same length as declarer. There are several clues pointing you in the right direction.

First, you know for certain that dummy holds four spades, but you don't know for sure that declarer holds four hearts. When you have a choice, guard against the suit you do know about, rather than one you don't.

Second, declarer would probably have responded 1♥, rather than 1NT, when holding a four-card heart suit. While there's no guarantee that declarer hasn't made an unusual choice of response, the auction can usually be counted on to provide some reliable information about the hidden hands.

Finally, for a heart discard to be costly, declarer would need to hold a strong four-card suit, such as ♥ A K Q x. If that's the case, declarer is making the contract anyway. It's more reasonable to assume that partner holds at least one of the high cards in the heart suit.

Discarding a heart is the only way to defeat the contract, since this is the complete hand:

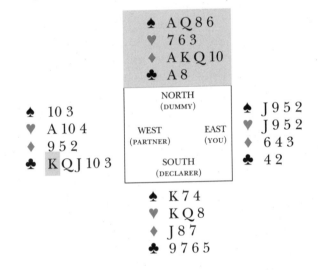

♠ A Q 8 6
♥ 7 6 3
♦ A K Q 10
♣ A 8

NORTH
(DUMMY)

♠ 10 3
♥ A 10 4
♦ 9 5 2
♣ K Q J 10 3

WEST
(PARTNER)

EAST
(YOU)

SOUTH
(DECLARER)

♠ J 9 5 2
♥ J 9 5 2
♦ 6 4 3
♣ 4 2

♠ K 7 4
♥ K Q 8
♦ J 8 7
♣ 9 7 6 5

If you were to discard a spade, declarer would be able to take four spade tricks, since dummy's last spade would become a winner. That would be declarer's ninth trick. By tenaciously holding on to all four spades, you prevent declarer from making the contract.

This example illustrates why you often have to hold on to the same number of cards in a suit as are held by declarer or the dummy. You are the only member of the partnership that can guard the spade suit. Partner will have to take care of other suits. The situation would be different if partner also held four spades. Then only one of you would need to protect the spade suit. The situation would also change if you were reasonably confident that partner held the ♠K. Suppose this is the layout you visualize:

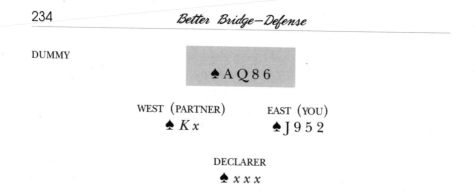

DUMMY

♠ A Q 8 6

WEST (PARTNER)   EAST (YOU)
♠ K x   ♠ J 9 5 2

DECLARER
♠ x x x

   Now you could afford to discard a spade and still prevent declarer from taking all the tricks in the suit. Declarer could finesse dummy's ♠Q and play the ♠A, but you would have the ♠J left to win the next trick. Note, however, that once you discard a spade, declarer could establish an extra spade winner in dummy through length by giving up a trick to your ♠J. That's why the guideline is to hold on to the same length as the dummy for as long as possible.

Guarding Against Declarer's Length

Of course, as the play progresses, you'll often be unable to hold on to everything. You'll have to do the best that you can. Consider this hand:

WEST	NORTH	EAST	SOUTH
			1♥
Pass	1♠	Pass	1NT
Pass	3NT	Pass	Pass
Pass			

♠ K Q 8 6
♥ A 3
♦ K Q J 10
♣ 9 8 6

NORTH
(DUMMY)   ♠ J 9 5 2
                                     ♥ J 9 5 2
LEAD ♣ K   WEST   EAST   ♦ 6 4 3
                (PARTNER) (YOU)   ♣ 4 2
                SOUTH
                (DECLARER)

Partner leads the ♣K, and declarer let's this win the trick. Another high club is led, and again declarer let's your partner win the trick. When partner leads another club, you have to find a discard. This one's easy. You can discard a low diamond, since you have nothing worthwhile to hold on to in that suit. Declarer wins the trick with the ♣A, plays the ♦A, and starts to take the rest of the diamond winners. You have to find discards on the last two diamond tricks.

This is a little harder. You want to hold on to four spades to keep the same length as the dummy, but you also want to hold on to your hearts because declarer has bid the suit. A little logic will help here. If declarer holds the ♠A, you can never defeat the contract. Declarer will have three sure spade winners to go along with the ♥A, the four diamond winners, and the ♣A. You have to assume partner holds that card, so it's safe to discard your spades and hold on to your hearts. Here's the complete hand:

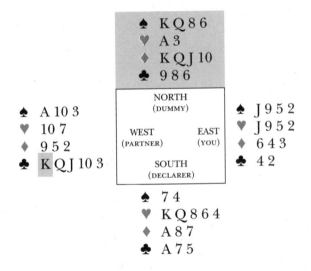

If you discard a heart, declarer will be able to take five heart tricks, making the contract with an overtrick. When you discard your spades, declarer can take only eight tricks. If declarer tries to establish a spade winner, partner wins the ♣A and takes two more club winners.

Getting Help from Partner

Although you could work out the best suit to discard in the last example, the choice is less apparent on many hands. Partner, however, may be able to help out. Consider this hand:

WEST	NORTH	EAST	SOUTH
		Pass	1NT
Pass	3NT	Pass	Pass
Pass			

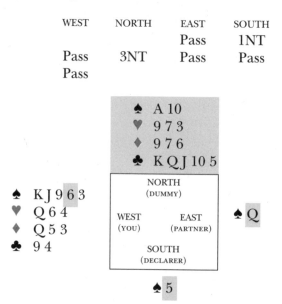

You lead the ♠6 against the 3NT contract, the ♠10 is played from dummy, and partner wins the trick with the ♠Q as declarer follows with the ♠5. Partner returns a spade to drive out dummy's ♠A. So far, so good—your remaining spades are now winners. But now its declarer's turn. Declarer takes a trick with the ♣A, and then proceeds to take dummy's club winners. After following suit to the first two rounds of clubs, what do you discard on the next three?

You need to hold on to all the spades. If you discard one, even if declarer gives your side the lead, you won't be able to take enough winners to defeat the contract. Without any information from the auction, there's little to choose between hearts and diamonds. It depends where the unseen high cards are located. If you discard hearts, declarer may then be able to take three tricks in that suit, and the same is true if you discard diamonds. Your only hope is that partner has some strength in at least one of the suits. You can then discard your cards in that suit, and hold on to the other suit. But where does partner's strength lie?

Partner may be able to let you know. Suppose partner also has no clubs left after the first two rounds, and on the third round discards the ♦2. What does that tell you? Partner is making a discouraging signal in diamonds, showing no interest in the suit. That warns you to hold on to your diamonds, since you're the only member of the partnership who can guard that suit. You discard your hearts, hoping partner has enough strength in that suit to prevent declarer from establishing extra winners.

It would be a similar situation if partner discarded the ♥8. That looks like an encouraging card, so partner probably has some strength in that suit. You can afford to discard your hearts, but you'll have to hold on to your diamonds. Here's the full hand:

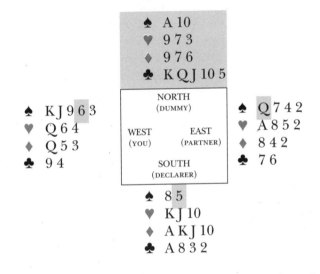

If you hold on to your diamonds, declarer can't make the contract. If declarer leads a heart, partner can win the ♥A and lead a spade to your winners. If declarer takes the ♦A and ♦K, or tries the diamond finesse, you will get a trick with your ♦Q and can take your spade winners. If you had discarded one or more of your diamonds, declarer could make the contract with an overtrick by playing the ♦A and ♦K, since your ♦Q would now fall.

Notice that partner had two possible ways to help you out when declarer led a third round of clubs from dummy. Partner could either discard a high heart—showing strength in that suit—or a low diamond—denying strength in that suit. Either signal would be enough to tell you which cards to hold on to. Partner could have afforded to discard a spade, but that wouldn't do you much good on this hand. The signal in hearts or diamonds is much more important. Partner has to recognize the importance of sending you the right message.

Declarer could have made things more difficult by winning the second round of clubs with the ♣A and then leading a club toward dummy. You would have to decide what to discard before seeing partner's signal. It would also be difficult if partner held three or more clubs. Partner wouldn't be able to make a signal in hearts or diamonds until it was too late. You won't always have the help you need.

If you did have to guess what to discard, don't make it an agonizing decision. Pick one of the suits, and discard a low card. The hand isn't over yet. If you did discard a diamond, declarer still wouldn't know which defender held the ♦Q and might take the finesse anyway. Sometimes, you just have to hold your breath and hope declarer also can't see through the backs of the cards.

Maintaining Communication with Partner

On the last hand, it was important to hold on to the winners you had established so that you could take enough tricks to defeat the contract when your side regained the lead. When partner is the one holding on to the established winners, it's often important for you to keep a card in partner's suit.

WEST	NORTH	EAST	SOUTH
	1♥	Pass	1NT
Pass	3NT	Pass	Pass
Pass			

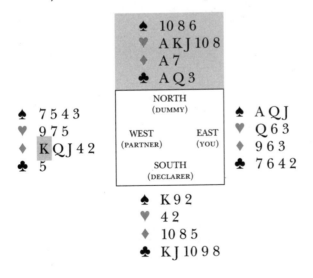

```
              ♠ 10 8 6
              ♥ A K J 10 8
              ♦ A 7
              ♣ A Q 3
              NORTH
              (DUMMY)
                            ♠ A Q J
LEAD   ♦ K   WEST    EAST   ♥ Q 6 3
             (PARTNER) (YOU) ♦ 9 6 3
              SOUTH         ♣ 7 6 4 2
            (DECLARER)
```

The opening lead is the ♦K, and declarer plays the ♦7 from dummy, letting your partner win the trick. Partner leads another diamond which is won with dummy's ♦A. Declarer then starts taking club winners by playing dummy's ♣A and ♣Q. Partner discards a low spade on the second round of clubs. That leaves declarer with three more club winners to take. What are you going to discard on the fifth round of clubs?

You can't afford to discard one of your hearts; otherwise your ♥Q will fall under dummy's ♥A and ♥K. You may not want to discard one of your high spades while you still have a low diamond left in your hand, but it's important to hang on to that last card in partner's suit. To see why, take a look at the complete hand:

```
                 ♠ 10 8 6
                 ♥ A K J 10 8
                 ♦ A 7
                 ♣ A Q 3
                 NORTH
                 (DUMMY)
  ♠ 7 5 4 3                      ♠ A Q J
  ♥ 9 7 5     WEST      EAST      ♥ Q 6 3
  ♦ K Q J 4 2 (PARTNER) (YOU)     ♦ 9 6 3
  ♣ 5          SOUTH             ♣ 7 6 4 2
             (DECLARER)
                 ♠ K 9 2
                 ♥ 4 2
                 ♦ 10 8 5
                 ♣ K J 10 9 8
```

If you discard your last diamond, the contract can no longer be defeated. Declarer can cross to dummy with a heart and lead a spade toward the ♠K for a ninth trick. Or declarer can take the heart finesse. Although the finesse loses to your ♥Q, the best you can do is to take your ♠A. Declarer has the rest of the tricks.

It's vital to hold on to your last diamond, since it's the link card to partner's established winners. Discarding the ♠Q or ♠J may seem extravagant, but it's far less costly than parting with your low diamond.

Discarding the Right Cards

You must not only be careful to keep the right cards, you must also be careful to discard the right cards.

Sending a Signal

The cards you discard can be used to send messages to partner. Usually, the most important thing to tell partner is your attitude toward the suit from which you're discarding. High cards are encouraging; low cards are discouraging. Be careful about discarding high cards in the suits you like. You want to avoid throwing away potential winners. Here's a typical example.

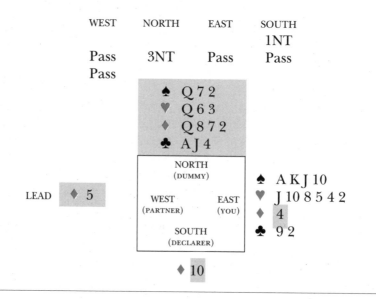

WEST	NORTH	EAST	SOUTH
			1NT
Pass	3NT	Pass	Pass
Pass			

Partner doesn't appear to have to have got off to the best lead for your side, especially when declarer wins the first trick with the ♦10 and leads the ♦J at trick two, which partner wins with the ♦A. You have to make a discard.

You have dummy's ♠Q trapped and would really like partner to lead a spade. It would be costly to discard one of your high spades as an encouraging signal, however, since that would be one of your potential winners. The best you can do is to make a discouraging signal in one of the other suits. Since the ♣A and ♣J are in dummy, partner is unlikely to consider switching to that suit. Partner's choice is likely to be between spades and hearts. By discarding the ♥2, you can send the message that you don't like that suit. Hopefully, partner can figure things out from there. Here's the full hand:

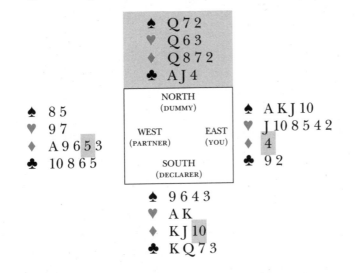

	♠ Q 7 2	
	♥ Q 6 3	
	♦ Q 8 7 2	
	♣ A J 4	

	NORTH (DUMMY)	
♠ 8 5		♠ A K J 10
♥ 9 7	WEST (PARTNER) EAST (YOU)	♥ J 10 8 5 4 2
♦ A 9 6 5 3		♦ 4
♣ 10 8 6 5	SOUTH (DECLARER)	♣ 9 2

	♠ 9 6 4 3	
	♥ A K	
	♦ K J 10	
	♣ K Q 7 3	

Looking at the West hand, you can appreciate that partner would have a problem after winning a trick with the ♦A, if you didn't send a clear-cut signal. Partner knows that continuing diamonds won't do any good, but needs to know whether to switch to spades or hearts. When you give a discouraging signal in hearts, partner can make the assumption that your strength probably lies in the spade suit. If partner switches to a spade, the contract is defeated.

If you had discarded one of your spades, you would no longer be able to defeat the contract when partner leads your suit. Notice that declarer tried to get a second diamond trick before the defenders had a lot of opportunity to exchange information. If declarer had taken some club or heart winners, it would become apparent to your partner that spades is the only source of tricks for your side. You were fortunate to have one chance to make a signal, and you had to make the most of it.

Discarding High Cards

When you lead from touching honors, you lead the top card. This sends the message to partner that you have the next lower-ranking card, but don't have the next higher-ranking card. The same is true when discarding from touching honors. Discard the highest of your touching cards. For example, suppose you're going to discard a heart in this situation:

```
                    DUMMY
                  ♥ A 7 3

   WEST (PARTNER)          EAST (YOU)
        ♥ ?                ♥ Q J 10 9 8

                  DECLARER
                    ♥ ?
```

All your hearts are equal, so you should throw the ♥Q, top of your equal cards. This will send the message to partner that you don't have the ♥K—the next higher-ranking card—but you do have the ♥J, and likely the ♥10 and ♥9 as well—otherwise you probably couldn't afford to discard one of your high cards. If partner doesn't hold the ♥K, partner can now infer that it's hidden in declarer's hand. If partner does hold the ♥K, partner knows it will be safe to lead the suit and promote winners.

Let's see how this type of information can be put to use during a hand.

WEST	NORTH	EAST	SOUTH
		Pass	1♠
Pass	2♦	Pass	2♠
Pass	4♠	Pass	Pass
Pass			

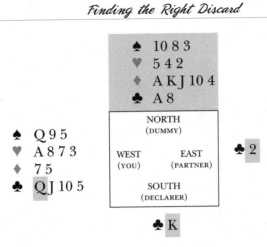

You lead the ♣Q against the 4♠ contract. The ♣A is played from dummy, partner plays the ♣2, and declarer the ♣7. Declarer now draws trump by playing the ♠A and ♠K and then another spade which you win with the ♠Q. Now what?

Partner has made a discouraging signal in clubs, and looking at those strong diamonds in dummy, the best chance is probably to hope your side can take three heart tricks. But suppose partner discards the ♥Q while declarer is drawing trump. This marks declarer with the ♥K, so you won't be able to take more than one heart trick if you lead the suit from your side. Your only hope is that partner can gain the lead and help you trap declarer's ♥K. Lead another club, or a diamond. Here's the complete hand:

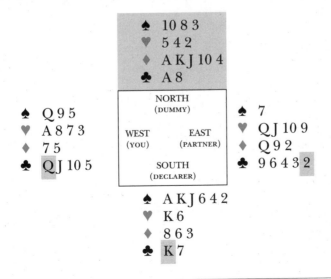

If you take your ♥A, declarer's ♥K becomes a winner, and your side will end up with only one spade trick, one heart trick, and one diamond trick. If you bide your time by leading another suit, declarer will have to lose a trick to partner's ♦Q, and partner can lead a heart through declarer. You'll get two heart tricks to defeat the contract.

Partner's discard of the ♥Q clarifies the situation. No other signal would do the job. Partner couldn't make a discouraging signal in hearts for two reasons: the ♥9 probably wouldn't look like a low card, and more importantly, partner can't be certain that a discouraging signal is correct. Partner can't make an encouraging signal in diamonds because partner can't afford to throw a card from that suit.

Suppose partner's heart holding were something like ♥ K Q 10 9. Then partner could make an encouraging signal by discarding the ♥10. Holding ♥ K Q J 10, partner could make an even more dramatic signal by discarding the ♥K. In either situation, you'd know to lead hearts and take your winners.

Thinking Ahead

In some situations, you must plan your discards carefully by predicting what is likely to happen. Consider this next hand.

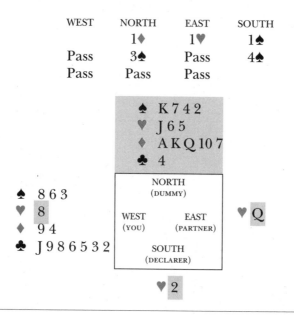

WEST	NORTH	EAST	SOUTH
	1♦	1♥	1♠
Pass	3♣	Pass	4♠
Pass	Pass	Pass	

You lead your singleton in partner's suit against declarer's 4♠ contract, and partner wins the first trick with the ♥Q. Partner continues with the ♥K, declarer plays the ♥3, and you have to choose a discard. Your first instinct might be to discard a low club. You've got lots of those, and you'll be able to tell partner you don't have much interest in that suit. Before doing that, consider how the rest of the play will go.

Partner will presumably continue by leading the ♥A. If declarer can't ruff this, that will be the third winner for your side, and you'll get to make a second discard. Since you have only two diamonds, you can discard both of them on partner's heart winners. Let's see how this works on the complete hand:

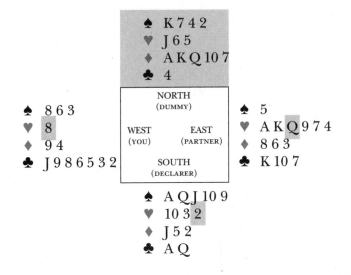

On the ♥K, you throw the ♦9, starting an encouraging signal. When partner plays the ♥A, you can finish your signal by discarding the ♦4. Looking at the high diamonds in dummy, partner will realize that you aren't make an encouraging signal because you have strength in diamonds. It must be for exactly the reason you planned. Partner can lead a diamond, and you can ruff it to defeat the contract. Partner isn't afraid that you have the ♣A, since you could have made an encouraging signal in clubs if you held that card. Only by thinking ahead—and having partner cooperate—can you defeat this contract.

Summary

When you have to make a discard, keep the following points in mind:

- Try to hold on to the same length in a suit as there is in the dummy or in declarer's hand to prevent declarer from establishing extra winners in the suit.
- Watch partner's signals for clues about which suit to hold on to.
- Decide on the message you want to send to partner with your discard.
- When discarding from equal honors, discard the highest-ranking of the touching cards.
- When making several discards, plan ahead.

Practice Hands

Hand 9.1

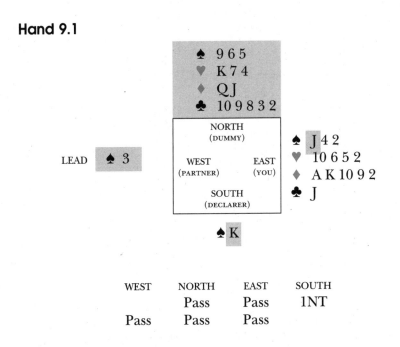

	WEST	NORTH	EAST	SOUTH
		Pass	Pass	1NT
	Pass	Pass	Pass	

Partner leads the ♠3 against declarer's contract of 1NT. A low spade is played from dummy, and you play the ♠J, third hand high. Declarer wins this with the ♠K and plays the ♣A, ♣K, and a third round of clubs which partner wins with the ♣Q.

Which two cards do you discard on the second and third round of clubs?

Solution 9.1

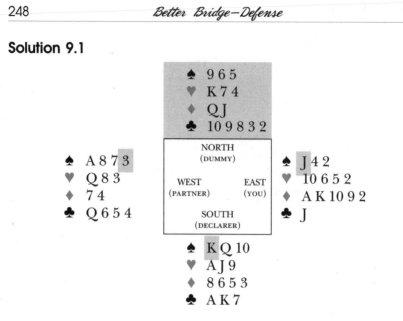

North (Dummy):
- ♠ 9 6 5
- ♥ K 7 4
- ♦ Q J
- ♣ 10 9 8 3 2

West (Partner):
- ♠ A 8 7 3
- ♥ Q 8 3
- ♦ 7 4
- ♣ Q 6 5 4

East (You):
- ♠ J 4 2
- ♥ 10 6 5 2
- ♦ A K 10 9 2
- ♣ J

South (Declarer):
- ♠ K Q 10
- ♥ A J 9
- ♦ 8 6 5 3
- ♣ A K 7

Once you see the dummy's diamonds, you really want partner to lead the suit, since you have several winners to take. You can't afford to discard a high diamond as an encouraging signal because you'd be throwing away one of your winners.

Instead, try to tell partner what not to lead. On the second round of clubs, discard the ♥2, warning partner not to lead that suit. On the third round of clubs, discard a low spade, asking partner not to continue leading that suit. Hopefully, partner will get the message and switch to a diamond after winning a trick with the ♣Q. You take five diamond tricks, and then lead a spade to partner's ♠A to defeat the contract.

If you discarded a diamond, you would be left with only four winners. In fact, if you discard the ♦10 or ♦9, you'll only be able to take three tricks in the suit. If you didn't warn partner not to lead another spade, partner might lead one, hoping you have the ♠Q. Declarer craftily won the first trick with the ♠K, leaving partner in doubt as to the location of the ♠Q. If partner leads either a low spade or a heart, declarer will make the contract with an overtrick.

Hand 9.2

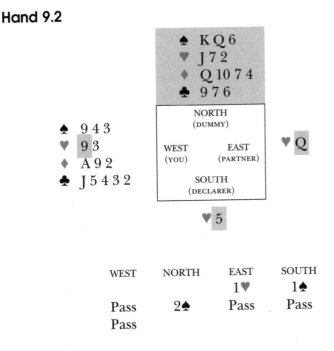

WEST	NORTH	EAST	SOUTH
		1♥	1♠
Pass	2♠	Pass	Pass
Pass			

You lead the ♥9 against the opponents' partscore contract of 2♠. Partner wins the first trick with the ♥Q and proceeds to take two more tricks with the ♥A and ♥K as declarer follows suit.

What are the possible messages you might want to send partner? Which card do you discard on the third round of hearts? How do you expect to defeat the contract?

Solution 9.2

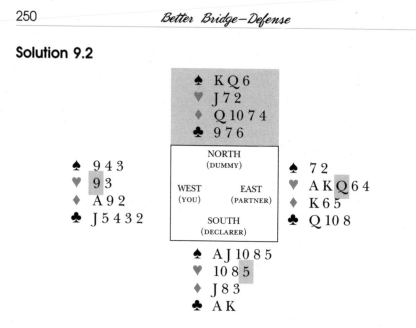

Partner wins the first three heart tricks, and you have an opportunity to send a message with your discard on the third round of the suit. There are two possibilities. You could tell partner that you don't like clubs by discarding a low club; or you could tell partner that you do like diamonds by discarding a high diamond.

Your side needs three more tricks to defeat the contract. You can see one more with your ♦A, so partner will need some high cards in diamonds or clubs to defeat the contract. If partner holds the ♦K, there's an excellent chance to defeat the contract if you discard the ♦9. This will encourage partner to lead a diamond. You win the ♦A, lead a diamond back to partner's ♦K, and partner can lead a third round of diamonds for you to ruff.

Looking at the actual hand, that's the only defense to defeat the contract. If you discard a low club, partner may lead a diamond, but you won't be able to get a ruff. You have to think ahead about how you might defeat the contract, and then choose your discard accordingly.

Hand 9.3

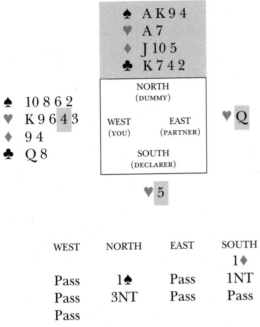

♠ A K 9 4
♥ A 7
♦ J 10 5
♣ K 7 4 2

NORTH
(DUMMY)

♠ 10 8 6 2
♥ K 9 6 4 3
♦ 9 4
♣ Q 8

WEST
(YOU)

EAST
(PARTNER)

♥ Q

SOUTH
(DECLARER)

♥ 5

WEST	NORTH	EAST	SOUTH
			1♦
Pass	1♠	Pass	1NT
Pass	3NT	Pass	Pass
Pass			

You lead your fourth highest heart against South's 3NT contract. Declarer plays the ♥7 from dummy, and partner wins the trick with the ♥Q, as declarer plays the ♥5. Partner returns the ♥8, declarer plays the ♥10, and you cleverly play one of your low hearts, since dummy is forced to play the ♥A. How do you think the remaining hearts are distributed?

Declarer plays dummy's ♦J, which wins the trick, and proceeds to take three more diamond tricks with the ♦A, ♦K, and ♦Q. You have to find two discards on the last two diamond tricks. If you're going to defeat this contract, which cards do you throw away?

Solution 9.3

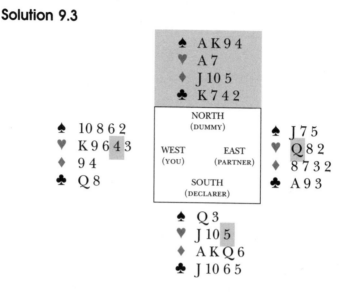

♠ A K 9 4
♥ A 7
♦ J 10 5
♣ K 7 4 2

NORTH (DUMMY)

♠ 10 8 6 2
♥ K 9 6 4 3
♦ 9 4
♣ Q 8

WEST (YOU)   EAST (PARTNER)

♠ J 7 5
♥ Q 8 2
♦ 8 7 3 2
♣ A 9 3

SOUTH (DECLARER)

♠ Q 3
♥ J 10 5
♦ A K Q 6
♣ J 10 6 5

When partner wins the first trick with the ♥Q, declarer is known to hold the ♥J because partner would play the lower of equal honors as third hand. When partner returns the ♥8 and declarer plays the ♥10, it looks very much as though declarer has only the ♥J remaining and partner has one more heart, the ♥2. Declarer would have played the ♥2, rather than the ♥10, holding that card. So you can visualize the heart layout as it is in the actual hand. Your remaining hearts are all winners if your side can regain the lead and partner still has a heart left.

When declarer now takes four diamond tricks, you must find two discards. You want to hold on to all the hearts; otherwise you won't be able to take enough tricks to defeat the contract when you regain the lead. Looking at the complete hand, you won't defeat the contract unless you discard both your clubs. If you discard any of the spades, declarer can take four spade tricks and make the contract. If you discard a heart, declarer can take a club finesse against your ♣Q to drive out partner's ♣A.

How can you work out to discard both your clubs? There are two indications. First, there's the general principle of trying to hold on to the same length as the dummy. Second, if declarer holds the ♣A, you can't defeat the contract anyway. Together with the ♥A and four diamond winners, declarer will have two spade winners and two club winners. You have to hope partner holds the ♣A and will lead back another heart upon winning a trick in that suit.

Hand 9.4

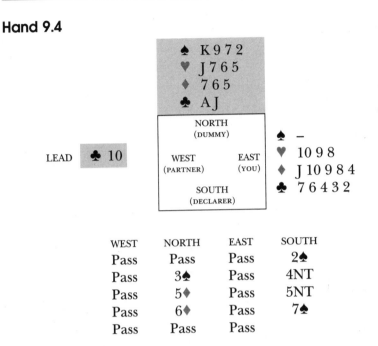

♠ K 9 7 2
♥ J 7 6 5
♦ 7 6 5
♣ A J

NORTH
(DUMMY)

LEAD ♣ 10

WEST   EAST
(PARTNER)   (YOU)

SOUTH
(DECLARER)

♠ —
♥ 10 9 8
♦ J 10 9 8 4
♣ 7 6 4 3 2

WEST	NORTH	EAST	SOUTH
Pass	Pass	Pass	2♠
Pass	3♠	Pass	4NT
Pass	5♦	Pass	5NT
Pass	6♦	Pass	7♠
Pass	Pass	Pass	

South uses the Blackwood Convention to find out that partner has an ace and a king, and then puts the partnership in a grand slam. Partner leads the ♣10.

This is no time to fall asleep, even if you don't have very much in the way of high cards. It looks as though partner is going to have to come up with a trick somewhere. Is there anything you can do to make partner's task easier when declarer starts to draw trump?

Solution 9.4

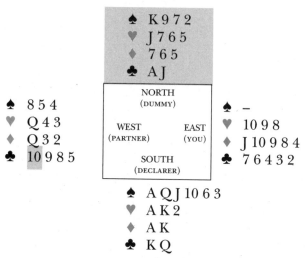

♠ K 9 7 2
♥ J 7 6 5
♦ 7 6 5
♣ A J

NORTH
(DUMMY)

WEST
(PARTNER)

EAST
(YOU)

SOUTH
(DECLARER)

♠ 8 5 4
♥ Q 4 3
♦ Q 3 2
♣ 10 9 8 5

♠ —
♥ 10 9 8
♦ J 10 9 8 4
♣ 7 6 4 3 2

♠ A Q J 10 6 3
♥ A K 2
♦ A K
♣ K Q

On the first club trick, you can play the ♣2 to let partner know that you don't have any help in that suit. That's not going to be much news to partner. When declarer starts to draw trump, however, you'll have an opportunity to help partner right away.

Your first discard should be the ♦J—the only high card in your hand! When you discard a high card in this fashion, you are letting partner know that you don't hold the next higher-ranking card, the ♦Q, but you do hold the lower-ranking cards.

On the actual hand, partner won't be very surprised to hear that you don't hold the ♦Q. But partner will be more than happy to know that you hold the lower-ranking cards in this suit. When declarer starts rattling off a lot of winners, partner can confidently discard diamonds and hold on to the ♥Q until the end of the hand. Partner is safe in the knowledge that you can guard the diamond suit.

If you don't discard the ♦J, partner may not know which suit to keep at the end of the hand. If partner discards a heart, rather than a diamond, declarer makes the grand slam. Any other discards you make would not be as clear to partner. If you discard all your low clubs, that's not much help. If you discard your "low" ♥8, partner may think that's an encouraging signal in hearts. Once you discard the ♦J, however, partner's worries are over.

10

Playing Detective

*"Contrariwise," continued Tweedledee, "if it was
so, it might be; and if it were so, it would be; but
as it isn't, it ain't. That's logic."*

— LEWIS CARROLL,
Through the Looking Glass
[1872]

To be a good defender, you have to think like a detective. When clues
are scarce, you may have to rely on your intuition. But there's usually
plenty of clues around. You have to search for them, recognize them
when you come across them, and draw the logical conclusion.

Using Your Ears

Assume you're sitting West and the auction goes like this:

WEST	NORTH	EAST	SOUTH
	Pass	Pass	1♠
Pass	1NT	Pass	2♣
Pass	Pass	Pass	

What do you lead? Oh, I suppose you want to see your hand first! Strangely enough, that's not always necessary. On an auction like this, you have almost all the information you need to make the opening lead without even looking at your hand. Let's consider all the clues that are available.

We'll start with North, the hand that's going to come down as the dummy. North passed originally, so there's your first clue. North has less than 13 points. North responded 1NT to South's opening bid. That shows a hand of about 6–10 points. Already, you're narrowing things down. North didn't raise partner's first suit, spades. Since most players would raise partner's major suit with 6–10 points and three-card or four-card support, it sounds as though North has at most two spades and could have a singleton or even a void. When South bid 2♣, North passed. So North prefers clubs to spades as the trump suit. North likely has four or five clubs. North is unlikely to have a long diamond or heart suit because North didn't mention one of them over 2♣. You can visualize the pattern of North's hand to be something like this:

NORTH
♠ x
♥ x x x x
♦ x x x x
♣ x x x x

Somewhere among those little "x"s are scattered 6–10 points.

How about our partner, East? Partner also didn't open the bidding. That's too bad, but it's also good reason to believe that partner has less than 13 points. Partner had other chances to come into the auction—after the 1NT response and when 2♣ came back around. With all this passing, you can draw the conclusion that partner doesn't have a good suit to overcall, or the type of hand to make a takeout double. Partner likely has some scattered strength.

Now for declarer, South. South did open the bidding and probably has a hand worth 13 or more points. South didn't make a strong-sounding rebid, so you can infer that South has a minimum-strength or medium-strength hand. South's opening bid of 1♠ likely shows a five-card or longer suit. The rebid of 2♣ shows a second suit of at least four cards in length. You can visualize South's hand to look something like this:

SOUTH
♠ *x x x x x*
♥ *x x*
♦ *x x*
♣ *x x x x*

Now you know almost everything. If you put the North and South hands opposite one another, how is declarer likely to play the hand? South has all those spades and North is short in spades and has some trump. Unless declarer has a very good spade suit, declarer will probably want to trump some of the low spades with dummy's clubs. How can you spoil declarer's plan? By leading a trump.

And there you have it! You haven't even looked at your hand, but can't wait to lead a club. Let's see how that works out.

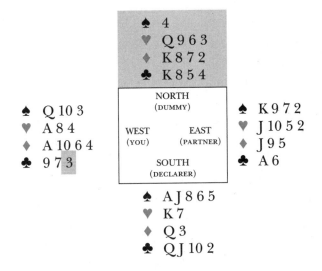

	♠ 4	
	♥ Q 9 6 3	
	♦ K 8 7 2	
	♣ K 8 5 4	

NORTH
(DUMMY)

♠ Q 10 3   ♠ K 9 7 2
♥ A 8 4   WEST   EAST   ♥ J 10 5 2
♦ A 10 6 4 (YOU) (PARTNER) ♦ J 9 5
♣ 9 7 3   SOUTH   ♣ A 6
           (DECLARER)

♠ A J 8 6 5
♥ K 7
♦ Q 3
♣ Q J 10 2

You lead a club, partner wins the ♣A, and seeing what you're up to, returns a club. Declarer can win this trick, play the ♠A, and ruff one of the low spades in dummy. When declarer now leads a heart or a diamond to try to get back to lead another spade, you win the trick and lead another club. With no trump left in dummy and only one trump left in declarer's hand, the contract will likely be defeated with careful defense. If you led anything but a trump initially, declarer would scramble home with at least eight tricks.

The play and defense in contracts like this can become quite intricate. There's scope for both declarer and the defenders. Nonetheless, the principle remains the same. Try to figure out what the unseen hands look like before making your opening lead. Most auctions will provide a surprising number of clues, if you take the time to listen.

The more you know about bidding, the easier it is to visualize the hands. Even if your opponents don't use exactly the same methods that you do, there's common ground. Often the auction screams for a particular lead, even if your not entirely certain what all the bidding means. For example, what would you lead as West after this auction?

WEST	NORTH	EAST	SOUTH
	Pass	Pass	1♥
Pass	4♥	Pass	4♠
Pass	5♣	Pass	5♥
Pass	Pass	Pass	

North-South agreed on hearts as the trump suit, and then went beyond the game level searching for a slam. South showed some high cards in spades, and North showed some strength in clubs. South decided this wasn't enough to carry on, and the partnership stopped short of slam. Well, did you lead a diamond? That's the lead world champion Bobby Goldman found when this hand came up in a match against New Zealand. This was the actual hand:

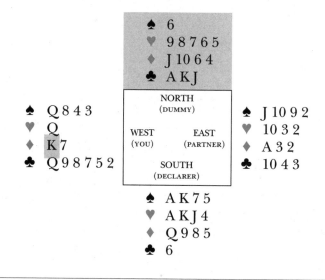

The opening lead of the ♦K is the only card to defeat the contract. A second diamond can be led to partner's ♦A, and you get to trump the third round of diamonds with your singleton ♥Q. A very dramatic defense, but you could find the same lead by listening to the auction and coming to the same conclusion based on the clues available.

Some auctions carry special inferences. A typical situation is when the opponents make use of the Stayman Convention—a 2♣ response to an opening bid of 1NT, asking opener to show a four-card major suit. For example, what conclusions might you draw from this bidding sequence?

WEST	NORTH	EAST	SOUTH
			1NT
Pass	2♣*	Pass	2♠
Pass	3NT	Pass	Pass
Pass			

*Stayman Convention

The 1NT opening bid tells you that South has a balanced hand with 16-18 points, and the 2♠ response tells you that South also holds a four-card spade suit. North holds about 10 or more points to have taken the partnership to the game level. But there's more. You can also infer that North has a four-card heart suit and doesn't have four spades. Holding four spades, North would have put the partnership in the eight-card major suit fit—4♠ rather than 3NT. If North didn't hold a four-card heart suit, North wouldn't have bothered using the Stayman Convention to ask partner to show a major suit. North would have gone directly to 3NT.

This sort of logic might sway your choice of opening lead against this auction with a hand like this:

♠ Q 10 8 5
♥ Q 9 7 3
♦ J 10 5
♣ A 5

This is probably not the time for fourth highest from your longest and strongest. A spade lead would be leading into declarer's strength.

A heart lead is equally unlikely to be effective, since that's dummy's four-card suit. Time to strike out and look for partner's long suit. Lead the ♦J, top of your touching cards in that suit, and hope that you can help partner establish some winners in the suit. It may not work out, but at least you're thinking!

Some auctions let you know that the opponents don't have anything to spare. For example:

WEST	NORTH	EAST	SOUTH
	1♦	Pass	1♥
Pass	2♥	Pass	3♥
Pass	Pass	Pass	

North opened the bidding, but showed a minimum-strength hand by raising partner to the two level. When South invited North to carry on to game, North rejected the invitation. So North has the barest possible opening bid. Similarly, South didn't jump right to game, but only offered an invitation. South probably has about 11 12 points. North-South are at their limit. Time to perk up—this contract may be beatable. You don't need to do anything spectacular. Just follow the basic guidelines—and keep on your toes to avoid letting an extra trick slip by.

Other auctions sound much stronger:

WEST	NORTH	EAST	SOUTH
	1♠	Pass	2♥
Pass	3♥	Pass	4♣
Pass	4♦	Pass	4♥
Pass	Pass	Pass	

This one sounds as though North-South were considering a slam contract. Time to get aggressive. Lead that singleton and go for a ruff!

Of course, you always do look carefully at your actual hand before making the opening lead. You put that together with the knowledge gleaned from the auction. Sometimes, you may come to a surprising conclusion. Suppose this is your hand:

♠ 10 9 8
♥ A
♦ 9 6 5 4 2
♣ A 8 5 4

WEST	NORTH	EAST	SOUTH
		Pass	1♥
Pass	2♦	Pass	2NT
Pass	4♥	Pass	Pass
Pass			

A reasonably strong-sounding auction, and it's tempting to lead one of the unbid suits—spades or clubs—hoping to establish and take your tricks before declarer wins the race. But take a moment to visualize the North-South hands.

North bid diamonds and then raised hearts, so North's hand might be something like this:

NORTH

♠ x
♥ x x x
♦ x x x x x x
♣ x x

South opened the bidding in hearts and then showed a balanced hand, so South's hand probably looks something like this:

SOUTH

♠ x x x
♥ x x x x x
♦ x x
♣ x x x

You hold five diamonds. That doesn't leave too many for partner—probably a singleton or a void. If you lead a diamond, partner may be able to ruff it. Even if partner has a singleton, you'll regain the lead with the ♥A before all the trump are drawn, and you could lead another diamond for partner to ruff. Let's see how a diamond lead works out on the full hand:

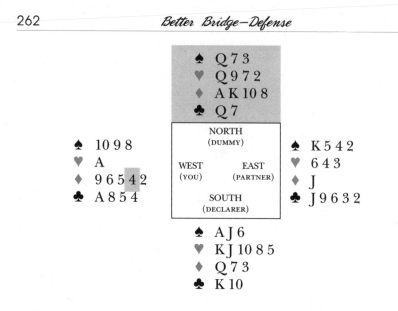

♠ Q 7 3
♥ Q 9 7 2
♦ A K 10 8
♣ Q 7

NORTH
(DUMMY)

♠ 10 9 8   ♠ K 5 4 2
♥ A   ♥ 6 4 3
♦ 9 6 5 4 2   ♦ J
♣ A 8 5 4   ♣ J 9 6 3 2

WEST   EAST
(YOU)   (PARTNER)

SOUTH
(DECLARER)

♠ A J 6
♥ K J 10 8 5
♦ Q 7 3
♣ K 10

The North-South hands aren't exactly what you pictured, but the diamond lead works out brilliantly. Declarer wins the first trick and leads a trump, but you win and lead another diamond which partner trumps. Partner plays a club over to your ♣A, and you lead another diamond, which partner ruffs to defeat the contract. How did partner know to lead back a club rather than a spade? Hopefully, you led a low diamond for partner to ruff, as a suit preference signal for clubs.

If you led anything else on this hand, declarer would have an easy time making the contract, probably with an overtrick. You'll amaze everyone—probably including yourself—when you find such a defense, but the signposts are there. It's not often that you want to lead the opponent's suit, but by listening to the auction, you can pick your spots.

Using Your Eyes

The importance of signals by the defenders has been emphasized throughout the book. You must be prepared not only to send signals when appropriate, but to receive those that partner is sending to you. Consider this hand.

WEST	NORTH	EAST	SOUTH
		Pass	1♠
Pass	2♠	Pass	4♠
Pass	Pass	Pass	

With nothing much to go on from the auction, you lead the ♦J, top of your sequence, and this is what you see:

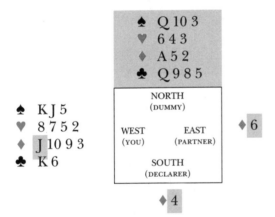

Declarer wins the first trick with dummy's ♦A, as partner plays the ♦6 and declarer the ♦4. Declarer now plays a low spade from dummy to the ♠A, as partner plays the ♠9. Now declarer leads a low spade toward dummy. There's not much point in playing your ♠J, so you win the trick with the ♠K. Declarer plays the ♠10 from dummy, and partner discards the ♥Q. What now?

On the surface, partner's ♦6 looks as though it could be an encouraging card. But you can see the ♦3 in your hand, the diamond ♦2 and ♦5 in dummy, and declarer played the ♦4 on the first trick. The ♦6 is partner's lowest diamond, so partner is sending a discouraging signal in that suit. What about the ♥Q? You discard the highest-ranking of equal cards, so partner is showing the ♥J and ♥10, but denying the ♥K. Partner probably doesn't hold the ♥A either. Holding that card, partner might have simply made an encouraging signal in hearts.

That leaves clubs. Partner hasn't made an encouraging signal in clubs, but partner also hasn't made a discouraging signal. Everything points to the club suit as your best chance. If declarer holds the ♣A, it doesn't look like you're beating this contract; if partner holds the ♣A . . .

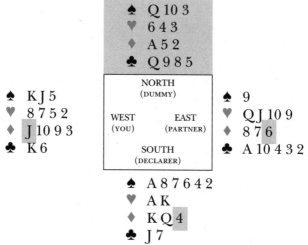

If you switch to the ♣K, it wins the trick, and you can lead another club to partner's ♣A. If partner leads back another round of clubs, you get to ruff the trick with the ♠J to defeat the contract. Will partner lead another club? Partner knows neither you nor declarer have any clubs left, but can visualize that you might have a higher trump than declarer—as on the actual layout. Hopefully, partner will come to the winning conclusion.

Sometimes partner hasn't had an opportunity to give you a signal. Perhaps you can find a way to give partner a chance. Take a look at this next hand after the auction has gone:

WEST	NORTH	EAST	SOUTH
	1NT	Pass	3♥
Pass	4♥	Pass	Pass
Pass			

Against this strong-sounding auction, you decide to lead your singleton club, and this is what you see after the dummy comes down:

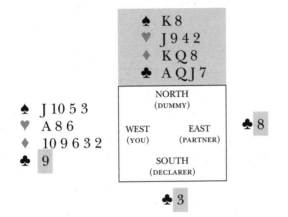

```
                        ♠ K 8
                        ♥ J 9 4 2
                        ♦ K Q 8
                        ♣ A Q J 7
                     ┌─────────────────┐
                     │   NORTH         │
     ♠ J 10 5 3      │  (DUMMY)        │
     ♥ A 8 6         │ WEST     EAST   │   ♣ 8
     ♦ 10 9 6 3 2    │ (YOU)  (PARTNER)│
     ♣ 9             │   SOUTH         │
                     │ (DECLARER)      │
                     └─────────────────┘
                        ♣ 3
```

The ♣A is played from dummy, partner plays an encouraging-looking ♣8, and declarer plays the ♣3. A low heart is led from dummy, partner plays the ♥5, declarer plays the ♥Q, and you play…?

Partner probably has the ♣K, based on the encouraging signal at the first trick. You'd like to get over to partner's hand, so that partner can take the ♣K and give you a ruff. You'll need to find an entry to partner's hand, but is it in spades or diamonds? Partner hasn't had a chance to signal. If you win this trick with the ♥A, you'll have to guess which suit to lead.

Some people will guess right in this type of situation; others will guess wrong. But you don't need to guess at all! There's no necessity to win the first trick with the ♥A. Declarer must hold a five-card heart suit for the jump to 3♥, so partner won't be following suit on the next round of trump. Wait to win the second round of trump. That gives partner an opportunity to signal. Suppose partner discards the ♠2 on the second round of trump, now you can lead a diamond, hoping the complete hand is something like this:

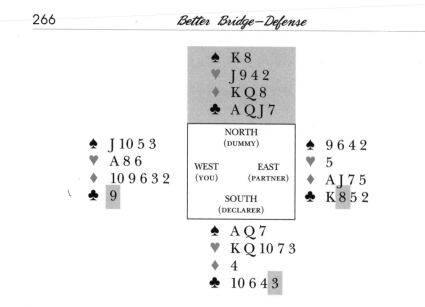

Partner wins the trick with the ♦A, plays the ♣K, and leads another club for you to trump. Partner had the choice of discarding a low spade or a high diamond to send you the appropriate message on this hand. If partner held the ♠A, rather than the ♦A, partner could discard a high spade or a low diamond. It's easy once you see the right signal—provided you give partner a chance to send a signal.

While partner's signals are valuable, don't forget to watch how declarer is playing the hand. Declarer's line of play will often give you a clue about the best defense. See if you can draw the correct inference on the following hand. The auction goes like this:

WEST	NORTH	EAST	SOUTH
	1♦	Pass	1♥
Pass	2♦	Pass	3NT
Pass	Pass	Pass	

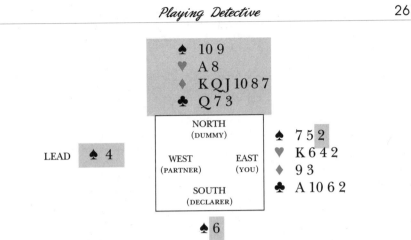

LEAD ♠ 4

NORTH
(DUMMY)

WEST
(PARTNER)

EAST
(YOU)

SOUTH
(DECLARER)

♠ 10 9
♥ A 8
♦ K Q J 10 8 7
♣ Q 7 3

♠ 7 5 2
♥ K 6 4 2
♦ 9 3
♣ A 10 6 2

♠ 6

Partner leads the ♠4 against the 3NT contract, and dummy's ♠9 wins the first trick as both you and declarer follow with low spades. Declarer now plays a low club from dummy, and you . . . ?

If you've fallen asleep on your job as detective, you might automatically play second hand low to this trick. If you're into your sleuthing role, however, you should be asking yourself what declarer is up to. With all those high diamonds in dummy, why is declarer leading clubs rather than trying to promote winners in diamonds? As Sherlock Holmes might say, "Elementary, my dear Watson." Declarer isn't promoting winners in diamonds because declarer doesn't need to promote winners in diamonds. Declarer must hold the ♦A!

With that inference, you can move to the next logical step. Declarer already has one spade trick and the ♥A in dummy to go along with six diamond tricks. If declarer gets one trick in clubs, that will be the ninth trick. No time to dally around. Play the ♣A, and lead back partner's suit. Here's the complete hand:

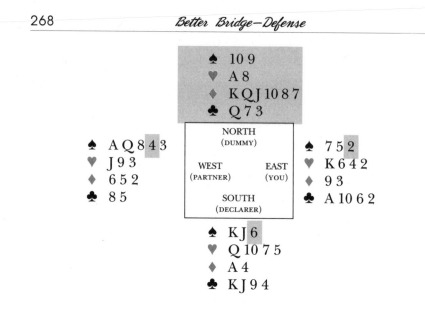

How many East's would let declarer sneak that club trick through and wind up shaking their head afterward, finding the burglar had slipped through their hands?

Counting

One of the most useful things you can do to improve your bridge game is to learn to count. You don't have to be able to count very high—thirteen is usually high enough—but you do need to do it on every hand, whether you're bidding, declaring, or defending. When you're bidding, you count your points; when you're declaring, you count trump; when you're defending, you count everything—if you want to play detective.

On the previous hand, you needed to count declarer's tricks before deciding what to do. That's always important. Here's a similar example.

WEST	NORTH	EAST	SOUTH
	1♣	Pass	1♥
Pass	2♣	Pass	3NT
Pass	Pass	Pass	

Against this auction, you start off with the fourth highest from your longest and strongest suit:

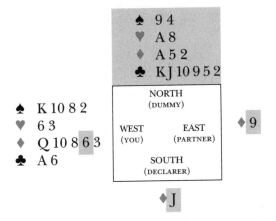

On your lead of the ♦6, a low diamond is played from dummy, partner plays the ♦9, and declarer wins the trick with the ♦J. Since partner has played third hand high, you now know declarer also has the ♦K. Declarer now leads the ♣Q.

Let's pause for reflection. Declarer is going to promote five club winners in the dummy. Along with three diamond tricks and the ♥A, that gives declarer a total of at least nine tricks. There's no point in continuing to lead diamonds. After winning the ♣A, it's time to quickly switch to spades. Here's the full layout.

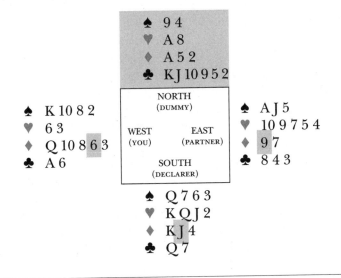

When you lead the ♠2, partner wins the ♠A and returns the ♠J. Declarer's ♠Q is trapped, and your side gets four spade winners to go along with the ♣A. You win the race. If you hadn't switched to a spade after winning the ♣A, declarer would have taken the rest of the tricks.

In addition to counting tricks, you need to count the number of cards in each suit. There's only thirteen, but that's important to remember on a hand such as the following:

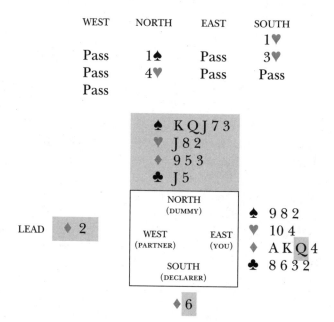

WEST	NORTH	EAST	SOUTH
			1♥
Pass	1♠	Pass	3♥
Pass	4♥	Pass	Pass
Pass			

NORTH (DUMMY)
♠ K Q J 7 3
♥ J 8 2
♦ 9 5 3
♣ J 5

WEST (PARTNER)   EAST (YOU)
♠ 9 8 2
♥ 10 4
♦ A K Q 4
♣ 8 6 3 2

SOUTH (DECLARER)

LEAD ♦ 2

♦ 6

Partner leads the ♦2 against the 4♥ contract and strikes gold in your hand—what a fine partner! A low diamond is played from dummy, and you win the first trick with the ♦Q. You take a second diamond trick with your ♦K, as declarer plays the ♦10 and partner plays the ♦7. You take a third diamond trick—hold on! How many diamonds are there in the deck?

The ♦2 appears to have been partner's fourth highest diamond from a four-card suit. There's three diamonds in dummy, and you have four. That leaves declarer with only a doubleton. If you lead a third round of diamonds, declarer will trump it. That's not going to do the defense much good. Unless partner has a heart winner and the ♠A, you're going to have to hope partner has some strength in clubs. This is your opportunity to lead through declarer's strength, and here's the complete hand.

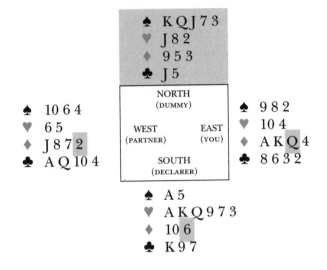

If you try to take a third diamond winner, declarer will ruff, draw trump, and take the rest of the tricks, using dummy's spade suit. You have to lead a club, trapping declarer's ♣K, and helping partner to win two club tricks. You're lucky to find partner with such a nice holding in clubs, but your defense would have been equally successful if the full hand were something like this:

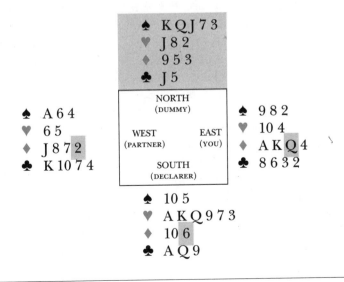

Your club lead would establish a trick for partner's ♣K before declarer has an opportunity to drive out the ♠A. If you led another diamond, declarer would ruff, draw trump, and establish dummy's spades before partner had an opportunity to get a club trick.

One other thing you can count as a defender is points. Let's see how that can help you on the following hand.

WEST	NORTH	EAST	SOUTH
		Pass	1NT
Pass	3NT	Pass	Pass
Pass			

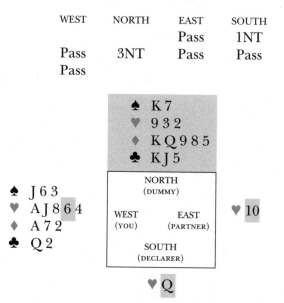

You start off defending North-South's 3NT contract by leading the ♥6. A low heart is played from dummy, partner plays the ♥10, and declarer wins the trick with the ♥Q. Now declarer leads the ♦J. What do you do?

Declarer still has the ♥K left—partner wouldn't have played the ♥K on the first trick holding that card. You'd like to find an entry to partner's hand, so that partner could lead a heart back through declarer, trapping declarer's ♥K. Is it possible that partner holds the ♠A or ♣A?

Not on this hand. Declarer's 1NT opening bid showed 16–18 points. You hold 12 high card points and can see 12 in the dummy. That leaves only 16 of the 40 high card points, and declarer must have all of them. Not only does that tell you that there's nothing to be found in partner's hand, it also tells you that declarer will have enough tricks after driving out your ♦A. There's only one possibility for the defense. Win the ◆A, and lay down the ♥A. With a little luck, this will be the full layout:

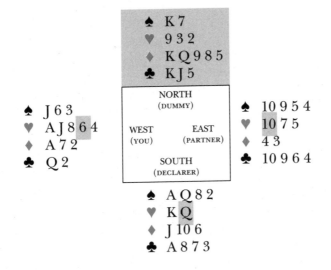

```
                    ♠ K 7
                    ♥ 9 3 2
                    ♦ K Q 9 8 5
                    ♣ K J 5
                  ┌─────────────────┐
                  │     NORTH       │
  ♠ J 6 3         │    (DUMMY)      │      ♠ 10 9 5 4
  ♥ A J 8 6 4     │ WEST      EAST  │      ♥ 10 7 5
  ♦ A 7 2         │ (YOU)   (PARTNER)│     ♦ 4 3
  ♣ Q 2           │     SOUTH       │      ♣ 10 9 6 4
                  │   (DECLARER)    │
                  └─────────────────┘
                    ♠ A Q 8 2
                    ♥ K Q
                    ♦ J 10 6
                    ♣ A 8 7 3
```

Your ♥A drops declarer's remaining ♥K, and you take the rest of your heart tricks to defeat the contract. You really are starting to see through the backs of the cards. You could tell where every missing high card was located as soon dummy came down! Sherlock Holmes and Columbo would be amazed—and so will your partners.

Summary

As a defender, you have to play detective and look for the clues to be found on each hand. In searching for clues, keep the following points in mind:

- Listen to the auction, and try to visualize the unseen hands based on the bidding.
- Watch for partner's signals.
- Look for inferences from the way declarer is playing the hand.
- Count everything you can: the number of tricks declarer can take; the numbers cards declarer has in each suit; the number of points declarer holds.

The better you become at identifying the clues and drawing the corresponding inferences, the more you'll enjoy being a defender.

Practice Hands

Hand 10.1

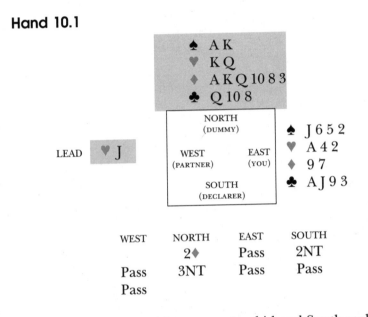

```
                    ♠ A K
                    ♥ K Q
                    ♦ A K Q 10 8 3
                    ♣ Q 10 8
            ┌─────────────────────┐
            │       NORTH         │      ♠ J 6 5 2
            │      (DUMMY)        │      ♥ A 4 2
  LEAD  ♥ J │                     │      ♦ 9 7
            │  WEST        EAST   │      ♣ A J 9 3
            │ (PARTNER)    (YOU)  │
            │                     │
            │       SOUTH         │
            │     (DECLARER)      │
            └─────────────────────┘
```

WEST	NORTH	EAST	SOUTH
	2♦	Pass	2NT
Pass	3NT	Pass	Pass
Pass			

After North opens with a strong two-bid and South makes a negative response, the opponents end up in 3NT. Partner leads the ♥J.

What do you think partner's heart suit looks like? How do you plan to defend?

Solution 10.1

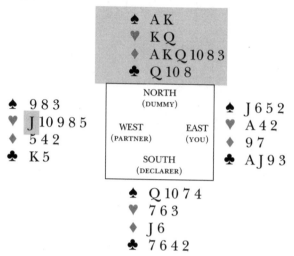

```
              ♠ A K
              ♥ K Q
              ♦ A K Q 10 8 3
              ♣ Q 10 8
                 NORTH
                (DUMMY)
♠ 9 8 3                          ♠ J 6 5 2
♥ J 10 9 8 5    WEST     EAST    ♥ A 4 2
♦ 5 4 2        (PARTNER) (YOU)   ♦ 9 7
♣ K 5                            ♣ A J 9 3
                 SOUTH
               (DECLARER)
              ♠ Q 10 7 4
              ♥ 7 6 3
              ♦ J 6
              ♣ 7 6 4 2
```

Partner has led the top of a sequence, probably something like ♥ J 10 9 x x. After winning a trick with the ♥A, you could return a heart to drive out dummy's ♥Q and establish the rest of partner's suit. Before doing that, however, count declarer's tricks.

Once you win a trick with your ♥A, it looks as though declarer has at least nine winners: two spades, one heart, and six diamonds. If you return a heart to establish partner's winners, declarer will run home with the contract. Your only hope is to take five tricks before declarer can take nine. To do that, you're going to need to find partner with the ♣K. At trick two, lead back a low club, and keep your fingers crossed.

On the actual hand, partner wins a trick with the ♣K and returns a club. Dummy's ♣Q and ♣10 are trapped, so you take the rest of the club tricks—enough to defeat the contract.

Hand 10.2

♠ 5 3
♥ J 10 9 7
♦ A 8 3
♣ A 9 7 2

```
                    NORTH
                   (DUMMY)

        WEST                EAST
        (YOU)             (PARTNER)

                    SOUTH
                  (DECLARER)
```

WEST	NORTH	EAST	SOUTH
		Pass	1♠
Pass	2♣	Pass	3♣
Pass	4♠	Pass	Pass
Pass			

It's your lead against South's 4♠ contract. Has the auction given you any clues? Can you visualize how the defense might go?

Solution 10.2

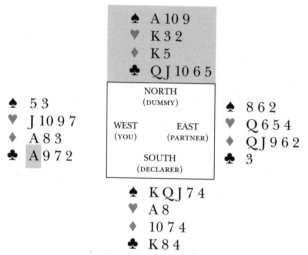

♠ A 10 9
♥ K 3 2
♦ K 5
♣ Q J 10 6 5

NORTH
(DUMMY)

WEST
(YOU)

EAST
(PARTNER)

SOUTH
(DECLARER)

♠ 5 3
♥ J 10 9 7
♦ A 8 3
♣ A 9 7 2

♠ 8 6 2
♥ Q 6 5 4
♦ Q J 9 6 2
♣ 3

♠ K Q J 7 4
♥ A 8
♦ 10 7 4
♣ K 8 4

If you weren't listening to the auction, you might lead the ♥J, top of your sequence. The bidding, however, has given you a good picture of the North-South hands. North bid clubs, and South raised the suit. It sounds as though they have at least eight clubs between them. Since you hold four clubs, that leaves partner with a singleton.

Lead the ♣A. Don't be discouraged by partner's ♣3. Continue with another club for partner to ruff. Partner leads back a diamond to your ♦A, and you lead another club for partner to ruff. The defense takes the first four tricks.

How will partner know to lead back a diamond, rather than a heart? When you lead a club for partner to trump, lead the ♣2, your lowest remaining club. This is a suit preference signal for the lower-ranking of the two suits between which partner will have to choose after ruffing the club—hearts and diamonds.

You can almost visualize exactly how the defense will go before dummy arrives on the table. Perhaps you can also visualize partner's applause when you find the winning lead.

Hand 10.3

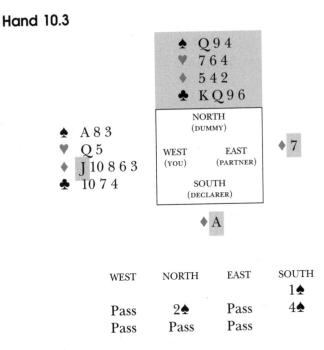

	♠ Q 9 4	
	♥ 7 6 4	
	♦ 5 4 2	
	♣ K Q 9 6	

NORTH
(DUMMY)

♠ A 8 3
♥ Q 5
♦ J 10 8 6 3
♣ 10 7 4

WEST
(YOU)

EAST
(PARTNER)

♦ 7

SOUTH
(DECLARER)

♦ A

WEST	NORTH	EAST	SOUTH
			1♠
Pass	2♠	Pass	4♠
Pass	Pass	Pass	

After South ends up in a contract of 4♠, you elect to lead the ♦J, top of your broken sequence. A low diamond is played from dummy, partner plays the ♦7, and declarer wins the trick with the ♦A.

Declarer next plays the ♣A. You play the ♣4, the ♣6 is played from dummy, and partner plays the ♣2. Now declarer leads a low spade toward dummy. What do you do?

Solution 10.3

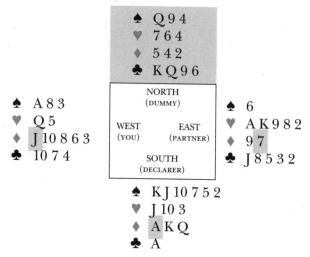

```
                    ♠ Q 9 4
                    ♥ 7 6 4
                    ♦ 5 4 2
                    ♣ K Q 9 6
                    NORTH
                    (DUMMY)
♠ A 8 3                             ♠ 6
♥ Q 5       WEST        EAST        ♥ A K 9 8 2
♦ J 10 8 6 3  (YOU)    (PARTNER)    ♦ 9 7
♣ 10 7 4                            ♣ J 8 5 3 2
                    SOUTH
                    (DECLARER)
                    ♠ K J 10 7 5 2
                    ♥ J 10 3
                    ♦ A K Q
                    ♣ A
```

The general guideline when declarer leads a low card toward dummy is second hand low. But that's only if you're not sure what to do. On this hand, you have all the clues you need to hop up with the ♣A and lead the ♥Q. First, there's partner's ♦7 on the first trick. At first glance, it might look like an encouraging signal, but you can see all the lower-ranking diamonds in your hand and the dummy. It's partner's lowest diamond, a discouraging signal.

Then, there's declarer's play of the ♣A before leading a trump. Declarer doesn't usually start taking winners until after the trump are drawn, unless declarer needs to discard some losers. If declarer wanted to discard some losers on dummy's club winners, why did declarer stop after playing the ♣A? The inference is that declarer has only a singleton ♣A. Declarer has unblocked the suit and is now trying to get to dummy to discard some losers.

Finally, if declarer is trying to get rid of losers and partner isn't interested in diamonds, you can deduce that partner's strength must be in the heart suit. Having done your detective work, you know how to thwart declarer's plan.

On the actual hand, if you played low on the spade, declarer would win the trick in dummy and discard two hearts on dummy's ♣K and ♣Q. The defense would end up with only two tricks, rather than four.

Hand 10.4

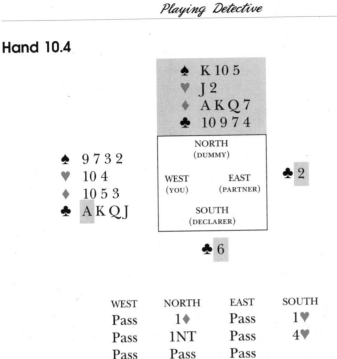

♠ K 10 5
♥ J 2
♦ A K Q 7
♣ 10 9 7 4

NORTH
(DUMMY)

♠ 9 7 3 2
♥ 10 4
♦ 10 5 3
♣ A K Q J

WEST
(YOU)

EAST
(PARTNER)

♣ 2

SOUTH
(DECLARER)

♣ 6

WEST	NORTH	EAST	SOUTH
Pass	1♦	Pass	1♥
Pass	1NT	Pass	4♥
Pass	Pass	Pass	

South reaches a contract of 4♥, and you lead the ♣A. A low club is played from dummy, partner plays the ♣2, and declarer plays the ♣6. You play another high club, partner plays the ♣5, and declarer plays the ♣8.

How are you planning to help your side get two more tricks?

Solution 10.4

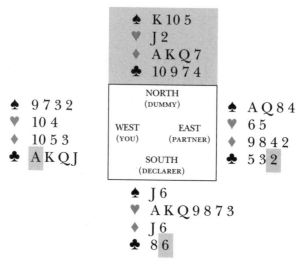

<pre>
                       ♠ K 10 5
                       ♥ J 2
                       ♦ A K Q 7
                       ♣ 10 9 7 4
                            NORTH
                           (DUMMY)
  ♠ 9 7 3 2   ♠ A Q 8 4
  ♥ 10 4   WEST   EAST   ♥ 6 5
  ♦ 10 5 3   (YOU)   (PARTNER)   ♦ 9 8 4 2
  ♣ A K Q J   ♣ 5 3 2
                            SOUTH
                          (DECLARER)
                       ♠ J 6
                       ♥ A K Q 9 8 7 3
                       ♦ J 6
                       ♣ 8 6
</pre>

Partner played a discouraging club on the first trick. That didn't
bother you, since you have all the high clubs, but you have to be
careful not to try to take too many tricks in the suit. When you lead
a second round of the suit, and declarer and partner follow suit, you
can draw the inference that your side won't be getting any more
club tricks.

With a doubleton club, partner would probably have started with
an encouraging signal—by playing a high club—hoping to get a ruff.
Since there's only thirteen clubs in the deck, if partner has three,
declarer has only two. You'll have to look for your two tricks elsewhere, and unless partner has a trick in the trump suit, the only
possibility is spades. At trick three, you need to shift to spades.

If you continue with a third round of clubs, declarer will ruff,
draw trump, and take all the remaining tricks. Only by leading a
spade, to help partner trap dummy's ♠K, can you defeat the contract. Did you draw the right conclusion from partner's message?

Glossary

attitude signal   A signal to partner about whether or not a defender would like a particular suit led. A high card is an encouraging signal; a low card is a discouraging signal.

blocked   A suit with no link cards to partner's hand.

broken sequence   A sequence of cards in a suit where the third card from the top is missing, but not the next lower-ranking card(s) (♥ K Q 10 9, ♦ Q J 9).

count signal   A signal by a defender to tell partner how many cards are held in a suit. A high card followed by a low card shows an even number; a low card followed by a high card shows an odd number.

ducking   Playing low cards from both hands to concede a trick that could have been won.

entry   A card providing a means to win a trick in a specific hand.

equal honors   Cards in a suit held by the defenders that are effectively in sequence.

finesse   An attempt to win a trick with a card when the opponents hold one or more higher-ranking cards in the suit.

forcing defense   Leading winners in an attempt to run declarer out of trump.

fourth highest   The fourth card ranked down from the top in a suit held by a player (♥ K 9 7 **6** 4)

guard   A holding in a suit which will prevent the opponents from taking all the tricks in that suit.

holdup play   Declining to take a winner at the first opportunity, usually with the intention of removing the link cards from one opponent's hand.

interior sequence   A holding in a suit that contains a sequence and a higher-ranking card that is not part of the sequence (♥ A J 10 9, ♦ Q 10 9 8).

link card A card which can be led to a winner (entry) in the opposite hand.

MUD (Middle, Up Down) The lead of the middle-ranking of three low cards (♥ 7 4 2). This is followed by the play of the higher-ranking card (up), then the lower-ranking card (down).

overruff Play a higher-ranking trump to a trick than one already played. Same as overtrump.

promotion Developing a card into a potential winner by driving out any higher-ranking cards held by the opponents.

rule of eleven A method of determining the number of cards in declarer's hand that are higher-ranking than the card led by partner when partner leads fourth highest. The pips (rank) on partner's card are subtracted from eleven to give the number of higher-ranking cards in the other three hands.

sequence Three or more cards of the same suit in consecutive order of rank (♥ K Q J).

signal A card chosen by a defender to send a specific message to partner.

splitting honors The play of one of two or more touching high cards by the second player to a trick.

stranded Winners which cannot be taken because there is no entry to the hand containing them.

suit preference signal A signal by a defender to tell partner which of two suits is preferred. The signal is usually given in a third suit. A high card shows preference for the higher-ranking suit; a low card for the lower-ranking suit.

sure trick A trick which can be taken without giving up the lead to the opponents.

top of nothing The lead of the top card from three or more low cards. Used to indicate that no high cards are held in the suit.

trump echo The play of a high trump followed by a lower-ranking trump to show a holding of three trump cards. Usually used when a defender is looking for a ruff.

uppercut A ruff by a defender intended to promote a trump trick in partner's hand.

Bi-Monthly Newsletter

Audrey Grant's Better Bridge Newsletter, which keeps you informed on what's happening in the world of bridge today. There are articles on a wide variety of topics including play, defense, bidding conventions, famous hands, bridge etiquette, and bridge history.

For a year's subscription, send $19.95 (U.S. dollars) and your name and mailing address to:

Better Bridge Newsletter
11333 Moorpark St., Suite 458
Studio City, California 91602

Cruises and Seminars

Audrey Grant's Better Bridge Cruises and Tours™, are offered regularly. Details can be obtained from:

Audrey Grant's Better Bridge Cruises and Tours™
Empress Bridge Cruises and Tours
1-800-724-1386; FAX: 607-785-9919

Bridge Supplies

Randy Baron produces a full-color catalog of bridge supplies, including a selection of cards and other specialties. The American Contract Bridge League also has a catalog offering bridge supplies.

Baron-Barclay Bridge Supplies
3600 Chamberlain Lane, Suite 230
Louisville, KY 40241
1-800-274-2221; 502-426-0410; FAX: 502-426-2044

The American Contract Bridge League
Order Department—The Bridge Source
2990 Airways Blvd.
Memphis, TN 38116-3847
1-800-264-2743; FAX: 901-398-7754